MW01194745

Charlotte Holzer

YEARS OF DEFIANCE

The Herbert Baum Group and Jewish Resistance in Berlin

Charlotte Holzer

YEARS OF DEFIANCE

The Herbert Baum Group and Jewish
Resistance in Berlin

Translated from the German by William Templer

YAD VASHEM
THE WORLD HOLOCAUST
REMEMBRANCE CENTER

THE INTERNATIONAL INSTITUTE
FOR HOLOCAUST RESEARCH

Charlotte Holzer
Years of Defiance
The Herbert Baum Group and Jewish
Resistance in Berlin

Academic Editors: Yaakov Borut (Yad Vashem),
Wolf Kaiser, Helmut Peitsch, Klaus Pistor
Language Editor: Susan Kennedy
Production Editor: Enno Raschke

Unless otherwise indicated, all photos in this book are courtesy of
Chava Kürer.

ISBN 978-965-308-668-5

Typesetting: Hava Salzman

Printed in Israel by Offset Natan Shlomo Press, Jerusalem

CONTENTS

INTRODUCTION

by Yaakov Borut

It is well known that during the Third Reich, communist Jews were doubly cursed—they were persecuted by the Nazis both for their political convictions and for their origins. But, as seen from her memoirs, Charlotte (Lotte) Paech (nee Abraham, later Holzer)[1] somehow managed to live in Berlin until 1942 while suffering less than most of the Communists or Jews who lived in that city.

Charlotte Abraham grew up in a family she described as *kleinbürgerlich* (petit bourgeois). Living in a working-class area, she encountered no antisemitism as a child.

Charlotte broke off with the Jewish religion at a young age. Later, after studying to be a nurse in the Jewish hospital of Berlin, she was determined not to be part of a religious (meaning Jewish)

---

1   The literature on Charlotte Holzer is mainly discussed in the afterword. In addition to the works mentioned there, see the partial biography in Beate Kosmala, "Zuflucht in Potsdam bei Christen der Bekennende Kirche," in Wolfgang Benz, *Überleben im Dritten Reich: Juden im Untergrund und ihre Helfer* (Munich: Beck, 2003), pp. 113–130, here pp. 118–129.

hospital. She tried to find employment in all of the Berlin hospitals, but each turned her down because she was Jewish. She was left with no choice but to join the Jewish hospital. The year was 1928/1929, and this treatment is a glaring testimony to the power of antisemitism already at that time; even more shocking since Berlin was the most progressive town in Weimar Germany. So it was that under Nazi rule, she was an employee of the Jewish community. This meant that— unlike the great majority of Jews—she did not lose her job. And later, during the time of the deportations, Jewish community employees, and especially those in highly needed professions, such as nurses, were protected better than most from deportation. What wouldn't most Jews have given to be in Charlotte's place, albeit against her initial intention.

Working as a hospital nurse before the Nazi era, Charlotte felt that the working conditions were unfair. She contacted the relevant Communist work union, which in turn created a Communist cell in the Jewish hospital, sending political instructors to organize and educate its members. One of them was Gustav Paech. Charlotte fell pregnant with his child, which led to her being fired from the hospital in January 1933 for immoral behavior. She subsequently married him and joined the German Communist Party—the KPD. In August 1933, when the Nazis were already in power, her daughter was born; her husband was arrested that same month.

In April 1933, the Nazis ordered the Jewish hospital to fire all Communist workers, according to a list of members of the local cell. Charlotte was not employed at the time as she was looking after her baby daughter and living on welfare benefits, and thus was not affected. In 1935, she was thus able to resume her work at the hospital. Her husband was released in 1935, but the two separated in 1936, and officially divorced in 1938. The divorce meant that she lost the protection given to couples living in a mixed marriage, but that seems to have had little effect on her life, except in one realm: she now had no choice but to send her daughter to a Jewish school. She continued to work in the Jewish hospital until her arrest in 1942.

Charlotte seems to have broken all ties to her family. She doesn't mention any help from them in raising her child, or even contact with them. Even the death of her mother is mentioned incidentally, insofar as she received a card from her posthumously.

Charlotte lived in a working-class neighborhood and did not encounter antisemitism in her immediate surroundings. She had to rely on her neighbors' help to carry her child's baby carriage to and from her fourth-floor apartment. As she describes it, she would simply go out into the stairway, yell "I need a man!" and some neighbor would come out and help her. The large majority of Jews living in the middle-class neighborhoods would never have received such help during the Nazi times—in fact, they would not have contemplated asking for it.

Charlotte did not even encounter the *Kristallnacht* pogrom in her vicinity. She only encountered its aftermath in her work at the Jewish hospital, as the staff there had to tend to the victims who returned from the concentration camps (to which tens of thousands of Jews were sent during the pogrom). Her description of those victims, broken people who—besides the physical injuries resulting from months of torture—lost their will to live and their human character, is an important testimony to one facet of the Nazi persecution that heretofore has received relatively little attention.

Charlotte, as she describes in some detail, was well fed in the hospital where she worked. Thus she did not need, as most Jews did, to go to a special store, during limited hours, to get the supplies allowed for Jews.

Her life changed when she joined a group of young Communists, mostly Jewish, led by the young and charismatic Herbert Baum. The "Baum Gruppe" (Baum Group) and its activities will be described later. Here suffice to mention that it engaged in underground Communist activities, until it was exposed and destroyed after some of its members tried to firebomb an anti-Soviet exhibition in Berlin. Almost all members were executed within a very short span of time.

When the group was broken up, Charlotte lived in hiding for a while, but was eventually caught by the Gestapo. In prison she was seen and treated as a Jew (rather than as a Communist), suffering limitations such as no contact with the outside world. But she had contact with other imprisoned Communist women (who, as non-Jews, could get parcels from the outside) and through them received warm clothing during the winter and important information on prison life and ways to get by.

However, another extraordinary combination of events occurred which saved her life. The authorities did not know that she was a member of the Baum group. She was instead tried for the relatively minor offense of illegally distributing ration cards and sentenced to 18 months, which she was supposed to serve not in Berlin, but in Leipzig. When the Gestapo caught on to her involvement in the Baum Group, she was in medical quarantine there and thus unavailable to them. Thus, she was not executed with the other group members after being tried and sentenced to death in absentia. When she was returned to Berlin weeks later, responsibility for all Jews had shifted from the court to the Gestapo and her case fell between the cracks in the system. The fact that she had been sentenced to death ironically saved her from deportation and extermination. Justice had to be done, so she was kept in Berlin. For a number of reasons, the execution of her sentence was delayed well into the year 1944. By that time, she was imprisoned in her former place of work, the Jewish hospital of Berlin. When the system caught on and her sentence was finally to be carried out, she was able to benefit from her detailed knowledge of the premises and from the damage caused by Allied air raids. Days before her execution, she escaped from internment and went underground.

Using her network of contacts, Charlotte received information as to where she could go to find a shelter and managed to be sheltered until the war's end (she—a Communist and atheist—received support by several devoutly religious women. One of them even told her she had a split conscience hiding an enemy of Germany). The final stage of the war was a time when it became easier to survive illegally due to the fact that many people had lost their homes and their legal papers in the frequent air raids. Germany was also filled with foreign forced labor. Charlotte used both these identity-hiding possibilities to survive after her escape, posing as member of a French forced labor column. Thus, she made it through the last months and weeks of the regime, testifying in her memoirs to the total collapse of what once was a seemingly invincible Reich, until she was liberated by the Soviet army.

The last part of Charlotte's memoirs describes her life immediately after the war: her return to Berlin and re-encounter with her former husband Gustav Paech, hospitalized with severe tuberculosis of which he died. On his deathbed he told her that their daughter Eva (who was twelve at that time) was being looked after by his mother. Charlotte writes of her contact with her daughter and attempts to regain her confidence, after Eva's grandmother had poisoned her against Charlotte during the time she was looking after her. She succeeded; Eva eventually chose to stay with her mother rather than with her grandmother. However, Charlotte adds that she refused to go to school with German children, because she remembered being beaten at school when she was a little girl.

Her life after the close of the book is described in detail in the foreword, including her daughter Eva's emigration to *Eretz Israel* in 1947, Charlotte's marriage to Richard Holzer, their move in 1950 to Communist East Berlin, Richard Holzer's death in 1975, and Charlotte's passing in 1980.

Charlotte Holzer narrated her memoirs to journalist Dieter Heimlich, in interviews that took place during 1966/1967, and "he wanted to craft [that material] into a book." But that plan did not materialize at the time. Upon reading the text, one can easily understand why it could not be published in Communist East Germany. For example, Charlotte Holzer spoke about Communist ideology as not being accepted by the Soviet people under Stalin: "the cult of personality produced a sense of fear and submissiveness, but no genuine bond with the idea, with the worldview." And then she went on to claim that this situation also existed in East Germany. In addition, she openly spoke about widespread rape and the spread of sexual diseases by Soviet soldiers. Such openness had no place in her country in those times.

Charlotte Holzer herself did not intend her memoirs to be published, at least not without being scrutinized. This can be seen by the following quote from the text concerning the "rug action" of the Baum Group: in which the group stole rugs from a wealthy Jewish couple who were about to emigrate, in order to get the financial means to acquire passports: "I was always against this action with the rugs and **under no circumstances should it later be published.**"[2]

2   My emphasis.

One interesting point in the memoir are the references to "Honecker's first wife." Erich Honecker was one of the main leaders of the GDR's governing party, the SED, and of the East German state, which he led from 1971 until his forced resignation shortly before the GDR's collapse in 1989. The wife mentioned here was Charlotte (Lotte) Schanuel, a warden at the notorious women's prison on Barnimstrasse in Berlin, with whom Erich Honecker fell in love in 1944, or early 1945, after he was assigned work there as a prisoner in forced labor in construction repair work after allied bombings. He married Schanuel in December 1946, and she died of a brain tumor six months later.[3] This episode was kept secret from the public all his political life and was known only to a few people in the Communist leadership at the time, as it seemed inconceivable that a high-profile Communist prisoner and leader would marry a warden of a Nazi prison. It only became public knowledge in Germany in 2003, long after Honecker's death. Now we learn from the memoirs that Charlotte Holzer was privy to that secret on account of her membership in the Baum Group. Perhaps other members of the group who survived knew this as well. Charlotte's reference to this secret was yet another reason why her memoirs could not be published as long as the GDR existed.

The memoir, however, provides us with important information on that point: It is not clear to this day if Schanuel was a Communist. Honecker arranged for her to become a member of the SED, the Communist leadership party. But she had many Communist prisoners under her in the prison and her personal views are unknown. In the memoir here we learn of her solidarity with the Baum Group prisoners and her passing of information, already in May 1942—an important hint as to her views, unknown to previous research about her.

* * *

As emphasized, various circumstances in Charlotte's life allowed her to survive the persecution and even to evade many of the restrictions

---

3   On that matter, see Ed Stuhler, *Margot Honecker. Eine Biografie* (Vienna: Ueberreuther, 2003), pp. 58–61; Martin Sabrow, *Erich Honecker: Das Leben davor* (Munich: C.H. Beck, 2016).

imposed on most German Jews under the Nazi regime. Various discriminatory rules were (dangerously) ignored by her and her friends, as they used public transportation, took trips into the countryside, and listened to music records. In addition, she was not the type to complain, not even about the restrictions that she did suffer. For example, the obligation to wear a yellow star was attested by many a German Jew as an especially painful experience. Charlotte mentions it only in passing, when she noted that her close friend (and later husband) Richard (Holzer), a Hungarian Jew, did not have to wear it while she, a German Jew, did. No mention is made of her own feelings regarding this public mark of identification.

For these reasons, readers of this book receive very little information about the sufferings and persecution of the Jews under the Nazi yoke. We would thus like to use this introduction to present a fuller picture of the treatment of Berlin's Jewish inhabitants under Nazi rule.[4] We would also like to present the reader with more information about the Nazi persecution of Communists and subsequently also about the Communist underground Baum Group, which Charlotte joined.

The Persecution of Berlin Jews

Berlin, the capital of Germany and a world metropolis, was the center of German Jewry. It was home to nearly a third of all German Jews and housed the leadership organs of almost all Jewish organizations at the national level. Berlin Jews were well integrated and prominent in various aspects of the city's economic, intellectual, and cultural life. In 1933 the 160,000 Jews living there represented about 3.8 percent of the town's inhabitants.

---

4   The major sources on this subject are Wolf Gruner, *The Persecution of the Jews in Berlin, 1933–1945. A Chronology of Measures by the Authorities in the German Capital* (Berlin: Stiftung Topographie des Terrors, 2014); Michael Wildt and Christoph Kreuzmüller, eds., *Berlin 1933–1945: Stadt und Gesellschaft im Nationalsozialismus* (Munich: Siedler Verlag, 2013); Beate Meyer, Hermann Simon, and Chana Schütz, eds., *Jews in Nazi Berlin. From Kristallnacht to Liberation* (Chicago and London: The University of Chicago Press, 2009).

Berlin was far from being a center of support for the Nazi party. In the last free Reichstag elections of November 1932, the Nazis received 26 percent of the vote there, a much lower number than the national average of 33 percent. The future propaganda minister, Joseph Goebbels, appointed by Hitler in 1926 as Gauleiter of Berlin, viewed it as his special mission to rid Berlin of Jewish influence.

The first persecutions suffered by the Berlin Jews were economic measures and violence. The town authorities began canceling contracts with Jewish firms. On April 1, 1933, which was declared "national boycott day," Nazi posts stood in front of Jewish businesses in an attempt to intimidate clients from entering, while trucks traveled through the streets disseminating anti-Jewish propaganda. The Jews, as is evidenced by memoirs, were shaken by this activity. But this was only the beginning of things to come.

On April 7, the Nazi "law for the restoration of professional public service" ordered that almost all Jewish employees of state agencies were to be dismissed. Subsequently, Jewish employees of Berlin municipal institutions were also dismissed, in a more brutal manner than stipulated by that law. Most Jews working in private firms were also dismissed. On May 10, the central event in the public campaign of burning books deemed "un-German" took place near Berlin University, with Goebbels delivering the main speech.

Municipal authorities also cancelled subsidies to Jewish institutions and demanded all contractors to be of "Aryan" origin. Until the end of 1934, the authorities issued fifty-five anti-Jewish decrees and regulations, which were not based on any official Nazi legislation. To those one should add anti-Jewish ordinances issued by other local bodies such as the police, courts, and the chamber of commerce.

In addition to formal steps, Jews were also subjected to violence. In the first months after the Nazi takeover the SA engaged in raids on the Scheunenviertel area, which contained a concentration of East European Jews (and was a target of antisemitic violence already during the Weimar period). Jews working in public institutions were also targeted in those months. Many of the victims of the wave of excessive Nazi violence against left-wing activists were Jews. Heavy anti-Jewish actions took place in June/July 1935. Those riots, which became known as the *Kurfürstendamm-Krawall*, were widely covered in the international press.

The Nuremberg Laws, promulgated in September 1935, officially stripped the Jews of equal citizenship rights, and forbade marriage or sexual intercourse between Jews and "Aryans." In addition, it severely limited the use of "Aryan" domestic help in Jewish households—a measure that had a profound effect on many Jewish middle-class families, especially those who were older and thus relied heavily on such help.

Following the Nuremberg laws, the Berlin municipality intensified its anti-Jewish policies. Berlin streets bearing names relating to Jews were renamed, municipal building societies began terminating rental contracts with Jewish tenants, and lease of commercial space to Jewish firms was limited.

In the beginning of 1936, a police report noted that, as a result of propaganda work, "the exclusion of the Jews from economic life was making ever greater headway." By the end of 1937, the number of "Jewish businesses" in Berlin had decreased by 30 percent.

Those developments signaled a large increase in the number of Jews unable to support themselves and having to rely on welfare support. But in 1936/1937 Berlin municipal welfare offices began cutting benefit payments to needy Jews.

The 1935 Nuremberg Laws signaled the active intervention of the authorities to enforce social separation of the Jews from the surrounding society. The Berlin authorities followed suit. In 1936, Jews were banned from most swimming pools and bathing facilities (except for Lake Wannsee, on account of the numerous foreign visitors there). In 1937, some district authorities began separating park benches for Jews and non-Jews.

By the end of 1937, the Jewish population of Berlin had decreased to 140,000, and by September 1939, to 82,788—about half of what it had been in 1933.

Violence against Jews continued. On May 30, 1937, a *Razzia* (raid) against Jews took place in the streets of Berlin, for all passersby to see. In May and June 1938, new anti-Jewish boycott campaigns were organized. Stores owned by Jews were vandalized or smeared with slogans and graffiti. In May of that year, during the national "action against asocials"—mainly people with previous convictions for minor offences—824 Jews were arrested in Berlin and sent to the Sachsenhausen concentration camp. Toward the end of June violent actions took place against Jewish businesses, in which windows and facades were shattered.

In the summer of 1938, the Berlin municipality acted to increase the social separation of Jews by having public benches in all districts with a high concentration of Jewish residents painted in pale yellow and marked "For Jews only."

In October 1938, Jews who held Polish citizenship were apprehended in their homes and forcibly deported to the Polish border. As the Poles refused to let them in, many remained stuck in no man's land, without any basic facilities, until international intervention led to an arrangement by which some of the deported Jews were allowed into Poland and others returned to Germany.

This was a prelude to the horrors of the November Pogrom, commonly referred to as *Kristallnacht* (November 9–10, 1938), a centrally organized wave of unprecedented violence against Jewish institutions, businesses, private homes, and individuals that took place across the Reich.

In Berlin, nine of the twelve official synagogues of the community were burnt down, and most of the other synagogues were demolished and looted. Jewish schools, the offices of Jewish public institutions, and Jewish medical clinics were also attacked. Jewish stores were ransacked, the merchandise thrown into the street, the shop windows smashed. In the eastern neighborhoods in Berlin, SA men forced their way into apartments, demolished furniture, slit open mattresses, and hurled household effects and pieces of furniture out of the windows. Dozens of Jews were murdered, 12,000 Jewish men were arrested in Berlin alone, and many of them sent to concentration camps.

The plight of the Jews sent to the camps in connection with the pogrom is a little-known episode in the history of the Holocaust, overshadowed by later events. They were subjected to the relentless sadism of the camp staff, living in overcrowded dwellings with minimal food and terrible sanitary conditions, performing backbreaking slave labor with no consideration for their medical condition or advanced age. In addition, they were tortured and punished without the slightest mercy. Many Jews did not survive, and many of those who returned were shattered, physically and mentally. Charlotte Holzer, as a nurse in the Jewish hospital, was a witness to their condition.

In the wake of *Kristallnacht,* the Nazi leadership decided on a uniform policy of persecution. That included a ban on Jews working in almost all professions and on conducting business, the exclusion of Jews from public schools, and restricting their social welfare. Of more than 6,000 retail shops owned by Jews in Berlin in 1933, 3,105 remained in April 1938. By the year's end, 2,570 of those had been liquidated and the other 535 sold to "Aryan" buyers.

Berlin moved ahead of the Reich in its persecution measures. Jewish children had to leave public schools a few days before that step was decided upon by the government. Welfare recipients had their access to consultation limited to special days and received only what was deemed "necessary maintenance." Jews were banned from attending public events and cultural and sport facilities. Religious services were permitted in four synagogues only (the number was increased to nine in early 1939). Dozens of Jewish institutions, including rabbinical seminaries and the Jewish community library and museum, were closed down. Their property, including valuable manuscripts, documents, and books, was looted or burned.

Toward the end of 1938 the town began employing welfare recipients as unpaid compulsory workers. Garbage collection was deemed especially suitable for Jews. In 1939 the municipal authorities began limiting the residence rights of Jews and banned several districts from receiving new Jewish tenants. These two developments began processes that were to have a profound influence on the lives of the Jews in the coming few years. In April and May 1940 all Jewish men aged eighteen to fifty-five and women aged eighteen to fifty were drafted into forced labor duties (for which they received hardly any pay). From January 1941, Jews were evicted from their homes and concentrated in "Jew houses" under extremely crowded conditions.

After the beginning of the Second World War in 1939, the Nazis confiscated all radios belonging to Jews, and forbade them to leave their homes after 8 P.M. By that time, almost a quarter of Berlin Jews were in need of economic assistance. Almost all the rest lived off their savings and pensions. Their food rations were restricted, as well as their possibilities to purchase food. In July 1940, they were allowed to shop for food only in a limited number of stores, and only for one hour in a day, in the late afternoon. Given the increasing food shortage later in the war, this meant that they could find only what was left over in the stores, if anything. They were also forbidden to use private telephones and had to cancel their phone numbers.

In July 1941, the Berlin labor office controlled 26,000–28,000 Jewish forced laborers (45 percent of them females) in 230 firms. The community arranged special prayer services for them on Shabbat (Sabbath) afternoons, as they could not attend the regular Shabbat morning prayers because of their work.

On September 19, 1941, all German Jews were required to wear a yellow badge, so everyone in the street could tell they were Jews. Of the many measures promulgated against them, this step was felt by many to be extremely harsh.

At that time, the Gestapo did not allow Jews to relocate to Berlin or to leave the town. On October 23, 1941, further emigration of Jews from Germany was prohibited. These were preparatory steps for the final act of persecution: the deportation of Jews to the East.

In early 1941, some 74,500 Jews were still living in Berlin; by the end of the year, some 1,400 had managed to emigrate. On the Day of Atonement 1941, top officials of the community were called out of the synagogue and summoned to Gestapo headquarters. They were told that a substantial number of Jews were to be evacuated from Berlin. The community was ordered to submit lists of the city's Jews, including their addresses, and to turn the Levetzow Street synagogue into a transit camp for evacuees. Later, other such assembly points, pending evacuation, were set up in community institutions.

The deportees were selected by the Gestapo and were ordered to fill forms about their private assets. The day before deportation they were given a few hours to pack their necessities, to a maximum weight of 50 kilograms. Then they were brought to the nearest police station, and from there to the assembly point in the synagogue.

The first transport left Berlin on October 18, 1941, taking some 1,000 Jews to the Łódź ghetto, and from there to their deaths. Until January 1942, 10,000 Jews from Berlin were deported in nine transports, to Riga, Minsk, Kovno, and Łódź. The first transport for the Theresienstadt ghetto left Berlin on June 6, 1942; the first direct deportation to Auschwitz from Berlin took place on July 11 of that year.

Hundreds of Jews committed suicide in order to avoid deportation. A special section was formed in the Jewish hospital to handle the suicide cases. Some Jews tried to go into hiding, whereupon the Gestapo activated a network of Jewish informants that succeeded in locating many Jews who had gone underground.

In early 1942, the Berlin municipality halted pensions and related benefits to Jews. The Interior Ministry tried to oppose these measures but failed.

In early September 1942, the larger deportations were concluded in most of Germany. There were no longer any sizeable regional concentrations of Jewish residents, apart from in Berlin, where 46,658 Jews still lived. They were spared because many of them worked as forced laborers in the armament industry.

In October 1942, Alois Brunner, who acquired the reputation of being a ruthless deportation expert, was brought from Vienna to Berlin for a few months (he left in January 1943) with some Viennese SS men to accelerate the pace of the deportations. Brunner was notorious for his brutality and cruelty, copying the Viennese methods of deportation to Berlin. The previous method of giving prior written notice to the deportees was scrapped. Instead, his men employed surprise raids. Specific house blocks were cordoned off, and *Greifkommandos* (seizure detachments) entered Jewish apartments, arrested the tenants, and sent them to the assembly camps from where they were deported. Brunner's men also raided places of Jewish assembly such as synagogues during prayer time or funerals. Another method was to drive through the streets and arrest anyone wearing a Jewish star. This had a fatal effect on the remnants of Jewish life in Berlin, as Jews were afraid to attend Jewish events or even leave their homes.

In February 1943, the SS managed to get authorization to also deport the Jews employed in the armaments industry, who were protected until then. They planned to arrest and deport them in a large operation that would be kept secret. The raid began on February 27–28, 1943, and became known as the *Fabrikaktion* (Factory Operation). It covered all the territory of the Reich, but was mainly centered in Berlin, where most of the remaining Jews lived. There, the action lasted a week. The Gestapo raided the factories and arrested the Jewish forced laborers, as well as arresting Jews at home, in offices, or out on the street. Out of fear of being deported, dozens committed suicide. As a result of the many warnings that circulated before the action, some 4,000 Jews managed to flee and hide in Berlin.

Up to March 6, 1943, some 7,000 Jews were deported from Berlin. Most were immediately murdered in Auschwitz. Some 1,000–2,000 Jews were deported later that month, mostly to Theresienstadt.

After the "Factory Action" and the March deportations, only 18,515 Jews were registered as residents of Berlin (not including those in hiding). In the following months, the remaining workers of the Jewish organizations and the Berlin community were deported. On June 10, 1943, the Gestapo terminated the Reichsvereinigung der Juden in Deutschland (Reich Association of Jews in Germany)—the representative organization of the German Jews since 1938—as well as the Berlin Jewish community and confiscated all their property. The last large transport left Berlin on June 28, 1943, with some 300 victims, most of them former employees of the Jewish organizations. Its destination was Auschwitz. The capital of the Third Reich was declared *Judenrein* ("cleansed of Jews").

But Jews did remain in Berlin, mainly those of mixed origin (*Mischlinge*) or those married to "Aryans." The Gestapo also kept some informers, whose task was to try and find Jews who had gone into hiding. Those hiding Jews (called submarines—*U-Boote*—in the jargon of the period) who were seized were deported in small-scale transports until the end of the war.

The last Jews in Berlin were organized in an organization called the Rest-Reichsvereinigung (the "rump" association). Its center was in the last remaining Jewish institution: the Jewish hospital, directed by

Dr. Walter Lustig, which was in operation up to the end of the war.[5] It served also as an assembly camp for Jews who were to be deported. From the spring of 1944, it was also used as a camp for Jewish forced laborers in the service of the SS. Charlotte, who served as a nurse in the hospital at this stage, provides a vivid picture of some of the characters, mainly informers, who were present there.

In July 1944, there were some 5,978 Jews officially residing in Berlin. On January 15, 1945, the Nazi regime started to also deport the "able-bodied" Jews living in mixed marriages. At that stage, the chaos in the town and the lack of transportation facilities enabled many Jews to avoid the deportation. Still, some were deported, and in February 1945, the number of registered Jews was down to 4,814. The last transport left Berlin on March 27, 1945, with forty-two people sent to Theresienstadt. In total, more than 50,000 Jews were deported from Berlin. Some 1,900 returned from the camps. About 1,400 survived in hiding.

The Nazi Persecution of Communists and the Baum Group

When they came to power on January 30, 1933, the Nazis first turned on their political rivals, first and foremost the Communists. After all, in the years leading up to 1933, those two movements had been fighting one another at the cost of dozens of lives. In this early stage of the Third Reich, the Communists were persecuted more severely than the Jews. They were fired from their jobs (Charlotte's memoir mentions the Nazi order to the Jewish hospital to fire all its Communist employees), many were murdered, and many others, including the whole leadership echelon of the movement, were sent to the developing network of concentration camps.

---

5   See Rivka Elkin, *Das Jüdische Krankenhaus in Berlin zwischen 1938 und 1945* (Berlin: Ed. Hentrich, 1993); idem, "The Survival of the Jewish Hospital in Berlin 1938–1945," *Yearbook of the Leo Baeck Institute* 38 (1993), pp. 157–192; Daniel B. Silver, *Refuge in Hell: How Berlin's Jewish Hospital Outlasted the Nazis* (Boston: Houghton Mifflin, 2003).

We have already referred to the horrendous conditions in the concentration camps in the context of the *Kristallnacht* pogrom. However, unlike the Jews, German Communists did not have to endure these conditions: they had the choice of giving up their ideology and serving the Nazi regime, mainly as informers.

Those informers proved very useful to the Gestapo. Undeterred by the persecution and arrests of their leaders, the Communists in Nazi Germany kept creating new underground networks of resistance. The informers, former Communists who were members of the movement and knew personally those involved in it, were able to infiltrate the underground networks, crushing them time and again, until the whole backbone of the organized Communist movement was eliminated.

But that did not stop Communists from trying to organize and act together, and Communist activities never ceased. One form in which they continued was in small groups of activists, who knew each other personally, usually centered around a leader, whose name the group bore. One such group was the "Baum Gruppe," led by Herbert Baum. Other Berlin groups, which were loosely connected with the Baum Group through personal acquaintances, are also mentioned in Charlotte's memoir.

Charlotte joined this group when it was already organized and active. Almost all of its members were Jews,[6] and many of them knew one another from childhood. Some had been members of Socialist-Zionist organizations, such as Hashomer Hatzair and Habonim—a fact that Charlotte does not mention in her description of the group members (she only mentions that Baum was sent by the Communist youth movement to the Jewish youth movement to recruit members

---

6   For modern studies on that group (apart from the sources mentioned in the afterword to this book) see Eric Brothers, *Berlin Ghetto. Herbert Baum and the Anti-Fascist Resistance* (Stroud/Gloucestershire: Spellmount, 2012); Regina Scheer, *Im Schatten der Sterne. Eine jüdische Widerstandgruppe* (Berlin: Aufbau Verlag, 2004); Wolfgang Wippermann, *Die Berliner Gruppe Baum und der jüdische Widerstand* (Berlin: Lichtwitz-Funk, 1981); and Rainer L. Hoffmann, "Jüdische Widerstandsgruppen in Deutschland—Die Herbert-Baum-Gruppe," in Michael Berger and Gideon Römer-Hillebrecht, eds., *Jüdische Soldaten - Jüdischer Widerstand in Deutschland* (Paderborn: Ferdinand Schöningh, 2012), pp. 241–258.

there). Regarding former youth movement affiliation, she mentions only the Kommunistische Jugendverband Deutschlands (KJVD— German Communist Youth Organization). As Jews, the group members were expelled from their workplaces, and were drafted into slave labor. Most of them performed this labor at the Siemens electric motors plant.

Most group members were in their early twenties. Charlotte, who was thirty at the time, was the oldest—and we know from other sources that the other members referred to her as "Grandma." The group members, as described in this book, engaged mainly in social activities, including taking trips out of town and singing together. They defied restrictions imposed upon Jews, such as using public transportation. Charlotte met Richard Holzer in that group. They became a couple and married after the war.

But the group also engaged in underground Communist activities. As mentioned in the book, they had a printing machine, and they published underground papers and leaflets, and put-up anti-Nazi posters on the street. When the deportations to the East began, the group managed to arrange false papers for some Jews and helped them avoid deportation. They also managed to acquire forged documents for themselves which identified them as French slave laborers.

As loyal Communists, the Baum Group members were enraged by the anti-Soviet exhibition "The Soviet Paradise," which opened in Berlin in May 1942. They attempted to firebomb it, were exposed, and arrested, and most of them were executed. Charlotte opposed the sabotage act in the first place, warning that because of the group members' Jewishness, their act would not be portrayed as a protest of the working class (as they intended) but as another Jewish crime against Germany. And this was precisely what happened, with the Jews of Berlin paying a heavy price. The Nazis executed 250 Jews in revenge, and their relatives were deported to Theresienstadt. Another 250 Jews were arrested and sent to the Sachsenhausen concentration camp. There some were executed, and the others deported to Auschwitz-Birkenau. For the Nazis, the members of the Baum Group were first and foremost Jews.

FOREWORD

by Klaus Pistor

C harlotte Holzer, or Lotte as she was known to us and other friends, was a Jewish anti-fascist in Berlin who survived the Nazi Holocaust. More than thirty years after her death, her memory is still alive. Lotte herself gave a detailed narration of her moving story to the journalist Dieter Heimlich. For the span of an entire year in 1966–1967, Heimlich interviewed her at greater intervals. The material he thus gathered he intended to craft into a book. Now Charlotte Holzer's memoirs are finally published for an English audience.

Lotte's narration of her story here comprises a period ending in the summer of 1945, at a juncture when she was caring for her terminally ill first husband in the Berlin Jewish Hospital and had been reunited with her twelve-year-old daughter, Eva. Challenges then arose with which she had to grapple in the second half of her life. She spoke about it in the interviews, too, but since it is not documented in this edition of her memoirs it will be described in the following from the perspective of a neighbor who had the privilege to become her friend.

Charlotte Paech, as she then was known, began a pre-med course in the autumn of 1945, and in the spring of 1946, entered into medical studies at the University of Berlin (today Humboldt University), which, unfortunately, she soon had to discontinue due to poor health. In addition, she was eager to investigate the fate of her murdered comrades and of those companions in suffering who were still alive, and to inquire into the work of the anatomist Hermann Stieve on staff at the Charité teaching hospital, who during the Nazi period had performed autopsies on many of her friends executed by the National Socialist regime.[1]

Her greatest concern was to care for her daughter Eva until the latter was placed in a Jewish children's home. In the spring of 1947, Eva emigrated from there to Mandatory Palestine, a fact which Lotte initially had difficulty dealing with. While talking with a neighbor in the house in Wedding where she lived, she learned this woman had made it possible for the Gestapo to eavesdrop on her Jewish comrades. The experiences she had planted grave doubts in Lotte's mind about whether the Germans had overcome the national socialist past.

Lotte endeavored to renew contact with Richard Holzer, who had become her close friend after they had met in the resistance group around Herbert Baum. Richard had fled to Hungary in 1942. Her efforts bore fruit in an unexpected way. Richard had been drafted as a Hungarian auxiliary soldier, defected, and was interned by the Soviets, who sent him, in poor health, back to Budapest. From there, he arranged his transfer to a camp for Displaced Persons in Ulm, which Lotte traveled to in the autumn of 1946. In a moving letter, she had impatiently asked him when he would finally be returning and whether he still felt he could love her. But in the letter, she also impressively described her current pessimism regarding political developments in Germany, and

---

1   Hermann Stieve (1886–1952), taught medicine at the University of Berlin and served as director of the Berlin Institute of Anatomy at the Charité hospital. He made important contributions to research on male and female genital organs. His merits later became contested since he also used the bodies of young women who had suffered the death penalty inflicted by Nazi courts. Though an ardent German nationalist, he did not join the Nazi Party and refused to make use of the bodies of the executed resistance fighters who had been involved in the attempt to kill Hitler on July 20, 1944. After the war, Dr. Stieve continued to teach at the University of Berlin.

her doubts concerning its socialist future, for which they both had fought and endured much suffering. She was living then in the divided city of Berlin, with all its staggering material hardships and diverging paths. Then came her marriage to Richard, unspectacular, followed by their return to West Berlin, and relocation into a former Nazi apartment in the Berlin district of Nikolassee.

In early June 1947, Lotte gave premature birth to a son, named Gerd, who passed away after but a few hours; there were further miscarriages, followed by prolonged illness. In her eyes, her close-knit contact with comrades constituted her nexus with the SED, but she had no formal membership card of her own—unlike Richard who, coming from the Hungarian Communist Party, was immediately accepted into the SED's ranks.

When he was no longer called upon to provide constant care for his ailing spouse, he obtained a position in a foreign trade organization, where he soon assumed a leading administrative role. Connected with that post was the Holzers' move to East Berlin, where they finally ended up in 1950. They settled into an apartment in Pankow-Niederschönhausen, where they remained until their deaths. Lotte was accepted into a "party group of the prominent," as she ironically phrased it, because that circle also included several members closely allied to the GDR government and the SED party apparatus.

Richard was politically active. He had been centrally involved in erecting the gravestone in the Jewish cemetery in Berlin-Weißensee in honor of Herbert Baum and his fellow combatants, executed in 1942/1943. The memorial site was dedicated in 1951; on the Day of Remembrance for the Victims of Fascism, commemorated annually in mid-September in the GDR, it became the place of gathering of the like-minded.

While the start of the Cold War in the 1950s threatened the world, socialist countries entered a phase of an increasing cult of personality and, in the view of the SED, of an "intensifying class struggle." In this atmosphere of intolerance, the regular internal SED "security check" on all party members in 1951–1952 began to pose a threat for the Holzers, arising from Lotte's hesitation to formally join the SED. She was also instructed to resign her membership in the Jewish community, which was deemed incompatible with membership in the party. She refused to comply. By the start of 1952, Richard, under a pretext, had been suspended from his post as director. In particular, he was reproached for having stayed on so long in Ulm in the West, but he was also berated because his stepdaughter had emigrated to Mandatory Palestine, where, it was alleged, she was totally "Western in her outlook." He was likewise criticized for his supposed close personal ties to "enemies of the party."

However, the Holzers were soon rehabilitated. Richard was able once more to work in foreign trade, even if in a lower, less prestigious position. In 1953, Lotte was medically classified as disabled. This notwithstanding, she remained active in the district of Pankow. She worked in maternity care, attended a course in 1959 to facilitate pain-free childbirth and took on voluntary tasks in the healthcare system. In addition, she was active for many years in voluntary jury service at the Pankow district court.

She also found time to look after her husband. Richard, a perfectionist who totally identified with his work, was so absorbed in it that, as Lotte opined, he had to be given requisite "guidance" at home. To that end, she would often jot down rhymes on slips of paper to remind him to eat, sleep, tend to the garden and flowers, and to take care of his health. She would then place these slips on the table for his attention when she was occupied with matters elsewhere. From 1957 on, Lotte was allowed to pay visits to her daughter Chava (Eva) in Israel; she arranged such a trip every three years or so, staying for a period of up to three months. Both mother and daughter were quickly able to overcome initial tensions; Chava had married and now had two sons. In Israel, Lotte visited friends, traveled around the country, and sent reports back home.

Richard completed a one-year course in foreign trade at the Higher Party School in 1959–1960. Subsequently, he was appointed deputy commercial attaché in the GDR Trade Mission in Stockholm in 1960, where Lotte joined him some time later. However, prior to that she had vehemently refused to accept a ban on having links to persons in non-socialist countries, even though both she and Richard were obliged to sign a written declaration that they would. Added to this were difficulties with the style of work in the trade mission and diplomatic etiquette. As a result of these issues, Lotte and Richard Holzer's stay abroad ended abruptly after less than a year in Sweden.

Richard continued to be employed in foreign-trade companies until 1966, when he was obliged to accept early retirement. He utilized the free time he acquired upon retirement to tend their beautiful garden at the house in Niederschönhausen, at times under the careful guidance of his wife. Above all he devoted himself to the treasures in their library.

Despite their disappointment with SED party politics, the Holzers nonetheless provided a room in their home to State Security where Stasi personnel could clandestinely meet to discuss classified matters. And they expressly refused to accept any payment for this service. Lotte and Richard, like other survivors, often traveled around the GDR to share their anti-fascist and communist outlook, giving lively presentations to the more than twenty groups that bore the names of members of the Herbert Baum Group, and to classes at school. In her preparations for these discussions, Lotte drew on chapters from her life to illustrate her presentations. Consequently, material was readily to hand for her "memoirs," which she then narrated.

Lotte first met her interviewer Dieter Heimlich in early 1964, when she accompanied the "Buchenwald child" Stefan Jerzy Zweig, together with his "camp fathers," on his visit to the former concentration camp on Ettersberg hill near Weimar.

I had the opportunity to meet the Holzers and other survivors of the Jewish resistance group around Herbert Baum at a memorial ceremony in Neubrandenburg in 1967. Some two years later, our family friendship with Lotte and Richard commenced after we moved near to them in Berlin-Pankow. Then in their late fifties, both had retained a youthful spirit, although their health was deteriorating. We visited them frequently, went for walks together in the public park near the Wall, or traveled together to the countryside. Books were the dominant chord in their apartment, and bright floral arrangements extended harmoniously into their well-kept garden. They enjoyed telling us about their experiences, some of which were difficult to accommodate within the armature of our firmly established political-ideological worldview at the time. The conversations with Richard, who had a great love for history, especially of the Middle Ages, were particularly interesting. However, his convictions were quite rigid and doctrinaire. They also prevented him from acknowledging the less ideal aspects of reality in the GDR, which his wife would then emend and correct.

Lotte—slender, warmhearted and a bit tomboyish in manner— was the vibrant heart of the family as well the vital center of attraction for the many friends and comrades who frequented the Holzer household. She was outgoing, quick to connect with others, and polite and friendly; by contrast, Richard initially was generally rather reserved. Their life experience encouraged us, when we were in personally difficult situations, to ask for advice which we generally followed. They also showed active concern for the needy members of the Jewish community in East Berlin. On the national holiday in October 1974, Charlotte Holzer was awarded the Patriotic Order of Merit of the GDR for her untiring social and political engagement.

Richard's final days came quickly. He passed away in February 1975 in Berlin. His funeral in the Jewish cemetery brought together many friends and comrades. Heinz Kamnitzer delivered the graveside eulogy titled "Requiem for a Man Indomitable" and bade farewell to the deceased comrade, as did we all, with a raised fist. Lotte had the epitaph engraved on his gravestone: "Born Jewish / became a Communist / that's what he lived for." The gravestone for infant Gerd Holzer, which we selected together with Lotte, later also found its place there.

Lotte survived her husband by more than five years. She continued to be active politically and in educational endeavors and provided decisive impetus for youth brigades of the Free German Youth and student groups to take on the maintenance of Jewish cemeteries. The latter included in particular a significant contingent of foreign students for whom a camp was organized in West Berlin by the Dutch Ecumenical Community for two weeks in the summer. This tradition continued for many years in annual Lotte-Holzer-camps under the auspices of Hendrik-Kraemer-House in Berlin-Kreuzberg.

To the extent her impaired health permitted, Lotte maintained close ties to her friends and to us. She felt a special bond to her daughter Chava and her family in Israel. Until the end of her life, she would assure herself of her daughter's well-being in long telephone calls, and she provided for Chava and family in her final will. However, Chava's family was only able to gain access to Lotte's estate in 1990, after the political turn in the GDR.

Lotte Holzer passed away aged seventy on September 29, 1980, in Berlin. She was laid to rest with a large number of friends and comrades in attendance, including her daughter and son-in-law. In his graveside eulogy, Franz Krahl honored her singular and exceptional life. He noted that as a German communist, Lotte had "never faltered in her worldview. But she had also always acknowledged being a Jew, an identity into which she was born, and her proud, angry protest simultaneously against fascism, antisemitism […] and racial hatred, against hate speech and genocide. […] Our Lotti, our mother and sister, our dear friend and steadfast comrade […] has returned home in this century-old cemetery, to lie in rest at the side of her unforgotten Richard, at the foot of the memorial stone for Herbert Baum and the comrades and companions of her youth, from which she will always be for us both a memory and admonition."

We were appointed by Lotte to administer her estate and entrusted by her daughter with the liquidation of her household belongings. From Lotte's papers we passed on almost all political documents to other survivors of the Herbert Baum Group and to Margot Pikarski, who had published a book about the group.[2] These materials are today partially housed in the Rosa Luxemburg Foundation in Berlin. Yet the pressing question also arose as to the location of Lotte's "memoirs." Only some years later was their history and whereabouts fully clarified.

Chava wanted to have her mother's "memoirs" published. Consequently, Lotte's typescript was secretly spirited across the border to West Berlin in early October 1980. Chava arranged to have it copied there, taking the original back with her to Israel. A photocopy was sent to the Röderberg-Verlag, the publishing house of the VNN (Association of Persecutees of the Nazi Regime) in Frankfurt/Main, which in turn contacted the SED. Research was initiated in the Central

---

2   Margot Pikarski, *Jugend im Berliner Widerstand–Herbert Baum und Kampf-gefährten* (Berlin: Militärverlag der DDR, 1984).

Party Archive during which it was established that Dieter Heimlich had been her interviewer. Heimlich was subsequently requested to hand over his material on this project. He responded in 1983 with a letter stating that his original typescript had not undergone any further editing. In addition, it also became clear from his letter that the fourteen pages missing from the middle of the "memoirs" were lost. With Chava's permission, the copy of the "memoirs" that remained in Berlin was used as the basis for the present publication.

As editors we wished to retain Lotte's original manner of narration. For that reason, we chose largely to disregard her subsequent handwritten alterations to the typescript.

We would like to express our heartfelt gratitude to Lotte's daughter Chava Kürer in Israel for her patient promotion of this project, for useful tips and supplementary commentary, for private photographs and photos, and for permission to publish these "memoirs."

We also wish to thank Gad Freudenthal for his mediation, and finally we are very grateful to the Yad Vashem Holocaust Remembrance Center for its willingness to undertake the publication of this book.

THE MEMOIRS

The following is a translation of the German transcript of an unpublished interview with Charlotte Holzer by journalist Dieter Heimlich, conducted in several sessions during 1966 and 1967. The original transcript also includes a section about Holzer's postwar life in the GDR. Since this publication focuses on the resistance against the Nazi regime, this part of the interview is not included here.

Family, School, and Training as an Infant Nurse

I was an unwanted child. But back then it was still common to carry a pregnancy to term. Probably there weren't as many abortions then as there are nowadays. But first of all, I think I should say something about my mom's background.

Mom was born into a petty-bourgeois family, with one artistic branch, Alfred Döblin.[1] Petty bourgeois as well from the side of my mom's mother, though the family was already pretty well-to-do. They could afford a private tutor for my none-too-bright grandmother, Therese. That tutor was Magnus, who became my granddad. When he met Therese for the first time, she was twelve years old. And he was her companion and guide throughout her life, until Grandma reached the age of eighty-two. It was love with a capital L, and they were always squabbling. Among her five living siblings, my mom was in the middle. Her father came from a poor home, his dad was a plumber. But Magnus was smart; he had really wanted to study at university. He lived in a basement somewhere in the Posen area. His future parents-in-law helped him obtain an apprenticeship with Salomon & Co., a large leather tannery on Lohmühlenstrasse in Berlin, and he remained with the company. That's where he started to work, and where he ended his long hardworking life, as authorized representative. So he worked his way up the ladder quite a bit.

Mom had attended junior high and normally wouldn't have been allowed to take up a profession. Nonetheless, she began to learn the millinery trade. But when they told her to sweep up the shop, Granddad pulled his daughter out of the place. Such work was not in keeping with her social status. When my mum turned nineteen, a very pretty woman and also intelligent, Granddad decided to marry her off. It was supposed to be a love match. A first meeting was arranged and the two became better acquainted in Treptow Park. My dad[2] stemmed from a family that

1   For more on the writer Alfred Döblin and the family connection, see the biographical entries in the appendix.
2   The name of Charlotte's father was Max Abraham. Notably it is never mentioned in the memoirs.

made shoe uppers and my mom's family made soles. So the match was perfect. Dad was fourteen years older than Mom, the second youngest of twelve children. There was no spare money left over for any kind of further training for him. Therefore, he became a sales representative. And he remained one all his life. He sold leather goods. He seemingly did have the potential to study and maybe of becoming an academic. Dad was never a good businessman. So there were good times at home, and bad times. He was a would-be coffeehouse regular. During the Nazi era he starved to death, in Argentina.

Margarethe (née Döblin) and Max Abraham as a young couple

My parents married, and my grandparents, as was the custom, provided a dowry and an apartment on Stuttgart Square. And right on time, after ten months, my sister arrived. Because money was running short, my parents decided to take a little break from having children. Instead, fourteen months later, I arrived. My mother was a modest woman and still quite naive. Later, talking to me, she claimed that never before had she seen a man naked. That notwithstanding, I was duly conceived. Of course, she was totally different many years later, and I'll say something about that: I was the one who made my mom into a nurse.

When my sister was about to be born, once the contractions started, my dad began walking Mom around the table, again and again, reciting the lines, "My *boy* in my arms, my hand on the plow … and that's enough of happiness." That's by the poet Liliencron.[3] Well, when it came to my birth, he just went off to the local café, didn't want to have anything to do with it. First my grandparents came in and said, "Oh what, another little Puschlotte?"[4] Then my other grandfather came and also observed, "Oh, what's this? A tiny Puschlotte?" After which my dad arrived, said the same and added, "OK, well then, we should name her Lotte."

Margarethe Abraham with her daughters, Charlotte and Rose Augusta, 1910.

3   A slightly misquoted part of Liliencron's poem Cincinnatus. In the original, it reads *"Meinen Jungen im Arm, in der Faust den Pflug, und ein fröhlich Herz, und das ist genug"* ("On my arm, my young boy, in my fist the plow, and a happy heart, and that's enough").

4   Translator's note: Puschlotte has some slang meaning, akin to "little baby doll."

My parents were Jewish on one side, but thoroughly petty bourgeois on the other, enamored of the middle class and loyal to the emperor. My sister's name was Rose Augusta. After the Empress.[5] And in my case, "Well, she should be named after Queen Charlotte."[6] Until I was three, we lived on Sybelstrasse, after that on Roscherstrasse. Quiet streets near the Kudamm.[7] Gradually the money from the dowry dried up and so we moved to Köpenicker Strasse in Berlin's southeast. That's where I grew up. World War I came, then the tuberculosis epidemic. And it had a significant formative impact on my life. I attended the Wagnersche Höhere Töchterschule (The Wagner Secondary School for Girls, named after Margarete Wagner), a girls' school at the corner of Köpenicker and Neanderstrasse. That was quite a long way for me to go to school, about half an hour. My sister and I always walked there. And what is barely conceivable nowadays, most children then went barefoot. After all, Berlin, and this corner of town too, was a huge metropolis. And the side streets—Wrangelstrasse, Zeughofstrasse— were workers' streets. There wasn't any unemployment at all, but the wages were terribly low. People looked very different from now. The old women wore shawls, which maybe they'd already received as a wedding gift back when they'd married, right down to the end of their lives. Yes, sometimes the shawls were even bequeathed and passed on to the next generation. That was not the popular fashion of the day, but an outcome of grinding poverty.

Ours was a five-story building, complete with mezzanine. We lived up on the fifth floor and had a five-room apartment. There was a long hall which connected the kitchen and the bathroom. Next to the kitchen was a room for the maid. Two rooms led off from the hall; these were sublet in order to gain funds for the monthly rent. Later on, they were used as a workshop. Then there was a large Berlin-style

---

5   A reference to Augusta von Sachsen-Weimar-Eisenach. For more on her, see the biographical entries in the appendix.

6   This refers to Sophie Charlotte zu Mecklenburg-Strelitz, the German-born wife of King George III of Great Britain and Ireland. For more on her, see the biographical notes in the appendix.

7   The Kurfürstendamm, colloquially known as the Kudamm, is the most famous street in central Berlin, comparable to the Champs-Élysées in Paris.

room,[8] very dark. That was our living room, and further on were the children's room and bedroom. We lived there for about twelve years. By the way, there were always bed bugs in the apartment. Mom could do whatever she wanted, it didn't help, the bed bugs belonged to the apartment and came with the rent. You couldn't get rid of them. It wasn't just in our apartment, and it wasn't because we didn't keep the place clean.

I grew up together with Trudchen Zedel, the daughter of the concierge, who lived down in the basement. She was probably born out of wedlock and had been passed on by her mom to her grandparents. Whenever my mother would start to scold me for something or other I used to say, "I'm going down to the Zedels! I'm moving!" I was happy there. Their apartment down in the basement had small peepholes in the front door because the building had once been the house of a wealthy gentleman. Right next to the entrance to the basement room there were two little night-potties, one for Trudchen, one for me. I was very much at home there. I can still recall that the water faucet was so high up, we couldn't even reach it. Then there was a very narrow courtyard area. It was just a bit brighter than the others because the fourth side next to the main courtyard was only closed off by a high stone wall. In the rear courtyard there was a small external wooden staircase. We used to play underneath it with our dolls. That was our little home. We took some blankets there and built a cave for ourselves just like all kids love to do. I think that's also a kind of atavistic thing.

Behind the rear building there was a wonderful beautiful big garden. It belonged to the Wölblings, our landlords. We children were not allowed to enter there. No, no you mustn't! We would crowd around peering in, but we had to play in the courtyard. We were also not allowed to play in the entrance hallway. And we could only get into the barracks yard to play if we teased the guard a bit and tried to persuade him. We kids managed to do that now and then. However, in order to do that, we had to go over to Zeughofstrasse, and Mom had forbidden us to do that. Actually, we kids hardly went out into the

---

8   A room that one had to pass through in order to get to the rear rooms of the apartment.

street to play. And my sister also didn't play with the Zedels; she was a little snobbish.

So we were hardly allowed to go out to play in the street, and Mom was right about that. Köpenicker Strasse was always quite busy. The streetcar went past there. Moreover, the street had lots of tall trees, so Mom couldn't look down and see us. In addition to that, we were simply not from among those barefoot children. And to boot, we were Jewish. But I only understood that once I started attending school. Not before that. The parents knew of course. I first became aware— probably through my parents—that there were a certain number of Jewish children in the class. That wasn't the result of negative statements by others, but due to our own positive perception, "Thank God! There are other lions in the class." Like the Schustermanns for example. We were four Jewish children. That was a lot. It was a kind of basis of support for us. And we were made aware of that by our parents.

In the first few years at school, I had very good teachers. And they, too, didn't let us feel that we were different. Our first teacher was called Fräulein Charice. I really loved her a lot. As a child I had many difficulties with discipline. I was very playful, and a little bit of a chatterbox. Once in the middle of the lesson I raised my hand and announced, "Fräulein Charice, it's my mommy's birthday, and I gave her a pot for wild chives!" I can remember: the war was going on. Some victory or other was celebrated once again. And like always on such an occasion, we were taken upstairs to assemble in the auditorium. There was a celebration. At some point I had to go out to the toilet. And I wasn't able to button up my pants by myself. I was wearing those long white pants, with some lace embroidery and buttons on the side. I mean, I just couldn't close the buttons. Miss Wittfeld, my second teacher, buttoned up my pants for me. I really liked her so so-o-o much for that. Because she helped me, I trusted her a lot. Teachers should take note what small deeds can earn a person the affection of children. She was teaching the higher grades as well. And just for *me*, she buttoned up my pants!

Already at that time we nailed up a "Hindenburg" wooden statue as a war monument. There were different colored nails for these

Charlotte Holzer as a young child, on her first school day, Easter 1916 (l.),
and with her sister Rose Augusta, 1918 (r.).

Nagelmänner,[9] at different prices according to donation: gold-colored,
silver, copper, and regular iron nails. Mom was not very enthusiastic
about Hindenburg and actually was probably already skeptical about
the war. We children were only allowed to hammer in iron nails. The
reason she gave us was: Hindenburg is an antisemite and Ludendorff

9 *Nagelmänner* (nail men) were a means of fundraising for members of the armed
forces in World War I. Those were wooden statues into which nails were driven,
either iron (black), or colored silver or gold, in exchange for donations of different
amounts. See Gerhard Schneider. "Zur Mobilisierung der 'Heimatfront': Das
Nageln sogenannter Kriegswahrzeichen im ersten Weltkrieg," *Zeitschrift für
Volkskunde*, 95 (1999), pp. 32–62; Dietlinde Munzel-Everling, *Kriegsnagelungen:
Wehrmann in Eisen, Nagel-Roland, Eisernes Kreuz*, Wiesbaden, August 2008
(http://www.munzel-everling.de/download/munzel_nagelfiguren.pdf).

even worse.[10] War is terrible, Daddy is away, and we don't have any money. I have to work very hard. What do you need to hammer in some nails for? But so that we didn't appear completely out of the ordinary, we were permitted to hammer in iron nails. Already back then it gave me a certain sense of pride. I can remember that.

Incidentally, my mom voted relatively early on after the war for the Social Democrats.[11] Daddy, by contrast, voted for the Democrats: I am a democrat, so I'm also voting democratically! That was totally separate from everyday politics. But when he returned from the war, he was in the Workers' and Soldiers' Council and had some kind of official function there. And he took us kids on over to Potsdamer Platz and talked to us memorably about Karl Liebknecht. He was burning with enthusiasm about the man. He respected and greatly admired him, especially on account of his speech against the war.[12] I think it is noteworthy that he was able to do that, that he was able to make that distinction. That he managed to entirely overcome his prejudices, to transcend himself. During the war, Mom had worked at the Office for Fat, a municipal office that helped distribute margarine. After all, there were ration cards for food. The fat was delivered in barrels. Up on top of each barrel was a round paper sheet. And the workers there were allowed in turn to scratch off the margarine stuck to it. Once a month. And then she would bring that margarine back home.

Mom found it very hard to deal with my TB. I came down with my first infection when I was four years old. It was osteomyelitis, a periostitis of the lower jaw. They operated on me. Today that's the spot where I always risk spontaneous fracture, for which the doctor placed a brace on my jaw. When I turned six, I got sick with glandular

10 For more on Paul von Hindenburg and Erich Ludendorff, see the biographical entries in the appendix.

11 German women only gained the right to vote after the *Novemberrevolution* of 1918.

12 This is a reference to Liebknecht's public speech against the war at Potsdamer Platz, which he gave on May 1, 1916, in the framework of a demonstration. The authorities reacted by charging him with high treason. He was subsequently sentenced to more than four years of prison. For more on Karl Liebknecht, see the biographical entries in the appendix.

TB. I have a scar from that under my chin. I was admitted at that time to the Friedrichshain Hospital. The children's ward was probably overcrowded. I was sent to a military hospital, to the surgery ward. I spent some nine months in bed there. That was marvelous for me. I learned a whole lot there! In particular there was a soldier there, a young guy. His name was Udo Leberlotz. He was in a wheelchair and always called me over to him. Udo taught me how to read the time on a clock. I'll never forget him for that.

I was in hospital for a long time. Maybe some of my love for medicine stems from that. It was a high barracks building. On the ground floor were the soldiers, and we were in the converted attic floor under the roof. We were a whole bunch of children, with our little legs suspended in a surgical boom, etc. Later when I was allowed to walk, I would move potties around and naughty stuff like that. As a six-year-old, I had a lot of fun doing that. At school I lost a whole grade as a result, a full year. My mom made sure I wouldn't develop an inferiority complex because of that. She said, "Look, you were sick for such a long time, but now you're already doing very well again." I had great gaps in my knowledge and abilities as a child. I learned how to read but found learning to write difficult. It was very hard for me, and even today I have terrible handwriting. And arithmetic, I didn't learn that at all. Even now I can only calculate if I have to do so for something concrete.

Later, when I became a nurse, I was able to calculate solutions just wonderfully. Things others never grasped correctly I understood immediately. But I never learned how to calculate in the abstract. After the war, my dad went to a lot of trouble trying to teach me multiplication tables, one to nine, but I never learned how to multiply from ten upward. I don't know whether maybe I'm missing some brain development there. My favorite subjects were German, history, and natural science. I was good at inventing stories and at putting my ideas into words. I was also able to sum up things nicely in writing.

But I have to go back and do some catching up in this story: until I reached the age of four, I grew up learning Bible history. My parents were relatively liberal in their thinking. Although they both still believed in the dear Lord, they no longer felt themselves bound by religion at all. Mom was a so-called "three-day Jewess." She went to the synagogue on three days during the year. Once for New Year and twice on the Day of Atonement.[13] She explained that saying, "That's really so beautiful. I'm finally able to rest, nobody disturbs me. And I can finally talk a bit with Aunt Selma. A chance for us to just chat." We kids were permitted to sit on the stairs in the gallery. On the Day of Atonement there was also something special for us as well: we had an uncle named Israel. You know, Jews go to pray dressed in a kind of shroud, so that before God each of them is equal. In fact, it's a prayer shawl with straps attached, which looks very beautiful. Now the Day of Atonement is a day of fasting, but Uncle Israel had a secret stash in his shawl. He reached down inside and then gave us kids some chocolate. Oh, was that lovely!

Dad was a sales rep and he had a lot of liberty in arranging his work time. In any case he didn't work all that much, because actually he spent his time in coffeehouses. Every day at noon he'd lie down on the sofa, seat his two little girls on his belly, and tell them fairy tales. And those were in fact the old biblical stories. He had a really extraordinary imagination and never was very precise in telling these tales. Rather he told them in a way that enchanted children. Added to that were the stories of Ali Baba and the Forty Thieves. Though in his case there were seven. And when he would start to feel tired, he'd announce with emphasis, "Time for a chocolate break!"

Originally, Dad was a sales representative for leather shoe uppers. When that was no longer possible, for a time he was a sales rep for chocolate. We sure ate a lot of sample packages, wow! That was really super!

---

13 *Dreitagejuden* (three-day Jews) was a common expression among German Jewry to denote the many Jews who had no connection with Judaism in their daily life but did go to the synagogue on the three most significant holidays of Judaism. Their numbers were so big that they did not only fill the synagogues, but the big communities had to hire extra halls to be used as temporary prayer halls in order to accommodate all those coming. The three days are actually Rosh Hashana, Yom Kippur, and Passover. The author's mistake in this regard shows how much she was cut off from Judaism.

Later we had a basement on the Engelufer—back then it hadn't been drained yet, there was still water.[14] Scraps of leather were stored there. We children had to sort them. So we weren't by any means without work. Later on, Mom made use of these scraps of leather, creating artistically crafted leather objects.

When the years of starvation came, 1917, 1918, we went to Treptow Park and collected acorns, to brew some coffee. We ripped bark off the trees and went to the bakers to beg for some bread. We, the middle-class kids! And Mom put us up to that, "Just go and say that your mom no longer has a bread ration card and that you're hungry!" I also remember eating a lot of rutabaga. And all that was after recovering from TB. After the war, even before the inflation, things were going somewhat better for us.

In the family I was known either as stupid Lottchen or good Lottchen. I was probably both good *and* stupid. Sometimes I also let my sister take advantage of me. That made no difference to me. And I liked to help Mom at home with the housework. For example, I really loved to peel or wash potatoes. Because while doing this I was always very good at what I called "denkeln" (thinkeling). That meant: thinking and also thinking up stories for myself.

Every noon I went out and got bread rolls for the family. The bakery was about ten houses away. On my way there I had to pass by the Herzsche Rubber Factory. Always sitting there leaning against the wall was an old woman, begging. Every day I'd ask Mom, "Mommy, please give me five extra pennies for a Chelsea bun." Mom gave me the extra money. And then I *always* gave the woman these five pennies. I never told my mother about that. Somehow, I felt ashamed, even though our upbringing had not discouraged charity. Just the

---

14 The Engelufer, today Engeldamm, is a street in Berlin-Mitte, in the very center of Berlin. The *Engel* (Angel) in the name was likely a reference to the Archangel Michael, to whom the nearby St. Michael's Church was dedicated. The second part *Ufer* (banks) respectively *Damm* (dam) references the Luisenstadt Canal, which ran parallel to the street until it was filled in and replaced by a garden from 1926 to 1932. This channel is referenced here by Charlotte Holzer. Later, during the separation of Germany, the garden was razed and replaced by the Berlin Wall. Today, it has been restored.

opposite: we'd been brought up to give, to be generous. But that was simply my secret. I would look forward to seeing the woman, to the look in her eyes, I still remember that. I recall that very precisely. And since my sister and I were both brought up the very same way, but my sister had a very different attitude, I think that does indeed belong to my unique character.

And already very early on I liked taking care of babies. From my eleventh birthday, I accepted that as my particular obligation. There was a small Jewish textile shop on Wrangelstrasse. The woman there had a small baby. But she couldn't take the baby for a walk. It was always outside in front of the shop. I felt sorry for it. Therefore, I pledged there and then to take care of the baby every day for a few hours. And that's what I did.

With an iron will, I played with dolls for a long time. And I always wanted to have twenty-four children, twelve boys and twelve girls. Later on, I reduced that figure to half. When I was half grown-up, what I wanted was: one Black child, one Chinese child, a Native American child, and a White child. I wasn't clear about the fathers. And didn't think about that either. I received my sex education relatively late. My sister got her education at school. I always turned to my mom. I was easy to educate, verbal instruction sufficed. Mom engaged an educational assistant—the good Lord. She claimed that it was the good Lord's will, and Lottchen believed that. And when I really misbehaved, she had a funny saying, "The good Lord doesn't come down, he punishes from up above." I'm sure I also asked where babies come from. But she said, "You're still too small. When you're big enough, the good Lord will tell you about that. Then you'll take note of it." But she warned me, "Don't let others tell you stuff about this." And strangely enough, I accepted what she said. At school I never listened to a single bawdy joke. And I made it over all the hurdles. For a long time, I didn't think about anything at all in that connection. I did fall in love though, very early on, as a small girl. My first love went by the name of Kurt Seldis. I was six years old. He wore a sailor suit with a very low-cut V-shaped neckline. That was the reason for my love. Kurt was a distant cousin of mine. And all I can recall is that neckline. Then I had a secret love for another cousin who was a little older than me. I always used to wallop him, beat him up.

I was always a relatively chubby girl. I didn't start thinning out until I was about sixteen. My sister was always a fine and proper little girl, always very neat and clean, well groomed, gentle, and tender. I was the heavyset, good, stupid Lottchen, who was always kind of dirty. Who always was digging in dirt. I also mingled with the street kids.

The difficulties with being Jewish didn't start until after I left the Wagnersche Höhere Töchterschule. I did have a confrontation at school with Mr. Wende, because I ranted about Theodor Körner.[15] Körner made me see red, with all his patriotism. And besides—I was around thirteen then—I just couldn't stomach his pathos. Probably at home there had already been some discussion about that. My parents must have sensed that elements there contributed to antisemitism. In any case, I didn't like that whole direction. And then I had my first clash with the teacher. I had joined the youth movement already at the age of twelve. My mom was in favor of coeducation. There wasn't much of that at the high schools. One day she read that the Central Association of the Jews[16]—a very middle-class affair—was organizing a youth group.[17] "Oh," she said, "that's very good, the girls should grow up together with the boys." So she signed us up. Once inside, I became acquainted very quickly with progressive things. Initially, we twelve-year-olds were involved only in social evenings, hikes, and singing. But we also had thousands of discussions about thousands of topics.

---

15 Theodor Körner (1791–1819), was a German poet. For more on him, see the biographical entries in the appendix.

16 The Centralverein deutscher Staatsbürger jüdischen Glaubens (Central Association of German Citizens of Jewish Faith) was established in 1893 with the aim of unifying the Jews of Germany in the struggle for their rights and to fight antisemitism. Its worldview was based on a commitment to the German nation. See Avraham Barkai, *"Wehr Dich!" Der Centralverein deutscher Staatsbürger jüdischen Glaubens (C.V.) 1893–1938* (München: C. H. Beck, 2002).

17 The author did not write the name of this youth group. The CV formed a few *Jugendgruppen* (youth groups) of its own but decided by 1931 (when the author was twelve years old), that it would be preferable to operate through political and religiously neutral youth organizations that attract a larger public.

As a twelve-year-old, I went through a religious period when I began to go to the temple. It was mainly the music that attracted me. My grandfather brought me a bit farther along in a humane-ethical sense in our extended discussions. While my dad withdrew ever more into himself, my mom became the driving force in the family. All he did at that point was learn and read English. He used to spend his time almost entirely at the coffeehouse, and let my mom become the chief breadwinner. Her wartime activity (in the Office for Fat) had made her an independent woman for the first time. And when he returned, he found in place of a girl-wife an adult woman who could care for herself and for the kids. She said, "I have two daughters. Why are they not going to have a confirmation?[18] Why should the boys be better? My girls should have that too."

At the time, a modern reform direction was emerging in Judaism that supported the provision of religious instruction to girls. I, too, was given a religious education. I had never had that at school. Aside from the fact that I'd known the biblical story from early childhood, I hadn't had any formal instruction whatsoever. And because of my TB, I had been excused from all minor subjects at school. Naturally, my mom considered religion a minor secondary subject.

I received religious instruction from one of my uncles, Rabbi Lewkowitz,[19] who was murdered as well. He was rabbi at the temple on Levetzowstrasse, which by the way was later on used as a collection point for the deportation of Jews. It was excellent religious instruction, very impressive. It brought me to a point where at the end of that year I said to myself, "I don't believe in anything. It's all a fraud, and the good Lord can't be genuine at all." I couldn't accept the contradictions. I was almost fourteen and I said, "I hereby resign from the synagogue." There were big arguments with the rabbi, who didn't want to force me, but hoped to convince me. Then I was called to go see my aunt, his wife, who had heard that I hadn't attended the consecration ceremony.

18   The Confirmation is the Lutheran–Protestant rite of passage for young teens, here it is likely used to refer to a Bat Mitzvah.

19   For more on the Lewkowitzes, Charlotte's aunt and uncle, see the biographical entries in the appendix.

I told her that was true and that I couldn't falsely pretend. Then she said to me, "Look, if you can't believe, I can't take that away from you. But you mustn't cause your mom heartache by not going to the consecration." And you see, once again something came from inside me and I thought, "I just couldn't do that. Cause my mom distress? No way!" So I said, "OK, Aunt Selma, I promise, I'll go to temple, I'll get confirmed. But I believe in nothing." And that was the last time I ever went to temple. And I stuck to that, aside from a few official things I had to take care of, later, like going to fetch a doctor from the temple. Or after the war, when I attended a wedding or a funeral. So that is a consequence of my childhood.

I left school twice. The first time was from the Wagnersche Höhere Töchterschule, from which I was expelled. I was probably guilty of umpteen violations of the middle-class ethos—or more: ideology—of discipline. I always spoke my mind. In addition, my previous education was not in keeping with the direction at school, which was decidedly German-nationalistic in orientation. But actually, the expulsion from school was only a pretext. Back then I was already in the youth movement. I knew a boy there, whom we called Heico, Heinz Cohn. He was older than me, and we were nothing but good friends. There was nothing sexual involved. Heico was an apprentice in a nearby shop, and we would meet every morning on my way to school. I would greet him happily, as was my custom.

One day—it was raining—he was waiting for me in the entrance hall of the school. He wanted to give me a book. I arrived, went toward him with my briefcase in one hand. With the other I kind of grabbed him at the hip. And sort of twisted him around a bit. And just then a senior teacher appeared, Fräulein Rostowsky, and she immediately reported to the school principal that I had broken the rules of morality. In the entrance hall of the school, I had had close physical contact, touching a boy. For that I was expelled. That was very difficult for my mom. What was she to do with me now? I was only fifteen, and my talents were quite diverse. I had no good grades to show, or only a few. She ended up enrolling me at the Luisen Oberlyzeum—a supplementary school for general secondary education—where, after an IQ test, I was admitted as a so-called "free student." After I'd been expelled from the other school! And I had to repeat a year in the tenth grade.

That year became crucially decisive for me. Just the trip to school: I had to take the train from Silesia Station all the way to Friedrichstrasse. At Silesia Station Wölfchen was always waiting for me. Wolfgang Roth,[20] a boy from our group, was the son of East European Jewish parents (later something more about that), and at home had already been exposed to significant political influences. His parents were left-leaning Social Democrats. We would travel together to Friedrichstrasse. The conversations I had with this boy had a major impact on me. He later became a set designer working with Piscator[21] and immigrated to Switzerland in the Nazi era. I liked him a lot, but it was also nothing but a genuine friendship between youngsters.

I was a late bloomer. From the age of fourteen on I had an educational assistant whom my mother selected. A boy from our youth movement called Heinz Deutschkron.[22] He was seven years older than me, an extremely decent fellow. He had bowlegs and marvelous black eyes. And I was very, very fond of him. He helped educate me. Because Mom was very clever and had said to Heinz, "You're my educational assistant. Help me to protect the child." I was indeed so very much like a child. In doing so she imposed a beautiful obligation on him, one that he also fulfilled. But he was my first conscious love. Later on, Heinz immigrated to England and married there. And sometime after that he returned to Germany as an occupation soldier. Then he had a fatal motorcycle crash. His influence on me when I was in my teens was not political but shaped me as a human being.

The Luisen Oberlyzeum was directed by Margarete Behrend,[23] a women's rights activist and Social Democrat, and by Elisabeth (Lilly) Abegg. She was a well-known historian who, if I'm not mistaken, lost

---

20 For more on Wolfgang Roth, see the biographical entries in the appendix.

21 For more on Erwin Piscator, see the biographical entries in the appendix.

22 The person referred to here is likely named Hans Deutschkron. For more on him, see the biographical entries in the appendix.

23 This refers to Margarete Behrens, a social democratic reform educator. For more on her, see the biographical entries in the appendix.

her life in Tibet.[24] She was my homeroom teacher and likewise had a powerful positive human influence on me. I loved her very much. She had a certain simplicity as well as goodness of heart and was highly intelligent. The female math teacher at this school was Trendelenburg, a known figure in education. But I hardly learned anything. I was always a poor student and lagged behind in math, except for geometry, which for me was clear and graphic. We called our French teacher Pilli because he was constantly downing pills. He was a small, heavyset man, who was a good person and very nice. And because he was so good, I always used to cut his classes. Instead I went next door to the Charité polyclinic where I "sat in" on the ward, because by then, medicine had become my great passion. To that end, I feigned some sort of surgical disease that I used to gain entry there.

My sister attended the same school and planned to take the final leaving exam for the secondary school diploma. She wanted to go to university. Only one person in our family could study. So the good Lottchen said, "OK, my sister's going to make it, she'll graduate." After all, I reasoned, she was much more intelligent than I was. Which is actually correct, she is indeed smarter. I said to myself, "OK, you'll just become a nurse." It was not at all difficult for me to make that decision. My dad was opposed to the idea. He still had terrible prejudices against nurses based on his experience in World War I. And my mom said, "The child will be exploited there." Actually, I was also still much too young for nursing. Back then you had to be at least eighteen to work in patient care. I said, "OK, fine, I'll convince you two that I can do it."

During my final school vacation, at the age of sixteen, I went to the baby nursery in Niederschönhausen in Berlin where I begged the doctor to let me work. He granted me the right to do so during the vacation period. Then Mom said, "Good, go ahead and do it, you'll see what it's like." So I went to work there, and right away was assigned a "daughter" to care for. The head was Dr. Mendelsohn, a well-known pediatrician.[25] In addition he was director of the infant welfare facility

---

24 Dr. Elisabeth Abegg (1882–1974), was a German educator and savior of Jews during Nazi time. For more on her, see the biographical entries in the appendix.
25 For more on Dr. Mendelsohn, see the biographical entries in the appendix.

on Badstrasse. He was a wise teacher and always assigned each young nurse one or two children to take care of, aside from the work on the ward. I was given Püppe (Dolly). One look at her and I fell in love immediately. She was already a year old, housed in the main ward where the toddlers were. She was completely bald and was always laughing; she would laugh and laugh. She stood there stretching out her little arms, and that was my child. Nicknamed Püppe, her real name was Vera Feldmann.[26]

There I heard for the first time something about children born out of wedlock, unmarried mothers. And to boot, they were Jewish! My mother could hardly believe that such mothers even existed. But I still wasn't clear yet about the role of fathers. I had in the meantime had my first kiss at age sixteen. Oh, no, correction: I'd kissed someone already when I was still fifteen. On the cheek. A boy named Herbert Simmenauer, from Breslau. We were together in the vacation camp. I was sitting alone in the dining hall, writing a letter. Then he came over to me. He was such a handsome dark-haired guy and he bent down over me. I don't know what it was, maybe a longing for home, but anyhow I immediately kissed him on the cheek. And then I started to cry something awful and felt ashamed. Then he said to me, "You don't need to be ashamed; I'll get rid of that." And he took a knife and cut a little into his cheek so that the kiss would be removed. I had good relations with him for several years, including a long correspondence.

After this first probation period in the baby nursery—work which was very strenuous—I said, "I'll begin." I made an agreement right away with Dr. Mendelsohn and was permitted—as an exception—to start even though I was still only seventeen.

The Jewish baby nursery was a facility for nurse trainees. It offered good training and was terribly exploitative. Training lasted one year, and we never had a single day off. Instead every second week we had a free afternoon. Working hours were from 6 A.M. to 7 P.M. with two hours off for meals, and "hospital porter" duty. We

---

26   For more on Vera Feldmann and her subsequent fate, see the biographical entries in the appendix.

also had a night shift, twelve hours. And there I got involved in my first solidarity action.

I was there with a girl from Stettin, Liselotte Meyer. In professional training we two were the best students. Liselotte was very organized, I wasn't. Not regarding my main tasks; those I also executed well. We were, however, required to do a lot of cleaning and to take care of a lot of extra stuff. And there, I refused to do what I didn't think was right. For example, in the kitchen for dairy products we were supposed to clean the table with Sidol decalcifier. I thought that was unnecessary given the huge amount of work we were assigned anyhow. So I said, "If you scrub the table well and keep it clean, that's enough. I won't do it. That's it!" We both had the highest grades in exams. I was actually second best, even though I was better at theory than Liselotte. Theory was always my strong point, likewise afterwards in training to be a registered nurse. In the end, I only got a grade of B, and ended up second in my class—because I had refused an order to work, by refusing to scrub down that table.

I lived together with Liselotte in a shared room. She was very pious, not Orthodox, but had a strong belief in God. And we had very long talks about God. Talking with her I got a better idea of what I thought. We liked each other a lot. One day Liselotte—otherwise very honest and proper—did something for which she was to be punished. Without justification, we all assumed. In any case, our head doctor, Dr. Mendelsohn, canceled her free afternoon that we all had every two weeks. I thought that was so outrageous that I spoke up in class and told Dr. Mendelsohn, "I think that is so unjust. If you don't cancel it, I won't take my own free afternoon either." He just laughed. But I was serious, and I refused to take my own free afternoon when it came. Moreover, I encouraged several of our sister nurses in training to join me in this protest. That was the first intentional protest action I ever took part in. And it helped. Dr. Mendelsohn was in all likelihood splitting his sides with laughter about our childish action. But he gave in, and Liselotte got her free afternoon back.

At that time, I came into contact with the German Socialist Party Youth movement, the Falken (Falcons). Initially we congregated in Castle Park in Niederschönhausen. There was folk dancing at the castle and we trainee nurses joined in. There we had conversations, chats, discussions. In the baby nursery in Niederschönhausen we were allowed to invite whomever we wished to. We had a very nice boss there. There were some nurses who came from the Bund, i.e. from Eastern European circles, some from Zionist circles, later on some too from the *Hehalutz*—meaning they were workers from the Zionist workers' movement. For a time, they also had a great influence upon me. I can recall one nurse called Puppele. She had a boyfriend, Mäxchen Tau, who was an anarchist.[27] We had hundreds of conversations and gradually my thinking became ever clearer. In addition, at the social evenings we began to read our first progressive literature, and finally, very slowly, we also arrived at socialist literature. However, during my time as a nurse trainee I didn't go to the social evenings very often. Because I just couldn't find the free time for that at all. And then I came down with diphtheria, a fairly serious case. I was confined in the Charité Hospital for a long time. I had soft palate paralysis and knee paralysis. The time that I lay sick I'd have to make up for and work off later. After all, we had had to pay for the time we had been trainees, by working. When I took my final exam, I still had three months' work to catch up on that I'd missed because I'd been ill. I took the exam together with the others, and managed to get an A. And then, despite being a trained nurse, I had to take unpaid work to make up for the three months I'd missed.

The baby nursery belonged to the Association for the Helpless Jewish Child. Dr. Mendelsohn, who also had a post with the municipality and a good private practice as well, worked in this welfare facility pro bono, on a voluntary basis. And we were exploited as unsalaried labor. We had sixty babies. In our free time we would have walks outside with, and care for, our assigned child.

Shortly thereafter I met up again with Marianne Baum, whose name then was still Marianne Cohn, and whom I knew from the youth movement.[28]

Then I started work in the Jewish Hospital as a trainee nurse. I absolutely did not want to go to a religious hospital, largely on account

27 For more on Max "Mäxchen" Tau, see the biographical entries in the appendix.
28 For more on Marianne Baum (Cohn), see the biographical entries in the appendix.

of my political views. I wanted to become a municipal nurse. I went to all
the municipal hospitals in Berlin and applied to all of them. Despite my
final A exam grade in baby nursing, I was accepted nowhere. Finally, I
went to see municipal councilor Schmincke.[29] His office was in Berlin-
Neukölln, in the local healthcare administration, and he was a socialist
comrade. I think he actually was the head of the healthcare department
in Neukölln. I had gotten this referral via our former subtenant Paul
Israel, also a socialist comrade. He sought to arrange that Schmincke
find me a position in Neukölln. He didn't succeed. Then I applied to
the Institute for Midwives in Neukölln. There I was told I was too
young. That was correct. But they wouldn't have accepted me anyhow.
Because I was Jewish. That's how I ended up in the Jewish Hospital.
That was 1928/1929.

When I became a baby nurse I left home, just before I turned
seventeen. For us that was early to leave home. My mom regretted that
very much, but she wasn't able to prevent it. Although at the time, I
tended to subordinate myself, I nonetheless felt that I needed to become
independent, to venture out on my own. Every two weeks I went
home for an afternoon. And my relationship with my mom was good.
My father at that point was already out of the house. My parents had
separated. Dad could no longer stand living with Mom. And Mom no
longer wanted to be together with Dad. He went to England, and later
returned for a time.

I didn't have any other relationship experience at all, nothing
sexual either. We were working much too hard for that. And time
was in short supply. I saw a whole lot of stuff back then. We had
in fact a whole load of moms who were unmarried, and women
whose marriage was on the rocks. Because wherever possible
Mendelsohn had taken in the mother along with her child. We had
a good maternity ward, where the moms could feed their children
themselves. When we put the moms under the sunlamp and "milked"
them, they used to tell us quite a few stories, though were careful not
to tell me too much, because I was still so young and childlike. You
can see on the photos that I was still very childlike, naïve, and even-

---

29 For more on Dr. Richard Schmincke, see the biographical entries in the appendix.

tempered. I heard all kinds of things. But my perspective was that of an uninvolved observer.

Charlotte Abraham (Holzer) as a young nurse, 1932.

The whole story of why I landed in the Jewish Hospital is certainly characteristic for those times. I don't think the rejections I got were personal, but rather because of some state regulations, even if they were not formalized. However, you have to take into consideration that the nursing profession in those years was still more than just a profession— it was an estate, a vestige of the feudalist era. Who after all became a nurse back in the days? Disproportionately, unmarried girls from noble or in any case wealthy families, or girls who were religious. For a long time, the whole institution of healthcare was in the hands of religious entities. The Friedrichshain Hospital, for example, was staffed by the most genteel women, the Empress-Victoria nurses. When I myself applied to their mother house, the matron virtually threw me out. I certainly looked very nice in my nurse's uniform, and back then was a rather good-looking girl. My professional skills were better than those of the other applicants. Still, I was Jewish!

During my initial period in the Jewish Hospital, I had seen six caesarian sections and many deliveries, but I *still* didn't know what the role of the man was in all this. The excellent theoretical instruction began with the genesis of the child in the womb. And at that time, I hadn't given it much thought. It's all quite revealing for the state of my own personal underdevelopment at the time!

In terms of the law, the Jewish Hospital was a private institution, but it was a hospital belonging to the Jewish community. We had a ten-hour working day, from 7 A.M. to 7 P.M., with a break of two hours for meals. Every two weeks we had one day off, and all the other weeks in between, one free afternoon. That already was a huge improvement for me. The theoretical instruction was excellent, two hours every day. We were under strict surveillance to make sure we did take a nap at noon. We were fed well, our weight checked once a week, and were not allowed to lose weight. The first year our salary was fifteen Marks a month, the second year thirty Marks. Clothing and everything else was cost-free. In return, we were contractually obligated to work for the institution for three years after graduation, at a lower salary. And if someone wished to marry—our hospital was famous for the fact that the nurses disappeared like hotcakes—they had to pay a contractual penalty. In the first year it was 500 Marks, the second 300 Marks, and the third year 250 Marks, something like that. That was a lot of money back then. But actually, during the time I was there, very few left before the required length of prescribed service. That obligation was generally adhered to. Moreover, after finishing the traineeship, we had just started to accumulate practical experience, although during the entirety of our traineeship, we engaged in practical work, because except for the two hours of instruction, we were on the job all day.

Our patients at the Jewish Hospital were for the most part not Jewish. Mainly they were workers from the district of Wedding. Naturally, this was of great importance to me. It was less about the patients exerting influence on me and more about the opportunity to learn about their situation. After all, this was a time of serious unemployment. What a misfortune to patch up some poor guy who then leaves, has no money to feed himself, and goes to the dogs!

Later on, when I myself and my husband were jobless, we used to take turns visiting each other so that we could pool the little dough we had and be able to eat our fill. In that way we economized on fuel for heating, light, and gas. It was the only way we could keep going: we shopped only on market day, and then just at the last moment, in order to buy up what was left and was being sold cheap. I bought a lot of damaged cucumbers that would have normally been thrown away, because those were very cheap. I bought pork rind to make soup. And I witnessed the same habits among our patients with TB, those sick with "internal" diseases, and also people with "surgical" ailments.

We certainly had a place to call home in the nurses' residence. But I felt it wasn't right that we should have to work so very hard! For years there had been a statutory eight-hour day, and we had to work ten hours a day, and got a real day off only once every two weeks. In my eyes that was not right. That was my first actual realization of the importance of banding together. I understood that the protest strike for Liselotte Meyer had actually been senseless. Sure, maybe it could help momentarily, but it could not change anything fundamentally. I understood that alone you can't achieve anything, that you are only a power when people unite and band together. So I joined the union. In keeping with my profession, I joined the Federation of Municipal and State Workers (VGSA). It was a very right-wing union at the time. But nothing else was available to me. Still, it led to some condemnation inside the nurses' residence. Like from our supervisor when she became aware of it. On the other hand, because of that condemnation there was a stronger sense of solidarity. In order to offer support, the Party came to our aid. Dr. Georg Benjamin was sent to help us. He was a communist doctor working in the municipal schools and had already been reprimanded.[30] So he became engaged in connection with our hospital. His task was probably to build up a cell among us.

---

30 Georg Benjamin (1895–1942), was a member of the Communist Party, a doctor, and the husband of Hilde Benjamin. For more on him, see the biographical entries in the appendix.

Right away I was very enthusiastic and ready to pitch in! Initially we comprised a small group of six nurses. Our group gradually expanded and joined together with the workers and technical personnel in the hospital. In 1933, we were a total of some 110 nurses. Of these 110, four returned after the war, others were murdered, a few emigrated. The way that Dr. Benjamin established contact with us: he placed his wife Hilde in the hospital maternity ward for delivery. That way contact was maintained at least with some of us. And he also acted from the outside. He spoke with some of us, instructed us to go here and there. Then they sent someone inside via the union: the man who would later become my first husband! But the cell was built up more or less from the outside. Georg spoke with a few of us, but never came directly to the hospital, as political leader. He spoke for example with Lotte Manasse and Nurse Beate, saying this or that had to be done. And that was what we did. I was the person appointed in charge of literature in our party cell, right from the outset. Every Sunday I had a quota of *Rote Fahne* newspapers[31] that I had to sell inside the hospital. That naturally was strictly forbidden! I also sold the *Arbeiter-Illustrierte-Zeitung*.[32] And I brought in other material as well.

Then we had Gustav there too, as an instructor from the Revolutionäre Gewerkschafts-Opposition.[33] I was never in agreement with that. But my thinking about it wasn't clear enough to speak up about this. And even today I still think that what was done was just not correct. Gustav gave us training lectures, with varying degrees of

---

31 Founded in 1918, *Die Rote Fahne* (The Red Flag) was the central newspaper of the German Communist Party during the 1920s and early 1930s, until it was banned by the Nazis in the wake of the Reichstag Fire. After the ban, it was published illegally.

32 The *Arbeiter-Illustrierte-Zeitung* (Illustrated Worker's Newspaper) was a socialist newspaper published in Berlin from 1921 until 1933, and from exile in Prague until 1936. It was one of the fastest growing magazines in Germany, its circulation grew from 10,000 copies in 1922 to 500,000 in 1933. The magazines influence waned after its staff had to go into exile.

33 The Revolutionäre Gewerkschafts-Opposition (RGO—Revolutionary Oppositional Union) was a labor union aligned with the German Communist Party that was founded as a competition to the large traditional unions which aligned with the Social Democrats. It failed to attract a significant following.

success. I was absolutely not in agreement with many things, absolutely not! The dictatorship of the proletariat gave me terrible stomachaches. And then there was the matter of class consciousness! Today I can define that concept very well. But right up to the present, it's still not clear to me how people can demand that I have a proletarian consciousness even though in terms of my background I am not at all proletarian. I profess to be part of the working class. However, I can't demand it...Hmm, maybe I can demand it after all. I don't know. I can demand it in terms of how actions are carried out. But can that be taken for granted? If a person doesn't come from that class, from where can he have it? Only from his or her sense of reason. The worker usually did not acquire it from the cradle onwards either. After all, his subjective outlook is often enough that of a petty bourgeois. Solidarity for me was always a great and self-evident concept.

In the hospital we had a ward system with twenty beds in the hall. That didn't stop me from going through the hall early on Sunday mornings and shouting, "*Rote Fahne*! The latest events. Well guys, get your copy now, I'll bring it over to your bed!" No one took that amiss, not even the Jewish patients. When it came to the women, there were only a few takers. But among the men... OK, sure, they liked me, yet that wasn't the reason. After all, it was a hospital for workers.

By the way, we also had some of the Immertreu people as well.[34] When they got into a scuffle down at their favorite bar on Schulstrasse, we prepared the surgery upstairs. They were always taken care of quickly by us. Once we had two young girls from that clique. One had a broken right jaw, the other a broken left jaw. They'd been walloped pretty heavily by their fiancés, the same day at the very same place. They stayed with us in the hospital for a long time. They remained loyal to their fiancés nevertheless.

---

34 A reference to the so-called ring associations, specifically the "Geselligkeits-Club Immertreu 1919 e.V." (Immertreu Social Club of 1919), led by Adolf Leib. These "social clubs" were actually criminal gangs, and membership was exclusive to people who had served time in prison.

Marriage, Birth of a Daughter, Unemployment, and Party Membership

Political and personal memories now sometimes overlap. Gustav had taken charge of the union affairs at the hospital. In 1931, at the May Day demonstration, that guy wouldn't leave me in peace. He continued to walk beside me, upsetting me something awful, telling me his life story. And then he more or less forced himself upon me. By the beginning of 1933, I was pregnant. In January 1933, I was tossed out of the nurses' residence for "moral misconduct." I was by then a fully trained nurse, but unmarried and pregnant—highly improper! But that actually worked in my favor, because back in December 1932, I had gone home with Hilde Benjamin and had cared for her infant son Mischa.[35]

When I returned in January, the supervisor noticed I was pregnant, and I was disciplined. I stayed one or two months at home. I took care of some personal matters and already in the fourth month fell ill. I had one phlebitis after the other and remained unable to work until after childbirth. As a result, I wasn't at the hospital when the Nazis took power. In April they filed a complaint with the Jewish community, demanding that all communists should be fired without notice from the Jewish Hospital and other facilities. Since our party cell existed quite officially and they had the list of members, on April 4 and 5, within a span of four hours, all the communist nurses were thrown out of the mother house. However, I was not included among them. Why? Because I'd been thrown out for "moral misconduct"! The consequence of that was that the hospital afterwards hired me once again. However, they didn't simply leave the others jobless; rather they moved them elsewhere, despite the Gestapo. That is much to the credit of the Jewish community.

In August I gave birth, and five days later my husband Gustav was arrested. For more than two years, I was alone. I assessed the

---

35 For more on Hilde and Mischa Benjamin, see the biographical entries in the appendix.

situation as follows, "Either I'll work at the Jewish Hospital, and then I'll earn exactly as much as I need in order to place the child in a baby nursery, and I won't be able to nurse her with my milk. Or I won't work, I'll have to survive somehow on social support, but then I'll have my child with me and can give her my milk." I chose the second option and didn't go back to work until two years later, in 1935. In the meantime, the regulation had been issued that the Jewish Hospital could only be permitted to admit Jews as patients. Among that group, there were few workers left.

Gustav Paech, mid-1930s.

I have to say something else about Gustav. He stemmed from the *Lumpenproletariat*.[36] Not from birth; in fact, he had descended into its depths. His dad was a potter. His mother was the illegitimate child of a

---

36 In Marxist theory, the term *Lumpenproletariat* (ragged proletariat) was used for the lowest strata of society, those unemployed or criminal, without class consciousness, who were impossible to organize effectively.

woman from the Spreewald. His grandmother received contributions, probably alimony payments from a Jewish merchant. I know that because one of Gustav's brothers was later repeatedly harassed by the *Sippenforschung*[37] because the authorities didn't believe his documentation of Aryan descent was genuine.

Gustav's mother was knocked around a lot. At the age of fourteen she ran away from her grandparents dressed just in her underskirt. From that point on she had scraped along on her own. Then she met this master potter, married him, and had three boys. She was a very energetic woman, liked to wear the pants in the family. Then she suffered a heavy fate: Her husband returned from World War I with a spinal cord injury. It left his brain intact, but the man was paralyzed for a period of twelve years. His wife had to support her husband and the three boys on her own. And she wasn't always discriminating in the means she used. She probably picked up extra cash sleeping with other men. And she probably did that as her paralyzed husband lay beside her. She was a strong young woman; her husband was able only to lie there and look on. The three boys too, since the family had only one room. And the boys resented what she did terribly. They were completely unable to put themselves in their mother's situation. She lost any influence, at least in the case of the eldest son, Gustav.

An autodidact, Gustav knew a lot and had many skills, but was convicted of a crime as a young man. He had stolen a bicycle, which was a serious criminal offence in my eyes since the bike belonged to someone from his social class. Over time, he was convicted several times. And then he started to drink as well. He was totally down-and-out. Gustav was six years older than me. But he gradually came into contact with the workers' movement. He was, by the way, the only one of the three brothers who had sunk to such depths. His last conviction before our marriage was already semipolitical. At that point he was already an instructor for the Red Union Opposition (RGO). He had found a Berlin public transport pass, had made a forged document complete with a

---

37 The Reichsstelle für Sippenforschung (Reich Office for Genealogical Research) was the authority in charge of certifying so-called Aryan heritage—or the lack thereof—in those cases where the regular method of drawing from church and administration records could not be employed.

Gustav Paech during the repair of a radio, early 1930s.

forged photo and was traveling around the city free of charge. Of course in the service of the Red Union Opposition. Since he had a criminal record, he had to serve a heavy sentence.

After he was released, he came to the hospital, which is where I met him. He had managed to get a grip on himself and was a loyal worker for the party. Yet he knew how to put a pistol to my chest, telling me, "If you don't stay with me, then I'm gonna start drinking again." And I was taken in by that ruse. I liked the guy. But it wasn't love, that was very clear to me. I understood how hard that would be for him and requested, "Listen, remain my friend, but nothing more than that." He wouldn't accept that. I became his wife. But then I met a very, very dear young man, a young party comrade, and fell head over heels in love with him. I told him right away that I was not free, so we went our separate ways. Gustav and I stayed together. We got married because of the apartment and the ration card for charcoal. Eva was conceived. That would not have been a reason to marry.

I didn't know exactly if I should go through with the pregnancy. I went to a doctor for some advice, also with the thought of maybe terminating the pregnancy. In his office I was crying so terribly that he asked me, "OK, what do you actually want? You want to have it or get rid of it?" And I told him, "I want to get rid of it, but I want so much to have the baby!" "OK, so if that's what you say, then I won't help you in that direction. I'll help in a different way. Go ahead, have your baby, I'll help you as best I can." That was Dr. Franz Hirsch.[38] I can still remember him. He had his office somewhere in the vicinity of Luxemburg Platz. I left his office and ran all the way home. The whole way—I was after all just twenty-two years old—I went skipping, jumping, singing, and laughing, "Wow, I'm gonna have a baby!" I was so very happy.

Then I went to the workshop. Gustav had rented a room where he was making our furniture. We had started in an empty room, where we spread our blankets on the floor and slept on them. He worked for some nine months making our furnishings. Exactly as long as I was pregnant. And then he said to me, "Well, OK, so I'm gonna have a child, together with you. Fine, I'll drink a bottle of beer to that. But it's your child! I don't want it, and you'll have to bear the consequences." At that point I could no longer be dissuaded, I would have the baby.

You ask how we spent time together before we had the empty room. We didn't see much of each other. My hours at work were very long, and he too was very busy working for the Red Union Opposition. He rented a small room for himself not far from the hospital, and I used to just drop by now and then. But that proved sufficient to conceive my daughter.

I've never gotten over his reaction. Down to this very day. It was extremely hard for me. And it was also very difficult for me then to marry him. My mom immediately broke off all relations with me, she didn't want to have anything more to do with me; that lasted until Eva was six months old. There were only two people who stuck by me. One was Rudi Goldstein, whom by the way I met up with again later on in Israel.[39] The second, Waldemar, was a trainee lawyer connected with Hilde Benjamin, who supported me in a fantastic way.

38 For more on Dr. Franz Hirsch, see the biographical entries in the appendix.
39 For more on Rudi Goldstein, see the biographical entries in the appendix.

Aside from the fact that now and then he brought along a piece of sausage from his mother's pantry as a gift, he also supported me with advice and assistance.

My acceptance into the Party was extremely straightforward, uncomplicated. We had been over on Badstrasse, Gustav and me. We were just passing over the *Damm*.[40] And right in the middle he says to me, "Listen, what do you say? I think you're ready for the Party. I brought you your membership card. Here, take it." It was very simple: You simply had to say that you wanted to join and then you were a member. The probation period actually came once a person was inside the Party, not before. And I can't recall that anyone was excluded from the Party back then. Not in our circle in any case. There were some who stopped being active. Then people simply said, "Oh, she's no longer involved." And someone went to speak with her. And if need be, they'd let her drop out, if people saw that there was no real basis for her to continue.

How were we guided? Well, we received literature, quite a lot of it and good stuff. It came from a literature office. That was a small basement on Exerzierstrasse. I had to go over and pick it up. Not only literature but also the "mail." That's what we called it. It consisted of instructions, tips on what had to be and should be discussed. Afterwards we received tasks to be carried out on the outside. I picked the material up regularly and passed it on to our political leader, Ruth Wendt, who still lives in the West (her name then was Abraham, like my family name as a girl). The head of this office was Comrade Kriebel, an old worker, a real nice guy. Afterwards in our cell there were about twenty, but not just nurses, but technical personnel— stokers, workshop staff, women who'd been on the ward. We tried to recruit among them, too. We had no cell members among the doctors. Among them were quite a lot of socialist doctors. They were members of the Socialist Federation of Physicians, the SPD Socialists and the KPD Communists were together there, but the SPD was much

---

40 In Berlin dialect, *Damm* (dam) is generally used to refer to the largest category of streets, comparable to the boulevard in English. In this case, it was likely a reference to the Osloer Strasse, a main street in the Gesundbrunnen neighborhood of Berlin.

stronger in number. Among those still alive I met one in Israel who in the meantime had joined the Communist Party. But on the whole, they all turned out very well. At least they are on the Left, also to the left of their government. In any case they haven't forgotten that you can't just patch up the human being, you also have to do political work. Of those who survived, no one has forgotten that.

I recall that we had contact with a man whose name varied: sometimes this, sometimes that. That was always a bit confusing, but I learned that he had some work where it was best not necessarily to have a personal name associated with him.

After I'd gotten Eva past the worst, I was not rehired full-time at the Jewish Hospital. Rather I was employed as a stand-in, as a temporary worker. That meant that I was paid each time for the night's work. I received five Marks for such night duty. And when I wanted to have some time off, I simply got nothing, no pay. They also didn't tell me, "You work now six nights and you'll be off work on the seventh, even unpaid." Rather, I was simply told I had night duty. The upshot was that in the subsequent years I only took off work on Eva's birthday, and on my own. Back then there was no longer free board and free clothing. I had to take care of all that myself. And the pay was meager.

The shift was always twelve hours. If you worked in surgery, there were operations to contend with; in the maternity ward childbirth was likewise part of the standard work. If my luck was running bad there were five deliveries in a single night. On top of that, in the following years, the Nazis proceeded to substantially decimate the number of nurses. They took them away for other forced labor work, sent them to their factories. On average I had some sixty to seventy patients to care for by myself. That was terribly difficult. Then you were really on your toes the whole night. One night I had to lift a woman onto the potty. She was in a pelvic plaster cast. Usually two people do that, because it's extremely difficult. But there was nobody else there, so I had to do it by myself. When I lifted her, I tore my ligaments around the womb. They operated on me immediately. After that I went quickly back to work, tearing the ligaments once again. And so they did another surgery.

I had started working again at the end of 1935; in 1941, I had the two surgeries. Then I went back to work again until shortly before my arrest in 1942.

Charlotte as a nurse in the Jewish Hospital, 1941.

I ought to add something here from my childhood. As a child of about five years old, I came down with late rickets involving a total curvature of the lower legs. I was scheduled to be put in splints. But my mom felt so sorry for the good little Lottchen that she didn't want to have that done. She took her good little girl Lottchen along with my little sister and reenrolled them for ballet lessons with Fräulein von Engelhard-Schnellenstein. That is how I came to have ballet lessons for a little over a year. Probably I had really demonstrated a gift for ballet, because I very quickly became the best pupil. That deserves a mention in my life story. I'm gifted with my legs! Musically I'm probably gifted as well, because I absorb languages more phonetically than grammatically and logically. I never had lessons in gymnastics, but at the age of fourteen I began to practice it. I continued until well into the Nazi period. I'll talk about that later on, especially about Adolf Koch, who taught workers' gymnastics. I studied with him for quite a long time. for as long as was practically possible. Later I myself taught gymnastics. And that proved to have been valuable for in 1960, I offered classes for mothers on how to give birth without pain. And these classes are still running today.

Why am I a comrade or a Marxist? Well, Marxist—that is probably a bit much, since in fact, I lack the education. There is a small number of reasons. One is that the means of production belong to one and all; a second is that all have the same possibilities for education, in keeping with their abilities and strength. And the third is the planned economy, which is derived and flows from all the rest. Those are the three things that make me who I am. Everything else is implementation. I am not always satisfied with how things are implemented. There is room for improvement. It needs to be worked on. But those three things are the essence. And they require that all essential powers join forces.

I've read very little [political texts]. First of all because I read a lot while training for my profession. Politically, I'm a bit "unmusical." My talents lie in things medical and pedagogical. I am quite certain about that. I always tried to gain a good professional education. And the Jewish Hospital offered the best opportunity for that. But then my reading of Maxim Gorky, whose writings I read extensively in my youth, influenced me a lot. Then as a young girl I read Ferdinand August Bebel's *Woman and Socialism*.[41] And after that a bit of Lenin, very little, only that which wasn't too difficult for me. Then on the other side, B. Traven,[42] Jack London. That extended to London's *The Iron Heel*, a book that confused me totally. And which, when I was

---

41 August Bebel (1840–1913), was one of the founding fathers of German Social Democracy. For more on him, see the biographical entries in the appendix.

42 B. Traven was the pseudonym of an anonymous bestselling novellist whose protagonists were mostly poor proletarians. For more on him, see the biographical entries in the appendix.

arrested, nonetheless proved a source of succor. I did a lot of reading of Freud's[43] works and learned a great deal from that. Although Herr Freud did not discover the be-all and end-all, nor did Mr. Pavlov. Freud told us things we didn't know before, and Ivan Pavlov created the material basis for that.[44]

To be honest: Certainly, there are questions I had a hard time understanding. For example, concerning the *type* of collectivization in agriculture. Publicly you defend that vigorously in the party meeting, but if you then come back home, and express a different opinion—I'd resent that and reproach you for it. However, if you—during or after a conversation—arrived at that conclusion (in my case I usually achieve a clarification in my own thinking): then no! It's historically correct and must happen. Then you can also publicly espouse that view. But then please do so at home as well, OK!? Think of Liebknecht during the first debate on war loans. He voted in favor of that for party disciplinary reasons. There is after all a party whip, an internal one. I can't in public oppose party resolutions. I can choose to say what I think or not. But I can't dissemble. I just can't. Nor do I wish to. And I'm fine with that. OK, if I have to raise my finger, I go ahead and raise it. Because it's simply on account of discipline. But this terrible hypocrisy is something awful, if in the privacy of your home you say one thing and in public something else. I cannot acknowledge these people as true comrades.

My attitude to war is feminine. Women bring life, they can't then say yes to destruction. It would be expecting too much to see my instinctive attitude strengthened by the experiences of World War I. I was still largely unconscious back then. I've meanwhile learned something about myself—namely that my own experiences have had less of a formative impact on me than what I've seen happening to others. In World War I, probably also in World War II, there were people who were so horribly wounded that they were not allowed to be seen in public. There was a kind of sanatorium where people were housed who no longer had a face and which couldn't be replaced cosmetically. To

---

43 For more on Freud and his fate during Nazi time, see the biographical entries in the appendix.

44 For more on Ivan Pavlov, see the biographical entries in the appendix.

see that was almost intolerable. There was a Jewish man in such a place who no longer had a lower jaw. He had heart trouble. He probably knew that the end was near and so he'd requested to be allowed to die with us in the Jewish Hospital. I was nineteen years old, and I experienced his dying. That was horrible. So very horrible. That rendered the theoretical abhorrence of the war so tangible and concrete, so real. How his windpipe was totally exposed! Everything else was gone. It was so terrible to see the man dying. Nonetheless, you had to pull yourself together in order to help him. This showed the concept of war in all its nakedness. And yet it was only the beginning of mechanical warfare.

In January 1933, as I already mentioned, I was thrown out of the hospital. Now we were both unemployed. In the beginning I had a few temporary jobs. In January I was in my third month of pregnancy. From February on I had phlebitis, vein inflammation, and was no longer able to work. With the money we still had, we purchased wood and Gustav began to construct furniture.

Things progressed slowly with the remnants of the former party groups. One segment joined the Nazi SA. That should not be omitted. One segment came together to engage in illegal work; we were in the ranks of those individuals. Initially this still involved the people remaining from the strike of the Berlin Transport Society (BVG).[45] Hilde Benjamin was dealing with the trial. She was a defense attorney; others had been arrested. And we started dealing with those who were still outside, to provide cover for them, and to maintain some kind of solidarity with the street cell on Koloniestrasse. But basically, it was a slow tinkering on this and that. In terms of organization there was still nothing. This went on until August 1933. That date was a watershed for me because it coincided with the birth of my daughter and my husband's arrest. I was in labor and went to the hospital; a day later my husband came to me and said, "Listen, there's Erich Fox, he was a

---

45 This refers to the 1932 BVG strike, in which the Communist RGO cooperated with the Nazi Party labor organization, the Nationalsozialistische Betriebszellenorganisation (NBZ—National Socialist Factory Cell Organization) against a compromise made by the mainstream unions aligned with the Social Democrats. The strike failed to achieve its objectives and was aborted.

leading functionary of the Berlin Transport Society. He's wanted by the police. Is it OK with you if he comes to hide at our place?" I said, "Sure, no problem." So Erich came to our place.[46] By that time, we were living in a one room apartment with kitchen on Zechliner Strasse.

When I was reprimanded, even though not for political but rather for "moral" reasons, I was left in practical terms without a home. I couldn't go home to my mom's because Mom disapproved of my involvement with Gustav. In her eyes her daughter had been destroyed morally, and on top of that, she'd become a communist! So that was impossible. Gustav had a place to sleep. But since it was with landladies—Bulgarians—who only let out a small place, I couldn't stay there. For one, two nights I nevertheless did stay with him. Then Gustav started looking in earnest for an apartment. After some time, we found the place on Zechliner Strasse. The owner was an old woman on a very small welfare pension. She moved into the kitchen and left us her room. The room was totally empty. The furniture had already been removed at some point. The kitchen was large and had a niche where the old woman's bed stood. So she had the bed and the kitchen, and we got the empty room. For my part, I was happy. It was a beautiful room with a large, tripartite window. But there was nothing inside. Initially we spread out blankets on the floor. The first piece of furniture was a couch made by Gustav. I helped out with making the second couch, since I wasn't happy to sleep together on the one couch all the time. That couch still stands in our place at home, is still in good condition. And then we constructed a table. So over time, he built…

I got very friendly with the old lady in the kitchen. One day, we'd only been there for six weeks, she said, "Lotteken, now dat ain't goin' on furder. I'z gonna probably die. Now just bring me to de hospital. And then you guys should have de apartment." All that happened so plainly. To the credit of that woman: So dignified! So I brought her to the hospital. But first I asked her whether she didn't want to stay on longer in the apartment. Because things could, I explained, still take a long time. But she said, "Nope, no, no, dat's not gonna be much longer!"

---

46   For more on Erich Fox, see the biographical entries in the appendix.

And a very short time later she died. So then we tried to arrange to formally procure the apartment. But we were not allowed to. No, the requirement was: only if we married. And that's how it came about that I married Gustav. Now we had the kitchen in addition. It was very nice, and I was really grateful to the old lady who'd shown herself to be better than my own mother.

Erich Fox moved in with us. Erich had quite a young wife who insisted on seeing her husband. He arranged to meet her somewhere on Zechliner Strasse in the evening. And bang, gotcha, the Gestapo caught him. And Gustav at the same time. Eva was five days old. I wasn't at home then, and Gustav probably covered for me. In short: In 1933, the Nazis did not think to immediately arrest me as well. Gustav was placed in the Columbia House camp, a prison at Tempelhof. He was initially treated "cordially."[47] He then got a sentence of two and a half years and served that in full. I was in the hospital—where almost everyone abandoned me. Except for a few colleagues who were kind to me, everybody around me was like a wall of ice. There was really only Rudi Goldstein, he was working with us in pathology. I was so envious of my sister nurses that they were able to care for my baby while I had to remain in bed due to my inflamed vein. But I fed her faithfully and properly, the little minx.

When I came back home, I was faced with a decision: To work and give the child away—or not to work and keep the child with me. I decided on social aid, nine Marks fifty per week. The rent was twenty-five Marks a month of which I paid nineteen Marks—the rest was a rent compensatory subsidy that you got. Times were very hard, but the doorbell kept ringing. Outside they were roaring, "Winterhilfe!"[48] Those

---

47 This is a reference to torture.

48 The Winterhilfswerk des Deutschen Volkes (Winter Relief Works of the German People), more commonly known by the abbreviation Winterhilfe, was an annual donation drive ostensibly aimed at relief for the poor but used by the Nazi Party also as a propaganda tool and to increase support in low-income households. Overseen by the Nationalsozialistische Volkswohlfahrt (NSV—National Socialist People's Welfare) and by the propaganda ministry under Goebbels, the organization employed volunteers to collect the donations. In many areas, a significant part of the volunteers were members of the party's youth organizations Hitlerjugend and

were our comrades from the Party. They came in and whispered, "Rote Hilfe!"[49] And then they gave me something, a hunk of bread perhaps. The other neighbors in the building also helped. Initially Rudi Goldstein often assisted me and the trainee lawyer Waldemar whom I mentioned, working with Hilde Benjamin. He helped not only economically, but also with advice and kindness. He was really concerned and took the trouble to help out.

In this proletarian quarter, the main work of the cell at that time was to provide aid for the relatives of the political prisoners. And there were plenty of those, God only knows how many. I saw Gustav for the first time again when Eva was about eight weeks old. I got a message from him that he was at Alexanderplatz. I picked Eva up and scurried over. I didn't have a baby buggy. And I also didn't have the cash for a buggy. So I went on foot, carrying everything, baby Eva in my arms. After all, the child had to get some fresh air. I was nursing her in addition and had nothing to eat myself. That went on for so long that one day I just collapsed at the Infant Welfare Office. They brought me back home. But because Dr. Mendelsohn was the head of that office on Badstrasse, he reported the incident to the Jewish Hospital, and then the former operating room nurse contacted me. She said, "Hey Lotte, listen! Somewhere around here there's a baby buggy, come and get it." My brother-in-law, Gustav's youngest brother, went by bike to Babelsberg. He returned with his bike and the baby buggy, passing through the Brandenburg Gate. Riding the bike, with his right hand pushing the buggy along in tandem.

So now I had a baby buggy. Back then the low buggies had become modern, and this one looked like a crate for charcoal. Nonetheless, I fixed it up as nicely as I could. And my baby looked very nice in it. She was a sweet little thing. I had gotten a baby bed from the baby nursery.

Bund Deutscher Mädel. Despite its claim to be donation-funded, a significant part of its finances was taken out of employees' salaries by employers.

49 The Rote Hilfe (Red Aid) was the relief organization of the German Communist Party. It provided legal and material support to Communists and operated officially from 1924 until 1933, when it was banned by the Nazis. Following the ban and despite persecution by the Gestapo, some of its members continued their activities illegally.

When, after keeling over at the Infant Welfare Office, I was brought home, my brother-in-law happened to be there. He said, "Lotteken, look, you must have something proper to eat." He fixed me a dish of some raw meat mixed with egg. He too was unemployed, but he went and got that somehow for me. I would never have thought of eating something of that kind. But I downed the food ravenously, I was so hungry, and then I felt better.

Later, while Gustav was detained in Moabit, he was allowed to have an account. And every two weeks I deposited three Marks for him there. I also told him: That's from the Red Assistance. Or at least told him some aid money from Rote Hilfe was there, because otherwise he certainly wouldn't have accepted it. I diverted that from my support money.

Before he was arrested, he visited me once more at the hospital after I'd given birth. But he didn't wish to see his child. He said it didn't interest him. He wouldn't deny the child. Said it was his, he knew that. But insisted the baby was my concern. Thus, he hadn't yet seen the child. I was the only wife who was allowed to go to speak with her husband at Alexanderplatz where they were being held, because I had this package in my arms. I can recall that as if it were yesterday: We were in the visitors' room. There was a huge, long table, on one narrow end I was seated, and he opposite at the other end. In the middle was a kind of small barrier, and on the broad side of the table sat a police officer. And then I kind of nudged the package over toward him. Well, then we both broke down in tears. And that's how he came to see his baby.

From there he was transferred to Moabit. It was open to visitors about once a month. He was still in what's called pretrial detention. I was in such financial straits that I couldn't travel from Wedding, from Gesundbrunnen, to Moabit. I was forced to economize with iron severity, in order to also be able to deposit the three Marks for him. The upshot was that I was always walking, never riding the tram. There and back, with the baby buggy. Nevertheless, it was nice that way, you could walk and think to yourself, and could always see the child lying in front of you.

In Moabit, a visitor wasn't permitted to take a child into the prison. But nonetheless I had to take the baby along. I invariably had to leave her outside, in the care of the police officer. Those in the porter's lodge took her in. I probably went there eight or ten times, and in the meanwhile, they got to know me. They were happy to watch the child. One fine day, she was already in her pushchair, it started to pour during visiting time. And when I came out, it was still raining, and the porters gave me my child. There she was, sitting in her pushchair, wrapped in a rain cape sewn together from packing paper, roughly stitched.

Yes, I had a pushchair. When Eva was six months old, my relatives decided to forgive me. After all, the child was so sweet. They saw what trouble I was having with the big buggy, because I lived on Zechliner Strasse in one of those "all-around" buildings, on the fourth floor. In the middle was a stairwell. Every half stairway there were apartments. The building was totally occupied. And when I sat in my kitchen with an ear to the wall, I could make out very clearly what people were saying in the kitchen half a stairway below me. That's how closely we were squeezed together. It wasn't permitted for tenants to store a buggy downstairs. I had to lug the buggy up and then also take it down again. But I didn't have the physical strength for that. Whenever I wanted to go out, I'd stand outside my apartment door and shout into the stairwell shaft, "I need a man!" Then doors opened, a few men came and helped me take the buggy downstairs. I'd do exactly the same when I returned, shouting, "I need a man!" And some guy would appear and help take the buggy upstairs. I had gotten the pushchair through my sister.

When Georg Benjamin was arrested in 1933, his son Mischa was six months old. Georg was sent to Sonnenburg concentration camp.[50] About a year later he was released. And about eighteen months later he was rearrested and put on trial. At that point, the public was still allowed into trials. I accompanied Hilde Benjamin. Hilde had also accompanied me to the criminal trial against my husband. On that occasion I made my first acquaintance with a rubber truncheon. I wanted to go inside, sit

50 Sonnenburg was one of the early concentration camps used by the Nazis to intern political enemies. It was situated in a former prison in Sonnenburg, today Słońsk in Poland and operational between April 1933 and April 1934. The site then served as a regular prison until the beginning of World War II, when it was used again as a concentration and penal camp, mostly for captured members of the resistance from German-occupied countries. At the end of January 1945, with the Red Army approaching, most of the remaining prisoners, 819 men, were murdered by the Nazis.

down, said I was the wife of the man on trial, but the guards couldn't have cared less. And then something came crashing down on me. Gustav was sentenced to two and a half years and was jailed in Brandenburg. And my travel money didn't reach that far. Time simply passed. Hilde, who now was also alone, placed her son Mischa in a baby nursery, headed by the Communist comrade Edith Fürst.

Initially, her nursery was located in the Nordend area of Niederschönhausen. Edith was the sister of Max Fürst,[51] who belonged to the KPD circle from Königsberg, had been in the youth group "Kameraden"[52] and then had gone over to the group "Schwarzer Haufen"[53]—i.e. they'd come from the Jewish youth movement to the Communist Party or to the Communist Youth Association. Edith was a baby nurse whose nursery contained only children (mainly Jewish) of Communists and those who had already been behind bars. Despite the fact that this was kept secret, the Nazis later found out and closed down the nursery. Naturally I went to visit Mischa, he was after all also a bit my little baby. That's when I met Edith Fürst. It was still in Nordend. Edith had managed to arrange travel with the children to the Baltic and wanted to have someone watch over her house while she was gone. She asked me, saying it would at the same time be a place for me to relax a bit. So naturally, I moved with Eva to Nordend. Out there she turned one year old. Edith had a sister named Rosa. Rosa Adler is still living today with her husband here in East Germany.[54] Her husband had just

---

51 For more on Max and Edith Fürst, see the biographical entries in the appendix.

52 Kameraden was a German–Jewish youth group that initially brought together young Jews with a variety of political leanings. The first chapter was founded in 1916 in Breslau, followed by several other regional groups that united in 1919 in a national organization. Around the mid-twenties, the Schwarze Haufen emerged as an independent subgroup, in 1927, its members were expelled. The rest of the membership split up in three ideologically different groups in 1932.

53 The Schwarzer Haufen (black bunch) was a social revolutionary youth group with antiauthoritarian and libertarian principles that existed for a few years during the 1920s. Many members subsequently joined Socialist or Communist organizations. The group was named after the Schwarzer Haufen, commanded by Florian Geyer, that fought against clergy and noblemen during the Peasants Revolt of the 1520s.

54 For more on Rosa Adler and her husband Siegfried, see the biographical entries in the appendix.

come from Esterwegen.[55] There I saw what had been happening. I saw the dog bites on his body. And he also told me plenty about that. So I knew what was going on.

There were a pair of rabbits that needed to be cared for. I had to fetch them from the basement shed and bring them out into the garden. A wire cage was there, that slowly had to be pushed along, so that gradually they ate up the lawn. It was very difficult for me to carry them into the cage and back downstairs. One morning, as they were being taken out, the male rabbit got away. That was very awkward. He returned now and again to the fence and begged for his mate. I felt so terribly sorry for him that I also let the female rabbit run off.

Rosa's husband had not gone with her to the Baltic, but had stayed on to work, so in the evening I also had to care for him. I wasn't able to stay the course in Edith's house. That probably should not be mentioned when these memoirs are published. It simply proved too difficult for me to be alone with a man. I was still a very young woman. A woman who had gotten together with a man only very late in her own youth. And then that had come to such an abrupt end. When I menstruated, the desire I felt troubled and upset me a lot. But I didn't want my housemate, who was after all Rosa's husband. I told myself, "I can't stand this situation." The desire was as strong as I could imagine it might well be in the case of men. I even told him, "I can't do that. And since I don't want something to develop between us, I'm going to leave." I went walking for nights through the streets. When I was finished with my last round of feeding the animals, I just left. I walked and walked, on and on, in order to get rid of that feeling. It was very difficult, and also a part of life. Maybe even a part of this story.

Initially in the early months Rudi Goldstein was still coming over to see me at home. I never had anything intimate with him. It would never have come to mind. One fine day he came over and said, "Listen, I'm going to Palestine. I didn't tell you anything about that

---

55 Esterwegen was, after Dachau, the second biggest concentration camps on German soil during the initial phase of Nazi rule. During its relatively short-lived existence as a concentration camp—from summer 1933 until the end of 1936—most of the inmates were political prisoners, predominately Communists.

before, because I wanted to spare us the big farewell. Today is my last time coming here." I was a bit baffled. But if he thought that he needed to leave... I had never had such an idea. At that time, I thought my place was here in Germany, in the workers' movement. I was probably still under the illusion that sometime soon the whole Nazi thing would come to an end. Another factor was that I would never have abandoned my patients, leaving them in the lurch. I knew that every person who had left this Jewish Hospital could no longer be replaced. And I knew how difficult and how necessary our work was. And why was my life worth more than anyone else's? But if that was what Rudi had decided, well, that was his decision. He wasn't a member of the KPD; he came from the Socialist Student Alliance and was later a member of the Socialist Physicians. As he was leaving, we embraced, for the very first time. And we kissed. At that moment we both knew we were in love. Without ever having said it. We said it afterwards, much later, meeting in 1957 in Israel. It was extremely difficult, even bitter for us. And when Gustav was released, I told him immediately that nothing had happened in the meantime, except that I had difficulties with myself during this period. And that I noticed when saying goodbye to Rudi that it was more than just a friendly relationship with him. Gustav could say nothing in response. In any case, that lay beyond the boundaries of our shared life together, which was always somewhat problematic.

By the way, how the sexual tension was released is another story: Edith had a gardener by the name of Tommy, a Communist comrade. He came running through the garden one day and lifted me up high into the air and said, "Well, how about it, Lotteken?" And then put me down. At that moment I felt clearly how I became a woman once more. When I try to see this more abstractly, thinking about myself, I find it interesting the way in which something like that can be triggered.

When Eva was ten months old, she came down with whooping cough and vomited up everything except my milk. And I continued to breastfeed her. In addition, my milk was the cheapest and best. I breastfed her until I had to tell myself that it can't go on, it has to stop. The kid was actually running after me to be breastfed. Then I got a first tetanus seizure, which however was not ever repeated. That problem was bound up with breastfeeding if a mother continues for too long. When I weaned her, she drank almost nothing for a week because she was so used to breastfeeding.

Georg Benjamin, by the way, who wasn't around at that point, had encouraged me to wean her and stop breastfeeding. He was found guilty here in the Berlin Court of Appeal, sentenced to six years, but afterwards was handed over to the State Police. Then I believe he worked in the Oranienburg camp on railroad track construction. Hilde saw him, I think one more time. Then he was transferred to Mauthausen, where he was murdered.

After Gustav was released, he had to report to the police every week. Naturally, he was jobless. But then he managed to arrange a job as a trained radio technician making small-scale repairs with a company in Gesundbrunnen. He did those repairs at home. Initially he was working illicitly, then as a properly registered worker. But our marriage was on the rocks, at breaking point. He held a view that perhaps some share. He put it pretty blatantly to me, saying that he wanted nothing more to do with anything political. Once the workers were victorious, he would be there again, would support them. But now—without him! On top of this, the burden of having a Jewish wife was too much for him. He wasn't so very blatant in telling me that but indicated this was a problem too. Gustav had drunk heavily throughout his youth but had stopped any alcohol during his politically active years. After his release, he started drinking again, a turn I could not tolerate. Half a year after his release we decided to split, but we stayed together for a while so that I could create the practical conditions for sustaining myself. I had to be working again and had to place the child somewhere safe.

At that point, the following transpired in connection with my mom: She had up to then been living with my sister. My sister had lost her husband when she was four months pregnant. Some two years later she married again, the cousin of her first husband. But at first, she didn't wish to take our mother in to live with her. That worked well for me. I told Mom she could come and live with me. Until the matter was clarified, Gustav and I lived together side by side in our one room plus kitchen apartment, quietly and peacefully. And when we finally separated, we both broke down in tears. Life over the course of the years had provided us with much that we shared. I'd had plenty of heartache on his account, but I also learned a lot from Gustav. He, too, had had good and bad experiences living with me.

Gustav was released from prison in 1935; we separated in 1936. During that period, I had three abortions. He tried to make up for the two years we had been separated. And I was neither in a position nor willing to have more kids. After all, things were not OK between us, not just the sex which was pretty terrible. One abortion was done by a communist doctor, in his apartment. Georg Benjamin administered the anesthesia, afterwards I went back home. I had the second—and the third—at home in the kitchen, without any anesthesia. I prepared the necessary instruments myself. But it was done by a physician, and competently... After that, I never dared to try to have another child.

Then Mom came to live with me, and I started working again in the Jewish Hospital. Eva was in the Jewish kindergarten. Then the Nazis shut down the Jewish kindergartens, one after the other, including Eva's. She was not permitted to go to another. Initially I took care of my mom's needs from my work on night shift. Then came the 1938 *Kristallnacht* Pogrom. Everything surged to a crisis level. I said, "Listen, Mom, we have to find some solution." At this juncture, given preparations for war, Hitler faced a huge lack of nurses. To counter that, they had issued a directive, I think in 1937, stipulating that caregivers with longer-term experience could make up their state nursing exam by taking a short crash course. Since in issuing the directive, they had not excluded the Jews, i.e. had not even given them a thought, I said to my mother, "Listen Mom, you're going to become a nurse! That gives us a chance for survival and even forced labor has some meaning." Very boldly, I falsified testimonials for my mom, signatures of persons who had emigrated whose names I knew, stating that she had cared for them for years in this place and that. And with these testimonials that were submitted, which others who knew us also signed, the plan worked out. Every night I took Mom along with me to the hospital and taught her everything. Mom was a good pupil. She soon took and passed her nursing exam. Armed with her new qualification she left my side for the Infirmary for the Incurable, a facility for those with incurable diseases that was attached to the Jewish Hospital.

Charlotte's mother, Margarethe Döblin, as a nurse (l.) and with
Charlotte's daughter Eva (r.), 1940.

After Gustav left me, he found a job at a firm at Kottbusser Damm. He
told me later—I still maintained loose contact with him—that he was
working on an invention whose aim was to disguise the muzzle flash of
cannons. When he told me that, he lost all credit with me. He was aiding
the war effort! It made no difference if it developed into something or
not! He hadn't simply become passive, he had in a sense keeled far
over to the other side. When we divorced, he hadn't stressed his Aryan
ancestry; the reasons for the breakup were invented. That's how decent
he was. As a result, child custody was granted to me. That was one of
those special regulations for the Jews: Until then Eva had, according
to Nazi racial law, been a *Mischling* (mixed race) of the first degree.
With the divorce she automatically became a "full Jew" according to

the same law. In that case "protection for mixed marriages" did not apply. And because that was the case, I immediately had her registered in the Jewish community. I told myself: To the extent that there can be protection of any kind at all, this is the only option for her now. I myself was always a Jewish community employee since I was a Jewish Hospital nurse. So now she was a full Jew and I had to deal with this terrible fate for a child.

Work and Relations at the Jewish Hospital

The hospital of the Jewish community was under the control of the Gestapo. The Gestapo had established a Reich Association of German Jews, with its head office on Joachimsthaler Strasse. The various Jewish communities were administered from there by the Nazis. The Reich

Charlotte's daughter Eva Paech (Chava Kürer).

Representation, for example, was directly subordinate to the Gestapo. Years before the "Final Solution," they were forced to register all Jewish assets, parcels of land, etc. Thus, Jews themselves had to take care of the preliminary work. Workers were continually being transferred from the hospital for use as forced labor. After all, the Polish Jews or the Jews of Polish origin were expelled very early on from Germany. That must have been in 1938,[56] and naturally among our nurses there were also some of Polish origin.

Our hospital had 400 beds, meaning that capacity was 500 to 550. Attached was an infectious diseases ward. However, even before 1933, the community no longer had sufficient funds and the infectious diseases ward—located a little way apart from the other buildings—had been rented to the Berlin Municipality, which housed various offices there. During the Nazi period it was reattached to the hospital as an infirmary for the incurable and for other purposes. Before 1933, most of the physicians were unmarried, because it was also considered a hospital unit useful for medical training and further education. It was not under university control, but we had graduate interns there. There were two residential wings—converted attics with perhaps thirty rooms—for these single doctors. Later in the Nazi period whole families were housed in one room. If they wanted to get to their room they had to go through the ward. At that time, I made the acquaintance among them of an older, old-fashioned bachelor, Henschel,[57] who also was a painter on the side. He had a somewhat pompous manner of speaking that I found very amusing. We used to have long arguments with one another. I mention him because after 1945, he helped me from America, providing me with necessary assistance that enabled me to survive.

---

56 From October 27 to October 29, 1938, the Nazis arrested approximately 17,000 Jews of Polish heritage who were living in Germany. Forced to leave nearly all their possessions behind, these people were placed on trains, transported to the German–Polish border, and expelled. Poland refused entry to many of the deported, and they remained stuck in camps in the vicinity of the border for months.

57 A reference to Hans "Henschel" Bernhard. For more on him, see the biographical entries in the appendix.

When I went back and started to work again, and took my mother in, things went relatively well. I was able to work the night shift and was calm, reassured. That regime began around 6:00–6:30 P.M. I got up and Mom fixed me something to eat, and then I said bye to my child and walked over to the hospital, some ten minutes away. How difficult the shift was depended on which ward you had to work in. In the meantime, we had gotten a new supervisor, the old one had passed away. She was a rather peculiar woman. Let me say a bit more about her. Outwardly, she was very strict, but inwardly, not at all. People said she had an illegitimate daughter, which probably was untrue. But that pointed to how we saw this woman, i.e. not at all how she presented herself. She did a lot for us, despite the exploitation. We had a place in the residence that we could call home. As trainee nurses she fed us well. And she even came to wake us up in the morning. She went from room to room and didn't budge until the trainee had jumped from her bed and said, "Good morning!" Then, as we stood there in our pajamas, she showered us with a stream of all the ignominious misdeeds we had committed that she had gotten wind of. After that we had to go together to breakfast. She supervised that. The registered nurses were allowed to eat in the ward. Then she paid very careful attention to how much butter we were putting on our bread. To make sure it was not too little. When a nurse had a problem with an ingredient included in our lunch, she knew about it. And had the kitchen prepare something else. At that time, I was vegetarian (for about four years). So they also cooked something different for me. And Friday evening, for the Sabbath, the nurses always looked their best for the meal.

There were about 100 of us, all dressed in black, with white skirts and nurses' caps. And Lotte got special food then, too! The supervisor incidentally had facial paralysis and a crooked mouth, and we imitated her mannerisms. When we came down early in the morning for breakfast, she used to say with a crooked mouth, "Nurse, your cap is on crooked!" In the social room downstairs, we were permitted to receive visitors. Including those of the opposite sex. She permitted us to have gymnastics lessons after we'd said we wanted them, twice a week.

One day one of our sister trainee nurses, Renate,[58] who was a close friend of mine, became pregnant. She was about twenty-three years old. The father was one of our younger patients, a guy of about seventeen. He had diabetes, was just about to graduate high school, a nice boy. She probably figured that he didn't have much longer to live anyhow, and so made life a bit more beautiful and bearable for him. We knew nothing about the pregnancy. One day the supervisor came and took Renate away. She often did that. Then she said to us, "I have to go with Renate to the ear doctor, trouble with her ears again." She accompanied her to the examination and also wanted to arrange for the pregnancy to be terminated. That was a lot for this religious nurse! But Renate did not want to have the pregnancy terminated. And the supervisor took care of everything. She ran around here and there, this old matron! So that the boy would be allowed to take an emergency final exam for graduation and then be declared of legal age early, and then the two of them could marry. In the case of Renate, she was able to hush things up.

I, on the other hand, proudly announced that I was expecting. I wore my bad habits on my chest, my immorality, I made no secret of that. For me that was part of public morality. Against all expectations, Renate's young diabetic survived, and may be alive today. He was a painter and went to England. Separated from Renate after a few years. She was an especially decent and stupid woman, a kind but simple-minded person. She stemmed from Bernburg, was the daughter of a cantor. I really was very fond of her. She left the hospital and had a lot of hassle and bother with her son Ralph. Sometime around 1938/1939 she placed the child in a Warburg residential home in France. During the war she was notified that during the occupation, the children had been evacuated to southern France; she was asked whether she wanted to officially transfer her power of attorney for the child. She did that. I would really like to locate this boy who is probably somewhere in the U.S. I've wanted to do so over all these years, and yet never did anything. You know what I learned in life: That whatever I did, there

---

58 A reference to Renate Moratz. For more on her and her son Ralph, see the biographical entries in the appendix.

wasn't much to regret. I only regret what I didn't do. It bothers me that some things can only be made up for by accident. That includes Ralph Moratz. To cut a long story short, Renate died because of us. She provided illegal accommodation to our people and was imprisoned with the others...

The old supervisor's name was Salinger, and the new one was called Salingré. She too is already deceased but was able to die a "normal" death. We were always happy when someone died "normally." My grandpa right at the end was placed in the home for the incurable where my mom was on staff as a nurse. He was eighty-five when he came to the hospital to die. He died of old age and exhaustion, because at that point he was no longer eating much. After his death I prepared him for burial and called Mom. Then we took him downstairs through the corridor to the mortuary where we laid him out. We were both so happy and pleased that probably, as we used to say then, he would be spared a great deal. In the case of Grandma, who had died two years before, also in the hospital, things hadn't worked out quite like that. We still had a normal mourning ceremony for her. She was an old woman, eighty-two, who for a few years had no longer been healthy mentally. Grandpa, however, made it to the end without any particular torments.

The new supervisor was already an old woman. She was very well known to us from the time she had been head nurse in the surgery ward, for decades. She was very well organized, extremely clean, and tidy. But she was stingy. You can't imagine what a tightwad she was. Her pantry was piled high with eggs and lemons, and the patients had nothing. That was still in the normal times. As for us: We obtained our main meal—and special dietary meals—from the central kitchen. But the nurses prepared supper and breakfast for themselves and for the patients. The ingredients for that were brought over separately to enable special meals to be prepared according to need.

The first breakfast was standard fare. Patients were only given a choice of beverage. We nurses had to prepare the food according to the dietary instructions for each patient and distribute it. We pushed the cart through the wards and distributed food at our discretion: rolls and butter, marmalade, honey, a choice of three different beverages. For the second breakfast, we would go through the wards beforehand

and ask what the patients wanted. On offer were eggs, cognac, red wine, lemons, cottage cheese, cream, and butter. You could do a lot with that—chaudeau, omelet souflée... And heaven help us if it wasn't nice and foamy! It was a lot of work for us. And to boot, we also had to deal with keeping everything kosher! Unfortunately, our hospital was still kosher. There were two sets of dishes, two kinds of pots and pans, two different tables for washing. But almost none of the nurses were Orthodox. And so we were quite diligent in mixing things up, again and again. Only when something was brought in for the patient was it truly kosher.

But the patients had little interest, if any, in that, because before 1933, we had very few Jewish patients. Every few weeks the kashrut inspection commission would drop by. These women were always called *Schamröschen* (little roses of shame); where that sobriquet comes from, I don't know. And if one of them discovered anything that was *treif*, she made sure it was kashered. There was always a lot of joking around. As I already said, Salingré was so stingy. Many edibles spoiled in her pantry, which did the patients no good. But despite everything, the excellent food made many who were jobless really overjoyed to get sick. Many a time they were very happy to have their appendix removed. In those days we were happy to indulge in the rolls that were available in the afternoon, thickly spread with butter. And we were allowed to indulge; we were part of the whole environment after all. Later on, of course this was no longer the case. After 1933, everything we had available to eat was stolen. I too was guilty of stealing. Of course not from the patients! Not because I thought there was anything wrong about that, but simply because I couldn't allow myself to get caught.

But once again let me go back to the narrative. After supper, that we also prepared, we would sit down on the beds of our patients—something strictly forbidden—and tell stories, lots of them! And that was also a period in which I learned things from many people. From men largely political stuff, and they also tried to court us a bit as well. That wasn't unpleasant. We learned about many things having to do with family from the women. Men by the way are easier to care for, they recuperate faster, while women are quicker to get depressed, stay longer, and can collapse. But then they are also grateful for any small act of assistance. In this period, I mean before 1933, I was still a virgin, still inexperienced. But I heard umpteen different stories about marriage which was helpful. Naturally, my sister nurses noticed the gap in my experience and teased me about it constantly. All I had was a rough picture. I can recall a trip we took in the youth hiking movement. We bedded down in a barn, boys and girls together. I'd been talking for a real long time with a boy outside, a med student. Everybody was already asleep when we went inside. So that we wouldn't disturb anybody, we just slipped under a blanket. He must have been sexually excited, and I also felt something. But what it was—I just didn't understand. I was like a child for such a long time. As a young woman, maybe I was around seventeen, I missed a period (I had menstruated from the age of eleven). I went to a doctor our family was friendly with, someone I had assisted during his visiting hours when I had been at school. He asked me about my encounters with boys and was dumbfounded at my reaction—namely that I didn't realize at all what he was getting at—that he immediately broke off that line of questioning. It wasn't until years later that I recalled that scene at his office.

I knew of course in the hospital that I was still a virgin. But I didn't know what the actual "procedure" was. We were just two nurses there who had never directly experienced sex and I started to feel terribly ashamed. Once a problem developed with my corpus luteum, leading to a critical lack of progesterone, and I bled for days on end. I went to our gynecologist, Dr. Levin. He wanted to examine me, but it wasn't possible yet from the front, so he examined me rectally. I felt so terribly ashamed! In fact, I was so ashamed that I went out to actually look for a boyfriend. And I met up with a young man I'd gotten to know a bit from the baby nursery. He was a relative of one of the nurses there. A nice guy, David Luft, an engineer, his brother was a doctor at the hospital. I decided to make him my boyfriend. I wanted to use him to get rid of my "deficiencies" in this regard. He got the idea and was quite ready to help out. But he was a bit clumsy and awkward, and in my opinion was not very experienced as a lover. Anyhow, we went out for a walk, and he wanted to "take care of that" somewhere in the park. For a girl like me that was totally impossible, out of the question. So when we were at the critical point, I just upped and ran off. That also spelled the end of our relationship. Then both of us were ashamed whenever we saw one another. But now the time was probably ripe. And then Gustav came along, whom I really didn't desire at all.

I was by the way always very proud of the fact that I had not come to the Communist Party as a result of some love relationship with a man. Some girls had, though it became irrelevant once the person in question had undergone political education. Nevertheless, in my case, it was the other way around—first I got involved with a political movement, and then with a man. I had also seen that when it was vice versa, once the relationship was over, the enthusiasm for the Party also declined.

When I was finished with the night shift, I passed the work on to my sister nurses, who now were all Jewish girls. And when our supervisor Salingré heard that I was going to return, despite the fact that she was very stingy and tightfisted, she nonetheless showed some sympathy and understanding for my situation. If some problem arose with my child or I wasn't feeling well, she sent me to an easy ward. Such an easy ward, for example, was the ENT care unit. And when we had no ophthalmology patients, it really was easy. Ophthalmology patients are always very difficult, it requires a huge amount of effort. You have to pay a lot of attention to them.

By the way, I once had an experience in the ENT ward that was terrible. My reaction was very educational. By nature, I can endure, experience, and tolerate a great deal, but afterwards I tend to collapse. We had a patient there who didn't feel very sick even though his condition was life-threatening. He had a tumor in his larynx, a polyp that was resonating, moving. We prepared him for an operation because he had a weak heart. As long as the polyp was in a good position, nothing bad could happen to the patient. But since it was moving and anyhow was big enough to block his windpipe, he was always in acute danger of death. We had to be careful and make sure nothing happened to him before the operation. But it had to be postponed for a few days because of his heart condition, so that he would be strong enough to tolerate the surgery. To this end we moved him to a small single room (we had only very few single rooms for the seriously ill or those in critical condition, and upstairs we also had a Class Ward with Class A and B). Directly next to his bed was the oxygen bottle and outside the door an intubation unit. Back then we were a lot less well equipped than we are today. There were big problems with intubation. Even though we were taught that in an emergency we could attempt anything, we nurses actually were not supposed to carry out intubation procedures—specifically not in our hospital, since we could always quickly summon a surgeon to do the job when necessary.

This patient made my job very difficult. The ward was very long, and I repeatedly had to cross it to reach his room to check on him. That disturbed him since he wished to sleep. But every ten or fifteen minutes I used to go to check on him, since I was after all aware of how dangerous, life-threatening his situation was. Yet everything was OK. I went to the kitchen to finish washing utensils after supper, a task we shared because of the lack of kitchen staff. We night nurses provided the nighttime medication as soon as we arrived, and we would ask patients if they had any special wishes. I was busy washing at the sink. His room was opposite. Now and then I went over and checked on him. Everything was alright. I was standing again over the dishes, and suddenly the man was there right behind me, he could hardly breathe. I grabbed him, put him back in bed, and connected the oxygen bottle. I ran to the phone to summon the doctor. And while I was still on the phone, he came up behind me and clutched me tightly. I lugged the heavy man back to his room. In one hand I took the oxygen bottle, with the other the intubation unit. Then the doctor arrived—and the man was dead. That was such a horrible death, this terrible wheezing...

The way he had clutched and embraced me, his fear of dying, his quite normal condition just a few minutes before and then this horror. I'll never forget that. Sure, I know my reaction was correct, I responded very quickly, I did everything that *I* could have done. But to plunge a knife into his throat that second—I wouldn't have been able to, no. I was an absolute wreck afterwards. I could hardly finish my shift. It was so terrible that I took special note of this, and the memory remains, even though I've seen a lot in my life.

I know from the following that I react well and fast: Later, when the doctors were no longer allowed to be called doctors if they were

Jews, we had some doctors who were there as caregivers. One doctor was sitting with a patient who had just undergone amputation. Such patients, recently amputated, usually suffer from mental confusion after a few days. That is a reaction I can well understand. The patient suddenly tore off not only his bandage but also ripped away the skin graft on his upper thigh that had been sewn over the stump of the leg. He sat there drenched in blood. And the doctor? He was standing next to him shouting. I rushed through the ward, entered the room, and reacted immediately. I took his leg and pressed it together and then put the skin graft on top. I stayed with the patient and sent the doctor away, telling him to telephone, to say the patient was being transferred to surgery.

I knew my reaction was right. But then I broke down a bit afterwards, started to tremble. That's the body. I found a nice sentence in the book *Pain Surgery*, "A human being has no fear, his body is afraid." That is exactly the way I formulated it for myself, "I feel no fear, but my body is not cooperating." Whenever I was on the easy ward, where you had to walk through and provide care, I had a time for conversation because initially we were two or three nurses on the ward. Later on, the state police allowed only a single nurse on the floor, and then naturally you never had any spare time. But next to it was the residential floor for the doctors. I already mentioned that the doctors had to pass through the ward on their way back from their shifts.

I've already noted here that much was missing in my life as a woman. Also when Gustav came back. On the ENT ward I was friends with Anja Drach, a Communist Party member.[59] She was close to fifty years old. A sensible woman. Her husband had been an actor. She had three children: Hans, Thomas, and Eva.[60] Hans was a son fathered by the dramatist Wedekind, with whom her husband had been close friends. The boy had arrived during their marriage, when her husband was in a TB sanatorium. He silently accepted the situation. It turned out

---

59 Anja Drach's first name was actually Anna. She survived the war in hiding, after escaping from Gestapo custody. For more on her, see the biographical entries in the appendix.

60 Charlotte Holzer remembered the name of Anja Drach's daughter wrong. Her given name was Rosa, not Eva. For more on her, see the biographical entries in the appendix.

OK. Hans became an actor, went to the Soviet Union, and died there.[61] Thomas probably also died, but I don't know exactly what happened to him.[62] Eva went to England and brought Anja there in 1946. But Anja's fate was similar to mine during the time of my imprisonment.

I confided in Anja about my troubles. And because she was sensible, she said, "Look, don't be so stupid, and don't torment yourself so much about that. It's simply part of life for a healthy human being. There are enough young men around here, just go and take your pick." That seemed very odd to me. Naturally, I rejected that advice. But it remained in my mind, nonetheless. There was a doctor, an internist, I liked him very much because he was always so well behaved and decent in dealing with the patients. Never was anything too much for him. He was the way you might wish a physician to be. In addition, he was very handsome. About my same age. His name was Schöngut. One evening he also came home to the hospital, and somehow, he had likewise probably sensed in conversations that I liked him. When he went back into his room, Anja read me the riot act. She said, "Come on, don't be so stupid. Just do something, say something. Cast aside your silly reservations, after all, they are so bourgeois!" And that's how, the next evening, I went with Schöngut to his room.

At that time Mom was no longer with me, and I never knew where I should put Eva. For the most part I took her along to the hospital. Subsequently I was really very friendly with Schöngut, things had developed... Of course it was clear to me it was nothing but a friendship with certain benefits. And Schöngut thought the same. There was never any talk about something more. But sometimes I didn't know where I should leave Eva. And then she slept in Schöngut's room. One day Eva saw the old supervisor in the garden. She would always say something to Eva who was so cute and small. She knew that Eva was being moved around a lot, here and there, and asked her, "Well, Evchen, tell me dear, where are you now?" And Eva replied, "I'm sleeping over at the place

---

61 Hans Eduard Drach was extradited by the Soviet Union and died at Niederhagen concentration camp. For more on him, see the biographical entries in the appendix.

62 Thomas survived and immigrated to the Land of Israel in 1947. For more on him, see the biographical entries in the appendix.

of my mom's boyfriend." For a long time, it went on that way. One day I arranged with Schöngut that he should take Eva again to his room and allow her to sleep there. But when I arrived around 8 P.M. with her, he wasn't around. He'd forgotten. It was then that I broke up with him.

I already felt that the relationship was not satisfying for me if it did not involve a genuine sense of affection. Because otherwise it slowly turns into disgust. In addition, it bothered me that our being together always had to be in hiding. During the day he had no time, and at night I was on my shift. At the most we were together very briefly in the morning. And then we would hide, and I felt that it was beneath my dignity. I'm OK with being outside of a legal relationship, but not for a long time and not in secret. And now there was, in addition, this breach of my trust for him as well. Yet I have never forgotten him and still like him. We didn't have any fight, but we broke up, from one day to the next.

When we were in the maternity ward, part of the ongoing care also involved the delivery of babies. I must say that I really used to enjoy that part of our duties. You had to care for the infants as well, so it was plenty of hard work. And on top of it all, you got to sit down for maybe half an hour at most during the night. When we were on duty in the surgical ward, along with the regular duties we also had to help out in the operating theater. Given this work overload and lack of personnel, another problem was that I ruptured the round ligaments of my uterus when I had to lift the patient up by myself.

My night shift was officially over at 8 A.M., but I usually did not finished until 8:30 or 9 A.M. Sometimes it was because by nature I'm a bit slow, at other times because I was just wasting time, dilly-dallying. And sometimes it was because there was really just so much to do. As long as Mom was living with me at home, things went very well. She would bring Eva to the kindergarten, which still functioned then. Then came a nice break for me: I didn't go home after finishing my night shift but would go out onto the sunroof. We had a sunroof on top of the hospital, reserved for the nurses. I used to lie there, all the time I was employed at the hospital, every day for one or two hours. That's how I am by nature. We would do gymnastics there. For that I would always wear something that looked decent and proper. We also had a shower area up on the roof that I'd make use of. And then I'd go on home. Mom would prepare something light for me to eat. Then I'd lie down to sleep until the afternoon. If I arrived home at 11 A.M. I used to sleep until 3:30 P.M., until Mom went to pick up the child. Then I was busy with my daughter. Around 6 P.M., I'd lie down to take a nap for another hour, and then leave for work. Later on, that was all much more difficult. Let me jump ahead: After the Gestapo shut down the nurseries and kindergartens, I would sometimes take Eva along to the hospital. She slept in the patients' beds. Later they were no longer unoccupied because the hospital had been reduced in size. She then slept on stretchers in the operating theater, where during the night she had to be removed. Then during the day, I would get some sleep, just for a short time. After all, she was at home with me. She was incredibly well behaved, it was touching, always quiet when I was asleep. Nonetheless, I had my duties in taking care of her.

On my political work: During my pregnancy, I remained involved and pitched in as much as I could. I came down pretty soon with one vein inflammation after the next. What was important for me was not the extent of my contribution but the attitude that I could express in doing resistance work. When I returned after the baby was born, the Party had "suspended me." After all, my husband was in jail. The threat for the other comrades would have been too great. I received visits from time to time though. I believe I already mentioned the Red Help. Then Gustav came back and had to report regularly to the police. As long as we were together, I was not allowed to engage in any activity either. Time passed, I was hard at work, but my political readiness lay fallow. And I took that very hard, it was a bitter pill. I started to search for something. That quest led me in 1939 to the Baum Group. And once again it was via the hospital that I established contact with them.

Meanwhile, *Kristallnacht* descended upon us. It revealed terrible things that I'd never seen before. In 1938, most of the Jewish intellectuals were arrested and taken away. They were sent to the Sachsenhausen concentration camp. During this arrest operation, one of the doctors who fled was Dr. Eichelbaum. He belonged to a group of socialist doctors, was already married then, and his wife had immigrated to the U.S. He already had an immigration visa for the States and had booked a place on a ship, with a few weeks until his departure date. During this time, he had to go into hiding somewhere. He stayed in my apartment, hidden in the kitchen for two weeks. Eva at that time was with the Londons. We had nicknamed Eichelbaum the "Nail King." He had dealt as a surgeon and orthopedist with the nailing together of fractures and had accomplished extraordinary work in that field. He also was a sculptor, highly gifted. He was also a large, handsome man, older than me.

Despite all the illegality and all the hardship, he gave me two beautiful weeks that I will never forget. When I would return from my night shift, everything was ready. There was something to eat on the table, and he cared for me in a very touching way. I was not accustomed to that, except from my mom. There were many, many conversations in those two weeks. When he was ready to leave, we got together once. I thought it was terrible because he was after all a married man. But I thought of my experiences with Wölfchen, Wolfgang Roth. I realized that it simply had to be that way if I didn't want to upset and offend him. He then continued to write me from the States and wanted to arrange to bring me there. I had already told him beforehand that I wouldn't do that. I said, "I won't do anything to upset your wife." What happened, happened. I told him, "You can tell her or not, I don't care. But I'm not going to come. Moreover, my place is here with the patients and here with my political work." I never answered his letters. In 1947, he tracked me down and provided me—it was very touching—with medicines, other things, and some food from the States.

Back to *Kristallnacht*: Those who were sent to Ravensbrück or Sachsenhausen were kept in the camp for six weeks. And after those six weeks, these people were brought in batches to the hospital in order to die. What I saw is difficult to describe. A lot of them had lost their mind. Many had frostbite, pneumonia, a lot were half-starved to death, others had been badly manhandled and abused. I really don't know what the aim was behind the decision by the Gestapo to release and hand these people over. Maybe they were trying to demonstrate something to the Jews.

It was terrible. The whole place reeked of all these festering wounds. We could hardly cope. In addition, a wave of suicides set in, of inconceivable magnitude. And those who had not quite succeeded in killing themselves were rushed to the hospital. Then you were left confronting the decision: Should you save them or not? What will you do? These individuals were nearly always devoid of any will to live, so despite all our efforts they died. We were no longer able to differentiate between men and women, they were placed side by side, wherever a place was free. We were no longer able to put fresh sheets and blankets on the beds. We brought in all our emergency beds. There were no more passageways at all between the beds. People lay there and died, lay there and died. You can't imagine what it was like.

That strengthened me in my resolve to stay here, as long as it is at all possible. Many who still were able to run away had done so. I told myself, "Look, you can never tell them anything, you have to accept it. OK, let them save their lives. But I can't. My child..." So, this matter went even further. Besides, where was I supposed to go, even if I'd wanted to? I had no money. I couldn't go to Eichelbaum. Gradually no other alternative remained. I had a chance to get to Newfoundland but that was very vague and uncertain. I tried to get to the Soviet Union. But they weren't accepting people. I went to the consulate. However, they told me immediately, "That's out of the question, it's senseless." And people at the Party said the same thing. They saw in the case of those who tried even harder: They weren't letting people in. In those years only one of our nurses made it out. Her name was Frida Rahel and she called herself in Yiddish Freide Ruchel. She was a Jewish woman of Russian nationality and she made it out to the Soviet Union.

But all that actually served to strengthen my will to resist and to search for some possibility to engage in resistance. It was very hard. And when a person believed they had found just the tiniest sliver of an option for comrades to operate illegally, and it came to the Gestapo's attention, well then the comrades shut it all down tight—because of the danger.

Herbert Baum and the Resistance

At this point in time, 1939, I was working in the urology ward. One evening I arrived to begin my shift. The patients there were nearly all elderly men. I opened up the door of one room, and some young guy was standing there looking at me. And I was looking at him. He said, "Yeah, yeah, it's really me!" It was Herbert Baum.[63] He was a few years younger than me, and I had been in the youth movement with him. Now he was suffering from a renal colic and had been sent from forced labor to the hospital. It was very nice for me to have Herbert there, but for him with his kidney infection it was less pleasant. Nonetheless, we had umpteen conversations. Finally, we started to question one another more directly and sensed that we had developed along similar lines. But neither of us said anything about this to the other. Maybe I to him a bit more than he to me.

In any case, I did tell him that I was terribly alone and really wanted to do something. And he said, "Listen, you know, I've got this circle of friends. Maybe you'll come over to us some time." And he had not yet said anything more to me than that. I did go to see them, and initially I went on excursions with them, although that had long been forbidden for Jews. Basically, in and of itself, that was already something illegal. But out in the countryside we still went hiking, we'd sing, we had conversations. I made the acquaintance of a few from the friends' circle, but not yet in any political respect. And when I was off work and could place my child somewhere, they also met over at my home. Then one day Herbert told me very openly, "We're a group that are dealing with this and that. Now you have to tell us if you want to be included as one of us."

And so, in 1939, I was accepted into the group. Initially work in the group was heavily concentrated on our own schooling. Opinions on current events of the day were worked out, and leaflets were prepared. I wasn't able to participate all that much because of my night shifts. When we decided to make a leaflet, each person made

---

63 For more on Herbert Baum, see the biographical entries in the appendix.

some statement themselves, then we checked the ideas each person had come up with and would work out an agreed text from that. At that time Herbert already had contact with other groups, but only later did we get instructions or material. We had a mimeograph machine that we then put to work. If you ask whether every one of us participated in such an operation, I can only reply: It wasn't structured and delimited in that way. It was a matter of time, possibility, courage. Whoever was able and wanted to participate, joined in. No one was ordered to do anything. For example, we did a few such leaflet actions, we left the leaflets in telephone booths. Then we tried to exert some influence on the forced laborers, the Jewish ones, sixteen- to eighteen-year-olds. And then we sent out letters to the front, to people that we knew as old friends.

My relationship with the Baum family became close very quickly because I'd known Marianne Baum earlier on, from before. She too had been in the youth movement, and then she'd worked as a caretaker for babies (i.e. without an exam as a qualified nurse) in the Rummelsburg Orphanage. I have a dim memory of one afternoon when I went over to the Baums. On that occasion Herbert said to me, "Too bad you can't come this evening. The meeting tonight is something more than our previous hikes..." Then he asked me if I wanted to join and let me understand that the group would accept me as a member. Because it was something mutual: being prepared to join in and being ready to be accepted into the group. And this after they had in fact looked me over, checked me out a bit. This was something dangerous, but the Jews were in danger in any case. To that extent we were the potential opponents of the Nazi regime right from the onset. There was no question among us about whether we supported the regime. It was self-evident that we were against it. But whether we were also ready to do something against it, that was the question. And at this point in time, when we knew about a "Final Solution" or had some inkling of that, a presentiment, and perhaps were still toying with the notion of emigration, that was a decision which tremendously increased the threat to our lives. You really had to make such a decision very consciously.

The mimeograph machine was kept for a time, as far as I recall, at Gipsstrasse 3, where today the Folk Music School is located. Back then it housed a Jewish children's home. Sala Kochmann was living there with her husband up in the attic in a "service apartment" for staff members.[64] She was a kindergarten teacher. They had a wonderful place; I can still recall that very vividly. And for a time, the mimeograph was down in the basement in Herbert's flat. After the arrest of the first group, Richard[65] had to destroy the machine, get rid of it. It ended up tossed into the Spree River. But more about that later.

Aside from sending letters to soldiers at the front, we also tried to send out letters here at home as well. We wrote to the population about the deterioration of the situation and the role of Hitler. We decided that each of us would write two or three letters and send them to distant acquaintances, non-Jewish. And that was designed with the aim of controlling the effect. But it was botched, and went very badly wrong. We were met with silence. We also could and should have told ourselves beforehand that it wouldn't turn out well. Many probably just destroyed the letters they got; they were so frightened. For example, I'd written to the owner of the local health food store. I had very cautiously wanted to question her. I sensed that she'd already noticed from my questions that I had something to do with these letters. And she immediately broke off contact, most probably because of our longstanding friendship. She'd been selling us things for a long time, items that were forbidden to sell to Jews.

The great strength of our group was that, after a test period for security reasons, we really got to know each other well. Partially from our contacts earlier on. Each of us knew very precisely the capabilities of the other. There was nothing in our lives that we didn't decide about in common, together, no concern or worry, no source of joy that was not shared. There was no informer in our group. That was impossible. But on the other hand, the group was far more endangered because of this close bond and contact. At this point we had for a long time been working in groups of two, three, or four. And then, in 1942, we divided up into groups of three. But the bonds of loose, personal contact throughout the

---

64 For more on the Kochmanns, see the biographical entries in the appendix.
65 Richard Holzer (1911–1975), Charlotte's future husband. For more on him, see the biographical entries in the appendix.

whole group continued. It was simply no longer possible for us not to know the others in the parallel group. Aside from Herbert Baum, none of us maintained contact with other groups. And his contact was via a go-between to the Steinbrinck Group, where the members were killed together with those in our group. Richard had connections to his earlier comrades. But the work was illegal and was kept clandestine so that not every member knew about the relations that other persons had to other groups. Only in the case of Herbert Baum did we know about that. Each of the Hirsch sisters still maintained relations to other illegal groups. And via these groups people were in contact with others. There were these loose contacts.

When we were still a single group, we basically dealt with our own internal schooling, with our position on events of the day, and also listened to music. It was actually forbidden for Jews to own gramophone records. And we really no longer had any radios. But we did manage to listen to records. We organized record-listening evenings, and we would sing a lot together. We went on excursions together out of town, something also forbidden for Jews. We tried to flout the restrictions that had been placed on Jews in their daily lives and attempted to live "normally." And then we established contacts with other forced laborers, the so-called "foreign workers." One reason was for the sake of political contacts. Another was because we'd recognized that the situation was getting ever more critical, and we needed to explore the option of being sent off somewhere as forced laborers. Where to? Well, that's something we still didn't really know. For example, we bought forged French passports. Herbert had arranged that. And we all studied French, and we planned to go into double illegality, as Jews *and* Communists. Our liaison to the French POWs was Suzanne. Our political work also went off tangentially in that direction. Then we set up working groups of three. In addition, we assigned our younger group members—Gerhard Meyer, Heinz "Buber" Birnbaum, Heinz Rotholz, and also Hella Hirsch[66]—the task of organizing and guiding younger groups within the ranks of the Jewish forced laborers.

---

66 For more on Gerhard Meyer, Heinz Birnbaum, Heinz Rotholz, and Helene "Hella" Hirsch, see the biographical entries in the appendix.

These younger groups did very good work afterwards, especially the Joachim Group that politically was already very advanced in its thinking. They developed along the lines of the KJVD,[67] and thus in the direction of the Party. It's very hard in retrospect to give an accurate number for those involved. Due to the conditions of illegality, Richard and I, for example, had no direct contact to those who were in the know. We knew the Joachim Group, because as the politically most advanced group, it was working together with ours. And I have to say: Hans Joachim and his wife Marianne—both were about twenty-one years old—were extraordinary.[68] He was *the* musician, a born artist. I don't know to what extent he'd had musical training. I don't believe he had any. He hoped to become a professional musician if he survived. Very sensitive, very tender. But he wasn't able to hold out either. He wasn't a traitor. Yet he didn't manage to hang on and bear up. Marianne was far stronger than he was. I mean in her mental attitude. She was clever and managed to hold out and survive exceptionally well. There's more to tell about both when we come to talking about the dissolution of the group after the arrests. If I venture a total count of the group, it included some sixty individuals. And they were young! I was the oldest in the entire group.

The influence on people naturally extended further. Thus, Joachim working at Siemens had already gathered a few others around him. The liaison for that was Gerhard Meyer. In the case of Richard's people, these were mainly friends and comrades who—like him—had been in the Jewish youth movement, in groups like "Kameraden" and "Schwarzer Haufen," and who still remained in Germany. Among others, that included Siecke Kahn.[69] And then there was the group he

---

67 KJVD—Kommunistischer Jugendverband Deutschlands (Communist Youth Association of Germany), the youth movement of the German Communist Party. The organization was founded in October 1918 as Freie Sozialistische Jugend (Free Socialist Youth), joined the German Communist Party when it was founded in 1920, and then renamed Kommunistische Jugend Deutschlands (Communist Youth of Germany). It received its current name in 1925.

68 For more on the Joachims, see the biographical entries in the appendix.

69 Sieke Kahn's real first name was Siegbert. For more on him, see the biographical entries in the appendix.

was in together with Irma. Irma Edom was her maiden name. That was a group of office workers from the insurance industry. Richard was steered toward that group as someone jobless. As an unemployed person you were told to go over to this group or that. From among those there was still an old comrade in Bernau, named Puwalla, who often provided us with a place to stay illegally.[70] Then there was another man, Ernst Jegelka.[71] He later went to the West, to West Berlin, and no longer played a meaningful role. But back then Ernst was a good political worker. He was a Communist comrade, and over at his place was a kind of center for listening in on radio stations broadcasting from England, but mainly from the Soviet radio. He was living on Holzmarktstrasse. Ernst gave me some assistance for a long time, even after I was in prison too. And after the war he was also still OK, reliable as a comrade. But then he kind of half disappeared. And now, well, he's totally lost his footing, gone to the other side. Probably it was the better pay that attracted him, who knows what!

But now I'd like to talk about how I met Richard, and how we became a couple. After all, I've mentioned to you that I was often alone, and that was a very bitter experience for me. When I found Herbert, I told him, "Pay attention, listen! I'm alone. And if you bring me together with other comrades, then you should know that. I'm not someone to say that people shouldn't get together. If you know some nice guy who's all alone, tell him about me. Because I can't always stay alone this way. And the child can't either." Herbert didn't respond. Richard, though, now was single. So Herbert told Richard, "Listen, man. You're all alone, after all. There is this woman Paech who comes to our group. So how about it?" I didn't know about this. Richard became really furious and said, "Hey, are you trying to play the matchmaker here?" He said he'd have nothing to do with that, it was out of the question. The upshot

---

70 The German system legally required and still requires citizens and residents to formally register their places of residence with the authorities. During Nazi time, this system and its records were also used for the deportation of Jews, and the persecution of those Nazi ideology regarded as undesirables or enemies. The only way to escape the system was to go into illegality, meaning to avoid registration and live in hiding.

71 For more on Ernst Jegelka, see the biographical entries in the appendix.

was that he behaved very coldly toward me. For a long time. We almost never spoke to one another. I had noticed him, I liked him. But he was simply so terribly quiet, always with a kind of silent strained look on his face. Now and then he would just sit there, smirking to himself. I liked him, but nothing more than that. And I was not thinking about him. I knew nothing about the fate of his brother.[72]

Little Herbert, however, couldn't leave things alone. And since he was a good organizer, and because I was constantly on the night shift and also couldn't always go along when they went for some short excursion out of town, he gave Richard an assignment: that he should take care of my daughter, Eva. Richard was always very kind and loving when around children. And he always came to pick up Eva when they arranged a short trip out into the countryside. And then he would also have to return her to me afterwards. And then Herbert very often arranged meetings in my flat, whether I was present or not. And Richard would sit there with this silent smirk on his face. I still recall very clearly: He would be sitting there on the couch in the middle of our long, small room, sort of smirking to himself in strained silence.

Now and then I also went out on a trip with them. And so that I could get some sleep after the night shift, I always left later and caught up with them. Then Herbert told Richard that he should wait and meet me at the train station. Because it was illegal for us to arrange such trips. It was a little dangerous. Or we would meet at the station. Then Richard would pick up my child beforehand. She was in childcare at the time. And one fine day—I recall it now as if yesterday—we all planned to meet at the Gesundbrunnen train station. I mean, that was the plan. I arrived, and guess what: Richard was standing there, holding Eva's hand, but no one else. I didn't know what had happened, neither did he—they simply forgot us! We then decided: OK, let's take a trip by ourselves. We went to Frohnau and during the whole journey, my Richard talked about himself, his brother. It was the autumn of 1940. We climbed up a hill. There was a bench. It was very calm; the leaves were rustling a bit. Beautiful, golden fall foliage.

---

72 Gerhard Holzer, Richard's brother and an active member of the Communist Party, was executed in 1937. For more on him, see the biographical entries in the appendix.

Richard had ever more to tell me. And little Eva kept bothering us with questions and talking. Like, well, a six-year-old little girl... We decided to put her in the big wastepaper bin behind us, it was full of leaves. She quickly became very busy, preoccupied with those golden leaves, and we too were very busy with ourselves. He told me everything about himself, in a way that was very different from before. He'd never behaved this way at all when around me. Then Richard asked me, "How about us becoming a couple?" And I said, "Yes." We arranged that he should come on over to my apartment... Then I asked him to move in and stay at my place, to live there. He was officially registered as living at his mom's address.

Probably that relocation was what helped save his life later on. Richard worked during the day, would come home from his job in the evening. He'd see me for about ten minutes, before I would have to leave for my job at the hospital. He had the child Eva there with him and would sleep the night in my apartment. When I returned early in the morning, Richard would have already left for work. Things went on that way for about a year. Altogether we only lived for just about a year together. We couldn't get married because Richard was a Hungarian Jew and I was a German Jew. Herr Hitler didn't allow that. Richard did not wear a Star of David. The law for wearing the star applied only to German Jews.[73] The non-German Jews did not have to wear a yellow star, presumably also because of a gap in the law, similar to the law regarding the training of nurses and its gap.[74]

---

73 The decree that regulated the marking of all Jews was based on the first amendment to the *Reichsbürgergesetz* (Reich Citizenship Law) and thus only applied to Jews with German citizenship.

74 This is a reference to Charlotte's use of a gap in an earlier regulation that enabled her to sign up her mother for training as a nurse. The *Gesetz zur Ordnung der Krankenpflege* (Law on the Organization of Nursing) of September 28, 1938, closed that gap and obligated (in section 3.1) applicants training to be nurses to prove their Aryan origin. See Herbert Weisbrod-Frey, "Krankenpflegeausbildung im Dritten Reich," in Hilde Steppe, ed., *Krankenpflege im Nationalsozialismus* (Frankfurt am Main: Mabuse Verlag, 2013), pp. 93–116. Apparently, as indicated by Charlotte Holzer, this limitation did not apply to non-German Jews. For more on that subject, see Hilde Steppe, "Nursing in the Third Reich," *History of Nursing Society Journal,*

But I think now I should go back and pick up again on presenting our group and those who were members in it. First, I have to speak about Herbert, a tall, slender young man, who when I encountered him again was about twenty-eight years old. He was smart, but not intellectual. From his youth he'd been attracted to things technical, and actually dreamed of becoming an engineer. But he wasn't able to during the Nazi period. As far as I know he attended the Beuth School for Engineering, but I'm not sure if he graduated or not. He was very active already before 1933, in political work, within the KJVD. His activity was both his source of happiness and his mistake in approach; he was careless, reckless. In normal times he was a wonderful political worker. Very useful under normal conditions—well, that's perhaps badly put. He was a good organizer; he knew enough about politics to also be able to explain it to others. With musical talent. At that time, he was already a forced laborer at the Siemens plant and was something like a foreman for the Jewish group of forced laborers. He was always the brains of the group. Always. But Richard was more the intellectual type. Nonetheless, Herbert was *the* leader of the group.

And then there was Marianne: likewise very active, not particularly smart, very careless, rash. Always wearing her heart on her sleeve, always having to say everything that was on her mind. Both she and Herbert were very hospitable. Their door was always open. Marianne, a bit taller than him. Somewhat rougher than Herbert in external appearance, and probably also in her inner emotions. Both the same age. I think their birthdays were only a few days apart.

Herbert came from a family that was probably petty bourgeois. His father survived in South America and contacted me once after the war. I don't know if he had any brothers or sisters. Marianne came from a so-called mixed marriage and had at least three brothers. Marianne's non-Jewish mother passed away here a few years ago. This very modest and kind old woman lost all her children. I believe one son died during the war. He was probably baptized and considered a *Mischling* of the first degree under Nazi law. Her second son, Lothar,

3 (1991), pp. 21–37; and Steppe, "Nursing in Nazi Germany," *Western Journal of Nursing Research*, 14:6 (December 1992), pp. 744–753.

was a relatively older Communist comrade. He wasn't in our group but had worked illegally in another. He had spent many years in camps, was released, and was mistakenly taken from Marianne's apartment when she was arrested. He was murdered. Marianne was executed. Her last son, suffering from the consequences of years under Nazism, died after the war.

Herbert and Marianne lived in an apartment on Schicklerstrasse, behind the big DIA building across from the *Damm*.[75] After the war there was still a corridor down below that now no longer exists. They lived in the rear building right next to Franz Krahl.[76] He also belonged to our group, during an earlier period of which Richard and I had no knowledge.

Martin and Sala Kochmann belonged to the inner core of the group. Both were a bit younger than Herbert and Marianne. Sala was a very special kind of person. Martin's dad had a tailoring workshop on Köpenicker Strasse. And Martin was also still living there. Later they were forced to vacate these buildings. They moved then to Gipsstrasse 3, where Sala worked as a kindergarten teacher. Sala was from a Polish–Jewish background, East-European–Jewish. There was a very close bond between me and Martin because we were together a great deal in illegal work and both of us went through a lot. He came down with a high fever, I took care of him in secret while Sala at that point had already been executed. He was a tall, good-looking young man, thick dark hair, his eyes constantly sparkling with happiness. He was always ready for a joke. He used to go out through the streets during the evening, with a potholder placed over his yellow star. He was always ready to do something risky. He worked as a forced laborer laying track with the Reichsbahn (German Railways).

I can't recall now what he had been trained in as an apprentice. He was a kind of show-off, what I'd call a "*Fliereflöter*." You know the expression? I think it stems from the Flemish writer Timmermans. That's a guy the girls like, who's funny, has a certain charm, a kind of

---

75 In this case, Damm likely refers to the Alexanderstrasse in the Mitte district of Berlin.

76 For more on Franz Krahl, see the biographical entries in the appendix.

playboy who lives life a bit simply and easily, but not too easily. He wasn't all that bright, and not intellectual at all. But in practical life he was always OK, he managed everything he had to, and well... By "not all that bright" I mean...; well, maybe today I'd have quite a different idea about him. Sala was very beautiful, her face very expressive, broad cheekbones, smooth brown hair, and her bosom was actually like that of a very young girl. But as a whole she was a very strong woman. Quite clever, likewise not intellectual, but very worldly-wise. There was something about her that people found attractive. Every one of the young guys was in love with her. Unfortunately, all we have now is a very poor photo of her.

We were almost all couples. The next couple that belonged to our group were Gert and Hanni Meyer.[77] When I first met them, they were still Gerhard Meyer and Hanni Lindenberger. Gertchen—you just had to like that man! He was a terrifically sweet young man, a good-looking guy. Relatively small in stature, maybe the same height as Richard, but slender. A very good athlete and sportsman, because, as Richard always used to say, his body weight was so very balanced. Beautiful eyes, average in intelligence, when it came to theory not too bright. Loyal, totally loyal to the cause! Despite the fact that he was younger than the others, he'd been active for quite some time in the workers' movement. In the group core he was among the very youngest. Along with him was Hanni Lindenberger—a pretty, dear, and somewhat stupid girl. Loyal and always trying hard to comprehend everything, so endearing. Later in detention, she bore up and hung on wonderfully. I'll come back to her later. The two married sometime around January 1942. Gert was executed on August 18, 1942, Hanni on March 3, 1943. When I was in such terribly miserable shape after the operation in November 1941, they took me into their young idyll of happiness. And all they had was a single tiny room. One couch here, another there. They gave me one and took good care of me as I lay there. I think that's really remarkable.

Then there were Hella and Alice Hirsch. Alice didn't quite belong to our inner core. She joined us later on. Still very young, both the girls. Hella, a very smart and quiet, calm girl, far too serious for her age. And

---

77   For more on Hanni Meyer, see the biographical entries in the appendix.

Alice, who hardly lived to the age of twenty, was so mature as only a person can become in times of great adversity.[78]

Another of the inner group core was Felix Heymann.[79] A very smart young guy who looked extremely Jewish. Like most of the core people he had been behind bars at some point. And he had returned again; in his basic outlook he was very, very pessimistic. He made the little bit of life he still had left very difficult for himself. He was the last one of us to be arrested. I was the next to last. His fiancée was Hella Hirsch, who was arrested the day before she was to get married.

Yes, and Richard: He was the intellectual of the group, very calm. He would only speak when he really had something to say. Very observant, probably still very depressed about his brother's execution. He had a younger brother, maybe two or three years his junior. Richard told me once that his mother was only about 150 centimeters in height. And that his brother was just as short with fire-red hair and looked completely Jewish. If I tend to use the expression "looked completely Jewish," it probably makes no sense today. But back then it was a factor that was life-determining. He probably joined the ranks of the KJVD at the same time as Herbert and the organization then dispatched him to the Soviet Union. They then sent him back during the Nazi period, to engage in agitation. A really short and tiny, fire-red Jew! That spelled his death sentence. He was involved in secret illegal activity working at Blohm and Voss in Hamburg.

I recently had a direct look at his files. He was picked up together with Bruno Baum.[80] In any case, he was the first foreigner to be sentenced to death. Richard tried his best to have him released. He went to Hungary since they both were Hungarian citizens. And Richard was given the assurance there that the Hungarians would file for his extradition. Horthy was already in power, but it still wasn't a situation like here in Germany. When Richard returned with this assurance and went to his place of work—in which he was already a forced laborer, but as a foreigner had certain small advantages—

78 For more on Alice Hirsch, see the biographical entries in the appendix.
79 For more on Felix Heymann, see the biographical entries in the appendix.
80 For more on Bruno Baum, see the biographical entries in the appendix.

he was surprised about the way everyone there that morning was looking so strangely at him. He didn't know why. During the break he went down to get something for breakfast. And then he saw the red placard stuck to the advertising pillar announcing the execution of his brother. That is how he got the news. He tried to obtain his brother's remains, and since he was a foreign national, he also got the urn with his brother's ashes, with a notification attached that only he was allowed to bury it. He had to be alone at the burial, and there could be no marker placed on the grave… He buried the urn in the grave of his father, in the presence of the Gestapo. So now you know why Richard is sick, what the reason is, as I see it. Because that is no simple matter.

After the war we arranged to have an inscription put at the gravesite of his father. The same as I did in the case of my mother. You know, I don't like any death cult. But a small something ought to remain. And then I also think that's something political. It ought to stand written there. People should read about what happened.

That was probably in 1938. Richard was just very silent and pent up as a result. Until that time, he had been very close to a girl named Irma, not from our group. Later on, I met her. I liked her very much. Due to the racial laws, due to the dangers, she had left him all alone precisely during the time of the execution. With some justification, yet it was nonetheless very difficult. She helped me a lot when I went illegal. Irma managed to hold out and survive, and today lives in West Germany. I also found her again after the war.

Another member of our group was Bobby or Buber. His name was Heinz Birnbaum. He was just twenty-three years old. Already at a very young age he'd played a role in the subdistrict Southeast. I only came to learn about the details of that after the war. He too was someone you could call a really good comrade. He came from a Polish background, I think, and had lost his parents. He got himself a girlfriend from the BDM![81] A working-class girl, Irene

---

81 The Bund Deutscher Mädel (League of German Girls) was the female equivalent of the all-male Hitler Youth, an organization designed to indoctrinate young girls and to prepare them for their role in Nazi society.

Walter.[82] She was the only non-Jewish girl in our group. She developed in an exemplary way, and became a truly good, loyal comrade. Irene had to learn a great deal just to be able join in at all in what we were doing, given her knowledge and abilities when she came into the group.

Another young guy in our group was Heinz Rotholz. He was the youngest of all. Aside from the fact that he was a decent person, there is nothing more I can say about him. He probably only reached the age of seventeen or eighteen, and then he was executed.

Another girl in our group was Suzanne Wesse. She was French, the second non-Jewish woman in our group. Her real name was Suzanne Vasseur. She had married Richard Wesse in Germany, was the mother of Kata, and probably came to our group somehow through contact with Richard Holzer. She stemmed from the French haute bourgeoisie, had had an international education, and was working here as an interpreter, and even more as a translator. She grew up very rapidly. For me though that is a somewhat bitter chapter. At the same time Richard became involved with me she likewise began to show a romantic interest in him. But that was the kind of girl she was. She turned Richard's head, confused him totally. He caused me lots of heartache and distress. And Richard still loves her today.

Later we attempted to transfer the two girls, Irene and Suzanne, to other groups, due to the huge dangers associated with being in a Jewish group. The other groups refused to take them in. That was the group of Hans Fruck... Then they continued to work with us right down to the end, and they were executed with the first group.[83]

Most of the members of the group came from the KJVD, only Richard and I were from the Party, the others were of course too young for that. Herbert had come to the Jewish youth movement very early on, to the so-called German–Jewish youth group, i.e. the non-Zionist one.[84]

---

82 For more on Irene Walther, see the biographical entries in the appendix.

83 For more on Hans Fruck, see the biographical entries in the appendix.

84 Baum was a leader of the German–Jewish youth group Ring — Bund Deutsch–Jüdischer Jugend. He joined the Kommunistischer Jugendverband Deutschlands (KJVD—Communist Youth Association of Germany) in 1931.

And that's also where I met him. He stemmed from a petty-bourgeois family (or so I think). Pretty early on he also joined the KJVD and was dispatched from there into the still existing Jewish youth associations in order to work for the Party among the Jewish youth. At that time, the threat to Jewish life was just emerging and was not at all correctly perceived. Not yet by many of our own comrades, either. But those who realized it or had a premonition of the danger tried to help people, us Jews at least, develop the will to survive...

In the course of the exacerbating dangers the local party organization of the subdistrict decided to remove Herbert from the area, along with all those who at that juncture had been working together with him there. That included Heinz Birnbaum—whom we called Buber—and Felix Heymann and other young persons who later emigrated and are still alive today. Thus, for example, Herbert Ansbach, who today is back together with us again.[85] They all at one time belonged to the Jewish youth group that Herbert helped to put together, which corresponded more to an illegal party group. On the whole, the differences between members of the Party and those with no party affiliation blurred under the impact of the same threat, the same living conditions working illegally... But at that juncture the group was still constituted somewhat differently than at the time when I was active in the Baum Group.

Segments of the group had already once before been discovered and people had been imprisoned (such as in 1938). And a few who had been ordered by the Nazi authorities to do so were at the point of departing from Germany. Remaining as the group's core were only Herbert and Marianne Baum, Sala and Martin Kochmann, Felix Heymann, and Heinz Birnbaum, who comprised the heart of the group. They were the ones who then very gradually had added a few more members, including Suzanne Wesse and Richard, the two Hirsch girls, and Edith Fraenkel.[86] However, Herbert had already "won over" those three from forced labor.

---

85 For more on Herbert Ansbach, see the biographical entries in the appendix.
86 For more on Edith Fraenkel, see the biographical entries in the appendix.

I've already said something about the group's actions—leaflets printed on our mimeograph machine, left between the pages of telephone books in public places, our experimental letter action, the discussions we engaged in initially to clarify our own views about issues of the day, the literary–musical evenings, the illegal excursions not wearing the yellow star on our coats, undertaken partially to strengthen our moral ability to resist, in part also to locate alternative temporary quarters to stay. Our activity among the "foreign workers" at the Siemens plant was so substantial and notable, for example, that it was also noticed.

It was a huge mistake, which actually sprang from Herbert's restlessness. But aside from the later consequences, it led to a situation where others who might have been able to join us, such as Ilse Haak (Stillmann),[87] in fact did not join our ranks. And then we obtained the "eighteen-pages material" (sometimes also known as the "seventeen-pages material"), likely assembled by the Gestapo. This is the story on that: Werner Seelenbinder had been abroad and had brought back this material from Scandinavia.[88] He was arrested in its possession. In all probability, this material was then distributed by the Gestapo, with added calls to join the activity of the individual groups mentioned. With the help of informers this material was then spread among groups, and we also received a copy. Heated disputes ensued among us regarding this material. Richard, for example, was one of those who rejected it. He said it was wrong, just couldn't be true. It wasn't possible to just move out into the light and undertake actions, something was not right about all this. But it was the first greater link with the KPD apparatus, that's what we thought.

The material probably came into our hands via the Steinbrinck Group. Herbert still had ties with this group from earlier on. There was a man by the name of Franke in the Steinbrinck Group who had been

---

87 For more on Ilse Haak, see the biographical entries in the appendix.

88 Werner Seelenbinder was a German wrestler who frequently traveled abroad to compete and used these opportunities to serve as an undercover courier for the Communist Party. For more on him, see the biographical entries in the appendix.

engaged in this as an undercover informer.[89] He was an old veteran Communist. I know all that only from being in detention myself, from the Gestapo interrogations, from secret messages and the little I was able to learn afterwards, or from the great deal that Margot Pikarski[90] learned about in the Gestapo files. Like most he'd already been arrested once before, together with his wife. His wife had been brutally beaten as he looked on. Both were released. And he probably had signed an obligation to cooperate. When he repeatedly brought nothing to them of interest, the Gestapo started leaning on him, issuing threats. He became a liaison for our group, and he probably helped promote and then betray the whole arson attack in the Lustgarten. He was executed together with our first group.

But I know from prison that our first group in Plötzensee was allowed to come together on their final night. Honecker's first wife was working there as a prison warden. We know a lot from her.[91] She said that on the final night, the guys and girls sat together and were singing. They also had cigarettes. Then they let Franke in, and the group rejected his presence. That must have been the reason. They knew it. The deportations of Jews had begun. We didn't wish to let ourselves be transported away in this manner. We wanted to stay alive and continue our resistance work against Hitler. Thus, part of our group activities was still the effort to acquire passports and to learn French. We had connections with the most diverse "foreign workers," who were selling their own identity papers. I think the asking price was 400 Marks, something in that range. That was raised through collections and then there was this "rug affair," which I will explain. That was in 1941. When the attack began against the Soviet Union, we had long since prepared those things, it was stored in the temporary secret quarters we'd arranged, because most of the group members had only temporary quarters. I was the only one who didn't

---

89 For more on Joachim Franke, see the biographical entries in the appendix.

90 Margot Pikarski is an archivist and author who researched the Baum Group. For more on her, see the biographical entries and the afterword.

91 Erich Honecker's wife mentioned here was Charlotte Schanuel. The indication here that she supplied information to communist prisoners already in 1942 is a very important, and previously unknown, fact. For more information on her, see the introduction and the biographical entries.

have all that. I didn't have 400 Marks. Later on, Herbert had somehow put together that sum for me at the expense of the group.

The "rug affair" was an operation undertaken by several members of the group. As was known, the Jews now could no longer possess any kind of jewelry or the like, that was forbidden. But we needed money for the passports, etc. Then a few came up with an idea: An older, formerly wealthy Jewish married couple still owned some rugs. The rugs had already been set aside for transport. So a few men went over to them, pretended they were Gestapo officers, and proceeded to confiscate the rugs. I didn't object to taking the rugs away from these wealthy people, items they hardly needed. But I was opposed to the fact that we had made use of Gestapo methods to seize them, and then the whole idea of this impersonation. What a shock that must have been for these people! Richard had kept a lookout in the operation, and my assigned task was to sell these things afterwards. A woman is probably less suspicious in such dealings. When later I was interrogated by the Gestapo, the room where they questioned me was draped full of rugs hanging on the wall... I was always against this operation with the rugs and under no circumstances should it later be published.[92]

Then came the point where Herbert was no longer satisfied with what the group had been doing, what it had achieved. It's likely he said to himself, "Time has advanced to such a point that more has to be undertaken in order to help bring an end to Fascism, in order to strike a blow from the inside." In addition, he had to try to lead the group out of the isolation we had stumbled into as a result of our singular fate. To that end he had to forge ties to another group. That was the group around Werner Steinbrinck whom Herbert had known for many years and knew as a safe person.[93] And in addition, he wanted to place the two non-Jewish girls elsewhere, because we no longer wished to pose a greater danger to them than that they already faced due to our illegal activities. But the Steinbrinck Group refused to take them in and so they remained with us.

92 The "rug affair" has been mentioned in detail in earlier publications, which is why it is included here as well.
93 For more on Werner Steinbrink, see the biographical entries in the appendix.

The front pages of the catalogue for the "Soviet Paradise" exhibition.

undergoing surgery. That was the second of two operations due to the injuries I'd suffered lifting the heavy patient at the hospital. Initially they said in the group that we should put stickers around the exhibition. But that idea was rejected because it was almost impossible. At that point Herbert contacted the Steinbrinck group, to which Franke had served as a Gestapo liaison. And then the idea was broached there to set fire to the exhibit, probably suggested by this liaison. Werner Steinbrinck declared his readiness to prepare the explosive charges in the Kaiser Wilhelm Institute, where he had access to the necessary materials. Our boys, who by trade were lathe operators, declared they were prepared to produce the containers.

One thing I should mention: Almost all our members were "couples." And members couldn't afford to have children. After all, Edith Fraenkel's baby had died... So our boys created caps for contraception, based on a cap, a cover that I'd provided for them. Some of them were discovered afterwards by the Gestapo, and they thought this was part of the explosive charge...

The idea was discussed, with only very few against the operation.

Inside the "Soviet Paradise" exhibition,
Yad Vashem Photo Archives, FA147/116.

Among those few were Richard and me… I was against it and I will
tell you why, though when you publish my memoirs, you mustn't say
anything against the operation! Not at this point. This operation was a
misguided undertaking, especially that it was executed by *our* circle.[94]
Because it represented a potential danger for the Jews as a whole. In

94 This remark was an expression of Charlotte Holzer's fears about the publication of
these details at the time, under the conditions of the GDR, and of the repercussions
that could result from it.

the case of any and every operation that was undertaken, people after all also had to consider that it might be exposed. For Richard all that was especially painful, because Herbert raised the question of party discipline, and Richard was then excluded from the group, and so was I. And for him this was especially terrible because Suzanne was extremely enthusiastic about it. Extended discussions arose between the two of them that dragged on for hours, and likely led to a certain sense of mutual estrangement. That undoubtedly hurt him a lot.

I said to myself, if it goes wrong, it would never be said that the German people or the German workers had turned against the exhibit. Rather, they'd say, "The Jews, the subhumans, were responsible." You know, don't you, that the exhibit hall was built by Jewish forced labor battalions, I think from the Sachsenhausen camp, they went and brought them in. And then I thought to myself, "It would be really horrible for the Jews in Berlin who were still there, if..." And that's what in fact happened in the end.

Richard went to speak with Herbert the night before the operation. Richard almost killed himself trying to prevent the arson operation. Well, Herbert had selected six individuals, from right across the groups, from all the mini-groups. Then he called them to come together and discussed the operation with them. Franke was also present and that was the first time he saw our people. And after everything had been discussed, Herbert excluded Heinz Rotholz from the operation at the last second. What motivated him to make that decision was not that Heinz was the youngest of us all. No, the reason was that Heinz had such a nose, a schnoz! And Herbert said to him, "You look too Jewish, so you're not coming along with us." Three days after the operation, everyone involved in it was suddenly arrested. And this young boy Heinz as well, even though he'd not been present at the arson attack!

I think, if you really undertake such an operation, how many should be directly on hand and involved? Three. That's the maximum! The one who does it, the one who covers as security, and maybe someone who observes the whole thing. But they did it as if at a masquerade ball. They dressed very conspicuously, as an entertaining, funny little coterie, and they brought along bouquets of flowers. And they went as an ensemble of ten. Five from our group and five from the other. Herbert lit the fire; maybe Steinbrinck did too, I don't rightly know. Then they left the place, came out. Herbert singed his coat in lighting the blaze. Richard knows the details more precisely. He discussed it for a long time with Suzanne, and then afterwards too, and Suzanne was also among those present. I only know that they all went together to the exhibit. And then Herbert went over to a kind of façade made of rags and set it ablaze. Then they made their departure as fast as possible...

Arrests and Illegality

Then they were all arrested and taken into custody. Heinz Joachim is the only one who managed to flee. Some were seized at their apartments, some at the Siemens plant. Heinz managed through a subterfuge to flee via the cloakroom. Afterwards the boy ran back inside and handed himself over, he'd lost his nerve.

I already told you that Sala had worked at the Jewish kindergarten located at Gipsstrasse 3. Another kindergarten teacher, Dorle Bahnmüller,[95] with whom I was later together in the detention camp and who also perished, immediately phoned Martin. He was not working at Siemens but engaged in forced labor on the railroad laying track. She somehow was able to reach him and told him, "Sala is in the hospital. I was asked to pass that information on to you!" Martin was not directly involved in the operation, but Sala was. However, he was aware of what was planned. He immediately took his forged Belgian ID, came over to our place, borrowed the bike from Richard, and cycled off in an attempt to get away. Martin looked very nice, with a small beard, brown hair. Such a fun-loving guy! But he couldn't really speak French. He got as far as Magdeburg with his ID papers. He had taken his bicycle along with him on the train. And at the station he was arrested.

But in the meantime, he had learned who he supposedly was. He told them who he was as stated on his Belgian ID. And they transported

95 For more on Dorle Bahnmüller, see the biographical entries in the appendix.

him back to Berlin; he was even allowed to take his bike along as baggage. At Alexanderplatz, he was placed down below in the huge hall for foreigners. He lingered there for six long weeks. And this kind and vivacious guy succeeded in not opening his mouth the entire six weeks so as not to reveal himself, because you did not know who the other people in that big hall were. He was brought for a hearing before the judge for summary proceedings and identified as Gustave so-and-so. There he said that yes, he was Flemish, a Belgian—this was substantiated by his identification papers. That's why he knew German, it was his mother tongue, and he wished to go back home. He said he didn't have any travel documentation. The whole matter unfolded very quickly. When he was asked where he worked, he answered referring to the plant from which his passport had been issued; and the court officials phoned the plant and made an inquiry. While the hearing was still in progress, someone had to come over from the plant in order to identify him. And a Belgian man, a steward, was sent over to the court. He looked him over from head to foot, and then said, "Yes, that's him alright!"

Martin was then released—naturally as a forced laborer. And this plant steward was supposed to escort him back to the factory. Then Martin said that first he wanted to go and get his documents of evidence that he'd left at the court. He went and got his bicycle. And then told the Belgian, "Listen, man, it would be unfortunate, wouldn't it, for you to have to pay my fare! Look, I'll come on my bike." And the Belgian plant steward gave an understanding grin and responded. "Sure, OK with me." Martin got on his bike and returned to our place. And we were living there illegally. We weren't living at our apartment at the time, which he somehow was aware of. We stayed at Renate Moratz's place. To boot we also didn't have much left to eat either. But in Herbert's quarters we'd managed to find some chocolate powder and sugar. And when Martin arrived, I stirred together all the ingredients we had, and first of all we ate that. Was that delicious, a delight!

Martin then remained in hiding together with us until we, too, were arrested. We were taken into custody at the same time, me shortly after Martin.

Listen, I told you once that I was trained here in Nieder-schönhausen, on what is now Wilhelm Wolff Strasse, to be a baby nurse. Our superior was Elsa Stein. A very decent but somewhat sloppy head nurse. She was a wonderful cook, but in my opinion not a good nurse. Anyhow, one fine day the furniture truck arrived. And the sixty infants who were there at our facility, along with some toddlers, were all loaded onto the truck and transported away. They were taken first to Gipsstrasse, before they were all sent on a transport to Auschwitz.[96]

Immediately after Sala's arrest and Martin's escape, the Gestapo came to Gipsstrasse, frightened everyone there terribly, and told them, "If you learn anything at all, have any information, you must report it at once to the Gestapo." And this silly woman, Elsa Stein, immediately called up the Gestapo and told them that Dorle Bahnmüller had warned Martin. I can't say whether Elsa phoned the Gestapo immediately or whether she told them this later in interrogation. And that certainly does make a difference. Anyhow, that's what Dorle told me. She was immediately arrested. And Dorle would have been one of those who might have had a prospect for survival, because she was married to a non-Jew, and had a child classified as non-Jewish. But she ended up in Auschwitz and was killed there.

In the meantime, I spent time with her for a while in the camp in Fehrbellin.[97] It was winter. We hadn't received any clothing, just a shirt and some kind of overall, something a garbage collector might

96 After the Nazis closed all Jewish daycare centers and orphanages in the Reich, the former kindergarten and daycare of the Berlin Jewish community at Gipsstrasse 3 was turned into an assembly site for minors. The children interned there were all deported to Auschwitz in the fall of 1942. Interestingly, the very same address seems to have also been the workplace of Sala Kochmann of the Baum Group, who worked there in the Jewish kindergarten (while it still existed) and apparently lived in the house with her husband Martin. It served also as a meeting place for the Baum Group. See Ulrich Eckhard and Andreas Nachama, *Jüdische Orte in Berlin* (Berlin: Nicolaische Verlagsbuchhandlung, 2005), pp. 23–24.

97 In the region of Berlin/Potsdam, there were two central camps for women: The KZ Ravensbrück and the considerably smaller *Arbeitserziehungslager* (corrective labor camp) Fehrbellin. The camp was used to punish foreign forced laborers for alleged misbehavior, but German women were sent there as well. They remained only relatively short periods in Fehrbellin, the imprisonment was initially limited to just three weeks, later to three months, after which the surviving women were returned to their regular workplaces. In Fehrbellin, prisoners had to perform hard labor in a factory that processed flax and hemp fibers, with insufficient clothing, starvation rations, and under the constant physical abuse of the guards.

wear. To complete the outfit, we had a piece of string slung around the stomach from which we hung our eating pan at the back. And our number. And we had a headscarf. Our legs were bare, nothing. Wooden clog-like shoes were available for some prisoners, but we hadn't been given any, none were left. We were no longer very strong, Dorle and I. But we were given a pallet bed. A genuine pallet, for the two of us. Nonetheless, we were both freezing so miserably, it was awful. Then pretty soon I began to try to find something against the cold. I'd located a few sacks, and we wrapped them around our legs.

In the clothing storeroom I then met a girl called Cilly (the girlfriend of a very well-known fighter in the civil war in Spain), and she gave me a soldier's green knee breeches. It was a very small size, must have been for a flak assistant of sixteen or seventeen years old. Probably it had belonged to someone who'd been killed, it was all bloody and covered with dirt. But alternating—one day me, one day Dorle—we always wore the breeches when we were required to work. But always underneath the overalls, because we weren't allowed to have such military knee breeches. And then we had to constantly make sure we were not searched, so that this would not be found on our bodies. If I had not gotten away from the camp, I would not have survived confinement there. Yet this was not an extermination camp, it was a labor camp. Dorle managed to hold out until Auschwitz but perished there.

Let me go back though, to talk about some other concerns: My tasks in the group included provision of a very special kind of care. When a person had to go on medical leave, contending he or she was unable to perform forced labor, I took urine from my prostate patents and then always instructed my comrades very precisely regarding how they could fake a kidney-bladder infection in order to have some alibi. In that way I managed to exempt Richard for many days even when he was wanted. Likewise Heinz Joachim, after he escaped—with a sick note buying him some time. He also had to have some form of ID on his person, because he could not go to the plant in any case. One day Heinz Joachim returned to the plant. He had a temporary clandestine place to stay, he could have ventured out once more. But instead he handed himself in to the authorities.

The people arrested were Werner Steinbrinck, Adler, Hilde Jadamowicz,[98] Herbert, Marianne, Sala, Suzanne, Irene, Gerd. There were five Jews among them. For each of the Jews involved in the attack, the Gestapo rounded up 100 Jews. Thus, a total of 500 Jews were removed from the street, wearers of yellow stars, and brought to Lichterfelde. There they were divided into two large groups, each of 250 persons. Half of them were shot immediately, the other half were sent to a concentration camp. The next day they seized 500 families. And nothing remained of these.[99]

A tiny sliver of hope for survival was always there. And if the arson attack in the Lustgarten had never come to pass...maybe among these persons one or another would still have made it. Some *did* indeed manage to survive. You see, and that's what I was afraid of.

When Herbert and Marianne were arrested, Marianne's brother Lothar Cohn was also seized and taken into custody with them. He had only been visiting his sister.[100]

---

98 For more on Hildegard Jadamowicz, see the biographical entries in the appendix.

99 Following the first arrests of the group members by the Nazis, hundreds of Berlin Jews were arbitrarily arrested and transported on May 28 and 29 to the Sachsenhausen concentration camp. Originally, it was planned to arrest 500 Jews from Berlin and to send two transports with 250 Jews each to the camp, but in the end, the first transport left with only 154 detainees. To complete the requested contingent, ninety-six Jews who were already imprisoned in Sachsenhausen, were selected in addition. These inmates were murdered first, in the evening of May 28, at *Station Z*, the execution site of the camp. The 154 detainees from the first transport were executed the following morning. The 250 arrested Jews who arrived with the second transport arrived in the evening of May 29 to KZ Sachsenhausen. They were initially admitted to the camp, where—according to witnesses—they were subjected to intense abuse. At least 126 of them perished as a result, another fifteen were murdered in the gas chambers of the euthanasia program in Bernburg. The remaining detainees were deported to Auschwitz on October 22 of the same year. There are no known survivors. For more on the state of research on the matter, see Günther Morsch's speech, given at the Sachsenhausen memorial on January 27, 2012, available online at: http://guenter-morsch.de/rede-die-ermordung-der-juedischen-geiseln-im-mai-1942-im-kz-sachsenhausen-27-januar-2012.

100 For more on Lothar Cohn, see the biographical entries in the appendix.

Sala Kochmann was likewise among the first persons arrested. I already told you she was someone very special. A calm and quiet person, well balanced. She had a certain aura—it was impossible to say exactly what that was. Not excessively jovial and happy, but nonetheless cheerful. Richard always said she was so at peace in herself. Yet Sala was a bit egocentric and had a very positive opinion about herself... She was arrested together with the first group, with which she had also been involved in the attack. And after three days and nights of interrogation...

But before continuing with Sala's story I want to first deal with something else, namely the taking of one's own life. There is, correctly, some ambivalence about that in the Party: Suicide is no solution to a problem. One can't affirm the idea of suicide, but you can accept suicide as seen from a certain psychological viewpoint. The reason I want to raise that issue is because some time back I had a conversation with Richard about this. I think Thomas Mann was angry with Stefan Zweig because he committed suicide. And I think that Thomas Mann had no right to be angry.[101] But you can never completely see into the heart and mind of a person. After all, you don't exactly know what Stefan Zweig's innermost state of mind was when he decided to end his life.

---

101 Thomas Mann initially reacted very negatively to the news of Stefan Zweig's suicide. In a letter to Friederike Zweig, Stefan's first wife, Mann disclosed his feelings, "Was unaware of his obligation toward the hundreds of thousands for whom his name was great and for whom his abdication must have a profoundly depressing effect? Toward the many who share his fate [of exile] throughout the world for whom the bread of exile is incomparably harder than it was for him, a man celebrated and without material anxieties? Did he regard his life as a purely private affair and simply say: 'I am suffering too much. Take care, I am leaving'?" Did he have the right to grant the archenemy the triumph of seeing yet another one of us give up in the face of the enemy's giant reshaping of the world, declare bankruptcy and take his life? This was how this act would predictably be portrayed and the value it has for the enemy. He was sufficiently individualist to not care about that." A decade later, on the occasion of the tenth anniversary of Zweig's death, he disclosed that he had changed his mind and that it took time for him to truly understand Zweig's despair over the state of the world and his severed connection to language and homeland. For more on Thomas Mann and on Stefan Zweig, see the biographical entries in the appendix.

The fact that we were dealing with this topic had other, very different reasons. Our adversaries had imposed upon us the thought of such a solution for the problems. And especially after our group had become really active, even before the whole matter with the Lustgarten, we had to deal with the likelihood of arrests by the political branch— or with being picked up as Jews. We told ourselves that—especially in the case of a political arrest—we had to be able to decide freely whether the interest of the matter was better served by ending one's life (possibly because further statements could be obtained by coercion) or by riding it out and surviving. After deliberating that issue, I came to the following conclusion: Since I after all was the only one who had expert knowledge of and access to chemicals that could end life, I should prepare something that could be taken without an injection and would be fast acting. I mixed something together—how I obtained these substances is another matter—and I gave each of us a small vial of it. I told people they had to stand on their two legs as long as possible after taking it so that it could penetrate as deeply as possible into their system. I knew all these things connected with flushing out the stomach very precisely. All of us had such a vial but no one succeeded in using it. I tried as well, and I tried other means as well, but none of us succeeded. No one.

When Sala was arrested, she'd already thrown the vial away, or they had taken it away from her. I don't know. But after five or six days, after all that she'd endured, and what she'd heard from the others—I mean acoustically, the screams—she couldn't endure it anymore. She and the others arrested were held on the fifth floor of the extension of the police headquarters and prison building at Alexanderplatz. It was a structure built around a vertical shaft in the middle, the cells laid out along each side with a wire-reinforced glass passageway in front of them; Sala decided to hurl herself down the shaft.

Probably that was a very common way for prisoners there to try to end their life, because rubber mats had been spread out down below in order to cushion the impact. But in falling Sala hit the banister. She suffered a fracture at the base of the skull and had deep lesions all over her body. Her basilar skull fracture was such that she was in dire mortal danger. She was rushed immediately to the

Jewish Hospital. She was a Jew, an Aryan hospital would no longer have admitted her, and besides, she was a prisoner. And she was the first prisoner to be treated in the Jewish Hospital. Later the whole hospital became one huge prison. The only non-imprisoned Jews who were admitted were in forced labor; they were mostly Jewish spouses in mixed marriages. Whoever was admitted never came out again. The Gestapo filled up its transport quota from the patients at the hospital. Auschwitz had requested a certain number of prisoners, say 800, and say they were fifty prisoners short for the transport, they would then take fifty patients from the hospital to round out the transport. Or say in the transit camps a transport had been full, but then a few had committed suicide. In that case, a few patients were taken to fill it again. Only very few patients were treated as such and later released.

Sala was the first inmate, and they prepared the first room for an imprisoned patient for her. It was a small room for the dying that had been enclosed with a lattice out front, and there was also a guard on duty. Later there was no guard, just a locked room. They always made it very easy for themselves. Sala in any case was not mobile, she lay there unconscious most of the time. They just kept it locked, and the Jews were made responsible. If not Sala, then it'll simply be you! She was operated on and her lesions were dressed. She had to be treated in that small room. If she'd been moved, it might have been fatal. I was a nurse in that hospital but wasn't there at the time. I had gone on sick leave in order to be out of the firing line for a while. But I was able to make contact with Sala, through the assistance of some colleagues. Twice I visited her during the night. The halls were kept empty, no one saw me come in. And since I'd been working there for fifteen years, I knew that there was a basement under the entire complex, and that I could access it from several spots. Sala was, to be sure, a bit mixed up in her thinking, yet nonetheless clear enough. Not everything she recounted was chronological and there were gaps in her memory. Yet I had to find out what we were facing. I was not able to care for or shield her very much. But she told me about the situation on the inside. She also informed me about what was already known [to the Gestapo], whose name had been mentioned, and who of those still on the outside they were looking for. That for us was very, very important.

Later I was able to send messages, or at least greetings to Sala via my colleagues who went there with the dressings trolley. And when she was in a slightly improved condition, when she was thinking more clearly, the doctors were no longer able to protect her by saying that she could not be interrogated, she was dying. Then I baked a small cake for her, the size of a cookie, with half a razor blade inside. So that she wouldn't have to suffer once again. And I placed a note with it, where I wrote, "For you to decide!" The nurse that was attending to Sala, Lucie—a very brave girl, maybe twenty-three or twenty-four, who was later sent to Auschwitz, and killed herself running up against the barbed wire—gave me a message from Sala that she didn't want it. She wanted to go with our other comrades.

Then they came and took her away, the Gestapo. And since they could not even place her on a stretcher, they took her lying in her bed. She was brought to a women's prison on Barnimstrasse. And from there we always had news from Honecker's first wife.[102] Then the first group came before the Sondergericht.[103] That must have been in August 1942. Sala was carried in her bed into the courtroom. They were all sentenced to death. Sala was returned to Barnimstrasse in her bed. Then they were brought to Plötzensee. All of them. And Sala on the last day of her life got up out of bed and said that she didn't want to be executed lying in bed. She wanted to go standing erect together with her comrades. And she managed, she did... That's Sala's story.

---

102 A reference to Charlotte Schanuel. For more on her, see the biographical entries in the appendix.

103 Sondergerichte (special courts) had been used in Germany before 1933, as a temporary institution, but they were massively expanded and installed as a permanent tool during Nazi rule. They were designed to process cases fast, and a defendant in front of such a court was stripped of the most basic rights that applied in the regular judicial system, including the right to a defense or the right to appeal the court's rulings. The special court system had two levels of hierarchy: regular special courts were used to try the less important cases of opposition to the regime, while the Volksgerichtshof (People's Court) mostly took on the high-profile cases, often in front of the cameras, to achieve maximum deterrence.

At this point, those still left from our internal core group were Richard, Martin Kochmann, Felix Heymann and I, and Heinz Joachim, who fled and then turned himself in again. Oh, and one more, Buber! We were all in contact with each other. I was living with Richard. We had get-togethers. In addition, Richard, Martin, and Buber, I think, had cleaned up the basement after Herbert's arrest. They threw the mimeograph machine into the Spree. He had initially used Renate Moratz's apartment as a first point of contact, and then as a last point of contact before he fled. We had only little contact with Felix. We also had contact with Buber. Buber too ran right into the trap. He had contact again with the Kaiser Wilhelm Institute, although Richard had already told him that was off-limits. Nonetheless, he phoned there, and this enabled his pursuers to place him under surveillance and subsequently arrest him. Oh, that is just so difficult! Of course, if you have a lot of experience over many years, like the comrades had in czarist Russia, then...

We had two more warnings sent to us. Once by Marianne Baum who alone was not in isolation as a prisoner, but rather locked up in the so-called Jews' cell, at Alexanderplatz. Later I was also placed in that cell for a time. It was a cell with double bunk beds. There was no more space in the room. We were crammed in, some fourteen to twenty women. We had to alternate sitting in order to get some sleep. We couldn't lie down at all. In the main there were women inside who'd been caught after fleeing and had been sent to a transit camp. Jewish marshals were on duty there, men who were in a so-called mixed marriage and who could go back home in the evening after work. In that way they had contact with the outside world. They also reported to us about things inside, likewise through contacts in a roundabout way. In addition, Suzanne had sent a warning via her mother-in-law, who went regularly to Alexanderplatz to bring Suzanne clean linen. As one of the two non-Jews in the group, she had permission for changes of linen. This is how we learned that Richard's name had already been mentioned inside and that they were looking for him.

When Richard learned that, he went underground. He was officially registered with the police at the apartment of his mom and was living with me. He went on sick leave and reported that to his place of work. Twice he was called to report to the health insurance office. We phoned up there to inquire and they told us he had not been called in at all. That must have been from the Gestapo who'd already searched for him at home. He had become totally illegal, and we told his mother she should cancel his registration and declare him missing.

At that point, my small daughter Eva had already been sleeping for some time over at Richard's mother's place. Later on, when she was with me and the threat was intensifying, and Richard was already underground, but I wasn't as yet, we had to train the child to deliver messages. She was eight years old, and I had to make use of her for such things. Under all circumstances it was imperative that we preserve contact with Richard's mother. That was in order to know who they were looking for and whether the Gestapo had appeared at her door. We had to send the child and it was a long distance. Then she had to return back home. Eva had to be able to deliver the message and in addition had to know that if someone approached to talk to her, she had to start running. Away from there! But she understood it. And she knew about the yellow star, she had to wear one. On one occasion she was attacked and beaten bloody. Which is one of the reasons why she's not here in Germany now. Her understanding at the time wasn't accurate, but childlike. She never forgot about those events, though.

Initially Jewish children were still allowed to attend Jewish schools. Eva went to a school on Kaiserstrasse. No, first she went to the orphanage in Pankow, then to the Auerbach orphanage on Schönhauser Allee, and then to the school on Kaiserstrasse. So in just less than a year that made three different schools, because they were repeatedly being shut down by the police, after the directive had been issued that Jewish children were only permitted to attend Jewish schools. It was like a witch hunt and became ever more constrictive. And then the ordinance was issued that these children were not allowed to attend any school whatsoever, and indeed that their parents were forbidden from giving them any education at home. At that point Eva was no longer going to school at all.

One day she came home with the message, "Mommy, Grandma said people were asking about the nurse." That meant me. That was the signal for me that I had to go underground. It coincided with the order that I should report to go into detention for quite a different reason. Let me describe what that case was:

I have already mentioned that I was late in becoming a woman. I went to a doctor, a gynecologist named Franz Hirsch, who belonged to the ranks of the socialist doctors. As was almost customary back then, he had a practice in two offices. One at today's Luxemburgplatz, where he helped anyone who needed it, free of charge. And a medical practice at Bayerischer Platz, where he also helped everyone who needed it, but charged a high fee. I went to his office after I had become a woman and asked him for some contraceptive. He said, "Well, you probably won't be needing that, you have a very infantile uterus. You're not yet at that point." I felt somewhat depressed about this. Four months later, I was pregnant with my Eva. He was the first, when I'd gone to him for a consultation, to give me some baby clothes as a present.

Then Gustav was imprisoned, and two years later returned, and I had several abortions. So I was familiar with that from my own personal experience. Then the ordinance was issued stripping Jewish doctors of their title and license to practice. Only very few were permitted to treat Jews, like for example those who worked in our hospital. Jewish doctors generally looked for a different profession. And at our hospital one of them was employed, a small man by the name of Dr. Laboschin. He was the one who back then had not known what to do when a patient just recently amputated and with a high fever had ripped open his bandage and wound. As a result of this episode we had had some contact with one another.

A short time thereafter, the Nazis sent Dr. Laboschin to work on the *Autobahn*, somewhere near Frankfurt/Oder. Later he came to me and told me that in his spare time he was still accepting former patients for treatment. He said now he had a particularly bad case on his hands. It involved a Jewish woman, formerly married to a non-Jew who was at the front, who'd had three children with this man. She was living with them, subletting a place. And now, he said, she was pregnant, from a Jewish man she'd been living with for some time. Maybe that was already 1941, and the deportations had begun in Berlin. She had written to her former husband, with whom she had split up amicably, asking him to revoke the divorce in the interest of the children and also for the sake of her own life. The former husband had said he was prepared to do that, but now this pregnancy had cropped up. And she had written to him about it. He had answered that this was her affair, but that she should not carry the child to birth. Otherwise he couldn't have the divorce revoked. So this woman needed help. With an abortion. But Dr. Laboschin no longer had a home, no place, nothing.

He asked if I could offer my apartment as a place for the abortion. I thought about it for some time. But it was important and had to be done. So finally, I decided: Before he does that somewhere else, my place would be the best option. I prepared for the abortion carefully as a surgical procedure in my kitchen. This woman came to be lying on my kitchen table, where I already had lain once before. Only I was able to administer some anesthesia for her. After the abortion, Laboschin drove the woman back home. And we got a promise from her that she would rest and stay in bed. But this woman, about whom all I know is her name, Gertrud, was concerned about her children, and told her landlady that she would be sick for three days. She probably also told her what the problem was. The landlady's husband was an air raid warden. The abortion was quickly reported to the police. She was arrested, along with Laboschin and me as well, on December 5, 1941. I remember it exactly, because it was my first birthday in jail, and then I had all my birthdays one after the next behind bars.

I had received a summons to report to Alexanderplatz for interrogation by the Criminal Investigation Department. Naturally, I didn't know why. But since I didn't have the impression that the Gestapo was behind this and that I would immediately have to go into hiding, I went to the police headquarters at Alex. I didn't foresee at all that I would not get out of there. Eva was at home because Richard at that time was living with me. I was able to get permission from the criminal police to phone Richard, at his job. So he knew that I had been arrested, but for what and why, I wasn't allowed to tell him. Then I was taken over to Kaiserdamm jail and was shoved into a cell all alone. I sat there for five days. The first five days behind bars. What was happening outside? What about my daughter? What's the situation with the group? We'd grown so close that this was extremely disturbing for me. What repercussion could this have for the group? I was well aware of course that anyone involved with the barest hint of illegal activity should never have done this whole thing. Though I considered it to be quite ethical, what I'd done.

I was brought then before the investigating judge, and he released me until my hearing date in court. When I exited the place, I had no idea at all where I actually was. They never tell you. I was standing there in the street and didn't know which way to go. I went to the next phone booth and called Richard. He was on forced labor but in a small shop. He left work early and picked me up right away. That's when I saw Richard cry for the first time. He brought me immediately home to his mother's place. Then he put me in the bathtub, and the guy, who was so shy, lathered me up and mothered me. And naturally I, too, broke down in tears. That I'd been released was indeed almost like a miracle.

My court hearing in this matter came before the Lustgarten arson attack. Laboschin was sentenced to two years, the woman to a year, and me to a month behind bars. And actually, I'd defended myself by pointing to what the Nazis called *Befehlsnotstand* (acting under the duress of orders). I said when a doctor gives me a job to do, then that is a legal order in my eyes, and I am not acting on my own responsibility. I did not know that that could be deemed illegal, I thought just that Dr. Laboschin had no place to perform the abortion. The court accepted that, which is why my penalty was only a month in jail. Later on, these judgments were totally rescinded (by then, however, I was in political detention), because this abortion amounted to the elimination of "valueless life" (a Jewish fetus) and for that reason was not punishable. But Laboschin was sent to the gas chamber, Gertrud was gassed to death, and her children probably as well.

Since the prisons were packed beyond capacity, I received something like a postponement of penalty, i.e. you were simply sent a notification later that you had to report for incarceration to serve your time. I got that notification when the first segment of our group had already been taken into custody. Then I managed to arrange quite a coup de main. Since I knew then that I too soon had to disappear into hiding, I told myself, "If I go to prison now, then they've got me. Because their file cards are probably without any gaps. However, the justice system still exists, even a proper justice system grounded in the law." And so I went with my daughter Eva, I took her along just in case, to Moabit to talk to the state district attorney. Eva still remembers that. She even recalls there was a placard hanging there on the wall, with a warning, where you could see people who had been hanged, because of espionage or who knows what and why. Eva told me recently that I said, "Don't look at that, little Eva, you mustn't see such a thing!" And I put her hands over her eyes. I then served up a very touching story for the state district attorney. "Listen, sir, I know I have to serve a month as a punishment, but I have this child to take care of! First I have to find some place for her." He granted me a two-week postponement. And during that time, I went underground, into hiding.

In addition, during those two weeks, Richard left Germany. A Jewish doctor gave me the address of a Hungarian couple, tailors. Richard went to them. They gave him a first point of contact in Vienna, via which he then went on to Hungary. They also agreed he could use them as a mail address when he was abroad. By the way, I never had a wedding ring. But in 1941, I once had a very nice patient. He knew that I was married, or had been. And asked, "You don't have any wedding ring?" It was the only item of value that Jews were allowed to wear. "After all, you must possess some object of value if you really are ever going to get out of here." And he brought me a magnificent pure gold ring. I gave this gold ring to Richard, and it really was the first means of payment that he had in his possession in Hungary.

I accompanied him over to the Gesundbrunnen subway station. There's an escalator going down, and I still recall watching him as he went down, getting smaller and smaller. That was terrible.

Before that I had found a place for Eva to stay, in Reinickendorf, with an old married, communist couple. They had a small cottage in a workers' settlement area. They told me they'd look after Eva no matter what might happen to me. They knew about everything. By the way, that was also the small house where Leni and Lucie, the communist sisters, had gone to live when they left the hospital and went to work in industry.

On that same evening when I accompanied Richard to the station, I returned home, around 9 P.M., and as I started climbing up the stairs, lo and behold: Standing there, I see a small sobbing eight-year-old, surrounded by her few pieces of luggage. The old married couple had brought the child back and left her in front of our door. It was too dangerous for them, that's what they'd told the child, after she had been three or four days with them. They didn't even bring her back directly, since they didn't know if I was still around or not. I'm not trying to accuse these elderly people. Even if it wasn't right what they did. But rather to show how deeply Eva was burdened by all this. Not yet the age of nine, you grasp that, and nonetheless still don't comprehend yet what is happening. And what a burden that was for me, psychologically!

Then I arranged an illegal secret meeting with Hilde Benjamin and told her, "Listen, somehow I have to find a place for Eva to stay, and I don't know how." Then she gave me a contact to the Confessing Church,[104] to Elisabet von Harnack.[105] She was a great woman, perhaps not so much in intellectual terms but in the concrete things she was doing. She had heard that I wasn't just a Jew but also a communist living in illegality. And she told me she would take care of the child. She would have her baptized and asked me if I could agree with that. I told her she should do what she wanted. For me that really was very much all the same. If she thought that's what has to be—OK, she should go ahead. She should try to save my daughter's life! What importance in such a situation does a bit of water and a blessing have? She told me she'd prepare everything. I was then to take the child to a children's home down on the Löcknitz River, just outside of town.

---

104 The Bekennende Kirche (Confessing Church) was a movement within the German Protestant Church that developed out of resistance to the Nazi regime's attempt to gain control of the churches and turn them into an instrument of National Socialist propaganda and politics. Its leaders and many of its members also opposed the Nazi treatment of Jews and were therefore more willing to help them.

105 Elisabet von Harnack was a leading member in German welfare and women's associations, a member of the Confessing Church, and helped persecuted Jews. For more on her, see the biographical entries in the appendix.

I had just a few more days to spend with Eva. During those days I also had to prepare her for being baptized, telling her that it had something to do with God. She was familiar with God from the Jewish school. I couldn't tell her, "Look, it's all a big fraud." Rather I had to tell her, "These people believe in that. You have to respect that. I have to put you there, even though I don't believe in it. But I don't know what might happen. You know how evil the Nazis are. And you must never ever talk about me again! Your mommy and daddy no longer exist, they're not around. You know nothing, understand?" That was all very, very difficult. Eva was very sensible and you always had the impression that she comprehended that.

Despite the fact that I'd already become illegal, I took my Eva and traveled with her to Grünau, and then took a really beautiful, wonderful motorboat trip to Löcknitz River, to the children's home. Frau Harnack had told me that the sisters shouldn't be told about anything. When we arrived, they said that yes, the child had been registered. But they didn't understand why Frau Harnack had told me to come since a children's illness had caused the whole place to go into quarantine; I could only bring the child at the very earliest in three or four weeks. I had to leave and return home. I couldn't beg or beseech them to take her then and there as it might have made me look suspicious. Little Eva naturally was very happy about this, and I initially probably was as well. But at that point I didn't know what else to do, how to go on, and so I turned to Gustav.

Richard had already established a relationship with Gustav. I'd asked him to… But Richard had already initiated something else—he was able to deal with Gustav: He'd convinced him to start a procedure against me at the Reich Office of Genealogy, the so-called Sippenamt. In this action he would try to claim that the child Eva had become Christian according to his wishes, making her a *Mischling* of the first degree, who then had been registered by me as Jewish. We knew that such matters always took a long time. Then I went to talk to Gustav and explained to him the situation. I told him that maybe in another two weeks he would have to help. I said he then would have to take Eva and bring her to the children's home. Gustav replied, "That's quite convenient. I'll go to your apartment [the apartment was still registered under his name so that it couldn't be taken away from me] and then report to the police department that you were picked up by the Gestapo. I'll take Eva to my place in the interim and then to the children's home." She was after all used to having to be alone all day. But I felt very queasy about the whole thing. Yet what should I do? Helping his child was to cost Gustav his life.

Then I left town completely. I went to Kummersdorf to the farmer where we had spent the night during our illegal excursions into the countryside with the Baum Group. We actually knew two farmers. One owned a large farm, but he was a really great guy. He knew we were Jews; probably also even knew we were anti-fascists. He always gave us his barn where we could spend the night. He would also tell us, "OK, now you have to go!" But he always behaved, probably for his own security, as if he knew nothing in regard to us. Nonetheless, we were certain he was aware. The second farmer had a totally dilapidated little farm. He took us in for the cash. Later on Martin stayed at the big farm, I was at the farm of the greedy one, paid for from the remainder of the group's funds. And then when I returned to the city again for the first time, because we had to have our meetings there in Berlin, just to know what was happening, there occurred the worst day I had ever experienced in my life. Though actually I can no longer really say what day was the worst one...

That was August 18, 1942. I returned to Berlin in order to meet with Martin and Felix at Rita Meyer's place (today Rita Zocher). Rita was Gerhard Meyer's sister-in-law, active in the KJVD, and specifically in the Baum Group.[106] She'd been arrested, and had behaved very ineptly in detention, though not intentionally. Therefore, she'd been excluded from the group. But living in hiding she'd been great in her dealings with us. She was the venue for the regular so-called "possible get-together." And yet all she had was a small kitchen in a so-called "Jews' house."[107] She had also taken Martin in when I had to care for

---

106 For more information on Rita Zocher, see the biographical entries in the appendix.
107 The Nazis evicted many German Jews from their homes and concentrated them in overcrowded conditions in special houses called *Judenhäuser* (Jew houses),which further increased the already high level of isolation. Together with the restrictions

him because he was seriously ill. We all had already run out of anything to eat. But she managed to put together some food and played the cook. And every morning she would place my bowel movement and that of Martin in some paper and flush it away outside, because she only had an outside toilet, and we couldn't leave her place. So on that August 18, I'd come into Berlin to see what was happening and to contact Gustav. And Eva was going to have her ninth birthday on August 21. I had collected blueberries for her in the countryside and wanted to give them to Gustav for the child.

Teddy Thälmann[108] was murdered on August 18, 1943. The first members of our group were sent to the guillotine on August 18, 1942.

I arrived in Berlin, went first to a telephone booth, and called the small place where Gustav was working, as we'd agreed upon. Those who answered the phone sounded strange. They told me I should come on over, but at the moment Gustav wasn't there. I said, "No, I can't." They said that I should phone again after a little while. I realized that something was wrong! The first shock: If something has happened to him, then my connection with the child has been ruptured. What's with Eva, what's happening? I left the phone booth and immediately noticed this red placard on the advertising pillars. A placard about the first group. I rushed over to Rita's place. How—I don't know at all. That must have been close by. And before they could say anything—they of course knew about it already—I just threw up, the first time I'd vomited so violently in my life. And Herbert, Rita's husband, he was so kind, and took care of it all, the whole mess. And I hardly knew the man. Such a mess... He himself was rather nondescript, a good young man. Politically a bit influenced by his brother and wife, but otherwise in thrall only to his wife.

Then we sat there together: Martin, whose wife had just been executed... What we talked about I can't recall. I left the city again. I had

of movement that Jews were subjected to, these *Judenhäuser* made it very easy for the Nazi authorities to round up and deport Jews.

108 Ernst Thälmann (nicknamed Teddy) was the chairman of the German Communist Party (KPD). He was executed in Buchenwald concentration camp in 1944 (and not in 1943 as is written here). For more on him, see the biographical entries in the appendix.

spent that night at their place, they wouldn't let me leave. Outside at that point everything became very difficult, because I had no information about my own loved ones, also nothing more from Richard.

Back in Kummersdorf, I used to meet with Martin now and then at the train station. The station was quite a distance from the village. And in the other direction, toward the village of Philadelphia,[109] was the large-scale farmstead where Martin was hiding out. That farmer by the way was shot to death after the war. That was in fact a mistake, they shot the wrong guy. It was a consequence of the war; people couldn't keep things separate. Richard visited and talked with his wife a few years ago. I met at certain intervals with Martin there. I told my farmer that I'd recently undergone surgery, was recuperating. And that was actually the truth. That was my second surgery on the round ligaments that hold the uterus, a consequence of lifting that heavy female patient from her bed. So I could readily make it credible that I was on sick leave. But for the sake of the farmer I repeatedly had to travel to Berlin, to say that I had to see my doctor. As much as I was able, I helped out at the farm with a bit of cooking and other stuff. It was a terribly run-down small wreck of a place. What was cooked to feed the pigs was also served to the people. They had a huge pot, and everything was tossed inside—potatoes, vegetables, meat... The people ate this mulligan, and the remainder was fed to the pigs. They had one of those flues, for an old open fireplace. You always stood in smoke and ended up covered with soot... Once I baked some potato pancakes, and boy, they were really very grateful for that.

The farm property went on in the back down to the canal. I often would go out back and lie near the water. Nobody was actually around there. But nearby was a glider air base, then already taken over by the Wehrmacht. A soldier came over regularly to the canal to do some fishing. Although the land belonged to the farm, it was already a public thoroughfare. He always used to try to chat me up. Now and then we had a conversation. He tried to question me, and I told him I was ill and on sick leave. I can't even say if he was suspicious about me, but I don't

109 A village not far from Kummersdorf, originally called Hammelstall, was renamed Philadelphia after the American city in about 1790. In 2003, it became a part of the town of Storkow.

think so. Yet I was very careful; in actuality, as it later turned out, that guy was my Gestapo informer.

One day, the farmer asked me, "Hey, don't you have to go to the city again? The farmers' leader[110] here is already asking: 'What sort of a woman is she?!'" I understood: He could not continue to host me. I had to leave.

Maybe I should add something, commenting on the "Polish" conditions[111]—you can be sure about that!—that existed on this farm. His daughter Lieschen, already an adult, still slept in her crib, until she had her own baby. Everything took place in the small room, also the creation of this child. I was not present. I had it very elegant, I slept on the floor upstairs, on sacks of fodder. And I even had to pay for that pleasure.

Sometimes I would take a hike out into the forest in order to get rid of the feeling of being afraid: afraid of people, afraid to be alone. I always headed over toward Storkow along the railroad line above. Once the ground in the forest caught fire. You can't imagine what kind of conflicts you can get involved in. After all, you have to go and report it! But on the other hand, you can't actually go and do that...

In Kummersdorf my food was secure. I paid, slept on the floor on top of sacks, worked, had my meals. The farmer must have noticed from all this that something was not exactly well and proper in my situation, otherwise I wouldn't have lived that way. But he did it for the money.

I returned to Berlin, and I no longer had any options, nothing anywhere. Wherever I inquired! In the end, I arrived back at Rita's small room. She took me in, yet also tried to create other options for me.

---

110 *Ortsbauernführer* (local farmer leader) was the lowest functionary position in the Reichsnährstand (Reich Food Society), a Nazi organization that was designed to organize and to control the farmers according to Nazi "blood and soil"-ideology.

111 *Polnische Verhältnisse* (Polish conditions), or *Polnische Wirtschaft* (Polish management) was an anti-Polish stereotype that alleged the country and its inhabitants to be inferior and underdeveloped compared to the German and Austro-Hungarian one. It depicted Poland as an inefficient, unclean, and unorganized country with lazy inhabitants. The phrase was commonly used, often thoughtlessly, by wider parts of the population.

But there no longer were any. We'd arranged one of those "possible get-togethers" at Rita's place. Initially there were just three of us illegals: Martin Kochmann, Felix Heymann, and me. Later I also made the acquaintance of Budzislawski. He was one of the younger members of our group whom I hadn't met before.

After some time had passed, we always wished to get together at Rita's in order to know if we were all still out and about. I knew about Martin from Kummersdorf. About Felix, we never knew where he was. Felix was in a relationship with Hella Hirsch. She was arrested the day before her planned marriage, before the registration of their relationship. He knew now that she was under arrest, and he became depressed. Everything now looked black to him; he no longer had his sense of gallows humor, the attitude of defiance that Martin and I still had: that sense of still, nevertheless! Felix probably was also afraid, so that's why he didn't let us know where he was. And actually, that was also the right thing to do. Yet in this interim period Felix also established a Party connection. Somehow. And they told him at one point that they wished to accept a certain responsibility for our group. And second, that possibly they'd find a place for me to stay and hide out. At least temporarily. I as a woman was after all less suspicious. Which is why I also had to arrange the meetings with the party comrades. In fact, I met with two of them. I didn't know the name of one of them, but the other was Bernhard Heymann; people called him Hardel. Those two I was supposed to meet and maintain contact with, because the boys in the group were always in danger of being seized by the "watchdogs," the Wehrmacht inspection squads. After all, it was in the middle of the war. And besides, in the eyes of non-Jews, I didn't look so Jewish.

By the way, I intentionally mentioned that for non-Jews I didn't look so Jewish. There was bitter proof of this, and the Gestapo exploited that by using Jews as informers, promising them their life in return—a Jew has a better eye for who's a fellow Jew than someone who isn't Jewish. And even more so in those times of emergency. Now that's not so much the case anymore. Probably a Jew has also experienced it very directly, this sense of being hounded, persecuted. I also see in many Jews that he or she's a "Persian," that's always how we used to refer to one another. How I can sense that, I don't know at all. That person is simply one of us, he doesn't have to have a so-called Jewish nose or something. And there are no "racial" features at play. Rather features acquired through shared experience. For that you simply have a better "nose." Maybe it was also a way, a certain manner of thinking. To think a bit outside the box. The way of approaching things differently from that of others. And the way of thinking must also express itself in a person's physiognomy. Like maybe it's the eye, the way of looking... But all that comes from situation and history, situation and environment.

When I had my first meeting with Hardel, he gave me an address over on Ackerstrasse. It was a building with seven rear courtyards, where a Jewish pharmacist lived, a Party comrade, and he was prepared to take me in. He was a nice guy. I spent three nights there, then had to change and go elsewhere. He'd given me the key. He wasn't at home when I returned, but there was a young boy sitting in the kitchen. I said something completely vacuous to him, I was a complete stranger to him. But he immediately said to me that he was in hiding, an illegal. That was Butz, Herbert Budzislawski, from the parallel group.[112] So there were four of us illegals. Despite the fact that we went our separate ways, we accepted concern and responsibility for this young chick of a guy. But the upshot of that was that I no longer could go to the pharmacist. This alternative accommodation was finished for me. He tried again to find a safe place for me, with Party comrades in Weissensee, probably connected with the Fruck Group. But that also didn't work out. Thus, there was no other option for me but to go back to Rita's.

I arrived at her apartment and Martin was already there. He'd also had to leave the farmer where he was staying. And to complicate matters, he was very sick. He'd gotten a terrible angina and was running a high temperature. We didn't know what to do, and now all were staying at Rita's. We were four persons in this small kitchen. In this situation, Rita was really terrific. She had only Jewish IDs, it was a Jew house. And all around us the Gestapo was dragging people away. One day there was a knock at the door—there was no doorbell— Rita opened the door. And there stood the Gestapo. But they only

112 For more on Herbert Budzislawski, see the biographical entries in the appendix.

inquired about Jews next door whom they wanted to pick up. And our apartment was full of illegals! Rita certainly also made mistakes... But I'll never forget what she did do for us then. And what her husband did in particular.

So then I took Martin into my care. One day Rita had a visitor, and she announced this ahead of her arrival, "Minna Harder's[113] coming." We knew she was an old Party comrade, someone who'd worked with Rosa Luxemburg[114] years before. For Rita, who'd known Minna for a long time, she was a role model. When she arrived, Felix happened to be on hand again. Rita said, "Aunt Minna, here are three illegals. Help me. I can't keep them here forever." Minna Harder took one slow look at us all, from top to bottom. And finally said, "I'll take that one along!" She meant me. Probably also because I looked quite unsuspicious. In the end it wasn't until the following day that I went to her place in Wilmersdorf. We had to be careful not to be seen together. I arrived and Aunt Minna was lying there, feeling somewhat ill. And it was very welcome for her to be taken care of a bit by someone like me. I was at Minna's for one day, old man Harder wasn't around. But since she was a veteran old Party worker, she didn't keep me longer. Rather she arranged something for me at Gertrud's... I have to recall the full name because it's important, it became my illegal name. But things that bother me so much—I keep noticing that—I repress and struggle to bring to the surface of my mind again. Ah, yes, Gertrud Richter was her name! Thus, a very unsuspicious name.

She was so very cordial in accepting me. And then I told her my story (it was safe to, Minna Harder had guaranteed she was OK) and that I absolutely needed ID papers, because in the meantime I'd had news from Richard via a cover address in Neukölln: He had arrived in Hungary and wrote that I should try somehow to follow him there as well. And she said, "Listen, I'll give you my work ID!" She was working at AEG. "Alright," I said, "Great—but how are we going to do that?" You always had to consider the possibility that you might be caught and arrested. "Oh yeah," she said, "don't worry! Pay attention:

113 For more on Minna Harder, see the biographical entries in the appendix.
114 For more on Rosa Luxemburg, see the biographical entries in the appendix.

You just have to stick to the story that you found the ID." And thus I became Gertrud Richter. We were about the same age, which was good. And for me it was after all a comforting feeling to have something in my pocket. I spent maybe two nights at Gertrud Richter's place. During the day I was running around a bit.

Rita had tried to change my external appearance a little. That was difficult, given my mentality. I didn't want to let myself be changed in that way. My hair was dyed blond, and I had to have some curls set, and to wear a hat with a brim that shaded the face a bit. That's how I walked through the streets.

At Gertrud's place and Rita's too I left very early in the morning and didn't come back until after dusk. Most of the time I didn't stop to eat. Like most of the illegals in Berlin, I traveled a lot on the elevated S-Bahn. One time when I was changing trains at Alexanderplatz I had the feeling I was being watched. And that was in fact the case. That was Fischer, the man who turned out to be my police inspector later on. Otherwise I never imagined that I was being shadowed, never! And I was someone who would turn corners, change directions, retrace my steps, and once I entered and passed through a building where I knew that you could come out on the other side…

In this period, I had another meeting with a Party comrade from among those whom Felix had arranged the contact for us, i.e. from Hardel Heymann. The man's name was Marksthaler—I learned that only later—and he lived here in Prenzlauer Berg.[115] I got notification for our meeting, and I met him out on the street, near Kollwitzstrasse. He brought me a pack of ration coupons for one person for a month and forty sheets of coupons for so-called traveler's bread, a kind of whole wheat brown bread. Whether the coupons were genuine or counterfeit I don't know. They were intended for the four of us. I was very happy because I thought maybe I'd soon be leaving for Hungary, and then the boys would at least have bread.

If I hadn't had these ration coupons I wouldn't have survived. But more about that later. I ran into a trap with these brown bread coupons. I wanted to give them to the boys. But the sheets were confiscated. To

115 For more on Wilhelm Marksthaler, see the biographical entries in the appendix.

jump ahead in the story, the forty sheets of traveler's whole wheat bread coupons had long before been stolen by my Gestapo inspector Fischer. I was only charged—aside from the political procedure—with having committed so-called economic war crimes, caught in the possession of a batch of illegal ration coupons.

Things were complicated with my roaming around town. I couldn't enter my old neighborhood, that was taboo. The life of the illegals, to the extent they had no money, always looked pretty much the same. You frequented coffeehouses, ran around a bit here and there, went to the parks. It was after all still summer. You sat down and relaxed for a while. Sometimes you tried to stay for the day at the apartment of old Party comrades who could be trusted. If possible, you should never during the day go to any place where you would be spending the night. During the day nothing to eat whatsoever. We had nothing. I used to eat where I was staying the night. In most cases they also had nothing.

For example, there was a place for illegals to stay that I haven't mentioned yet at all, in Neukölln. It was the apartment of a Jewish woman whose baby I'd taken care of. The child died. Accidentally I bumped into her on the street, and she felt very close to me, because the two of us had together experienced the death of her baby. She took me in. In the case of Jews, that was always dangerous for both sides, but we all had nothing more to lose. In any case, they were always opponents of the Nazis.

So mainly I was walking the streets. I took the S-Bahn when my legs were too weary. And I was frightened. I tried to push those fears away from me. However, especially burdensome for me was that I didn't know where my daughter was, and also was unable to inquire anywhere. I likewise could no longer go to speak with Fräulein von Harnack.

In the initial period we still had some money from the group. But with ration coupons there was hardly anything to buy. Martin had a very kind and winning way about him. He'd been sweet-talking a salesgirl in a drugstore. And she agreed to sell him, although it wasn't free to just purchase, malt extract in a powder form. So we had some dry food. The dust would rise whenever we went to the john... I went back to Rita since once again I had nothing at all, also because I wanted to see how Martin was doing. That was on one of the last days of September 1942. It was about 6 P.M., still light outside. I walked up the stairs. Rita lived one flight up. I rattled on the letter slot as we had agreed as a signal. The door opens—and there's the Gestapo! I can only say, I don't know now what occurred. Only that it was pitch-black all around me and my tongue was on fire, almost a pain of death, and burning in my throat. That was the last thing that I remember. If I fainted—I just don't know.

When I regathered my senses, I was sitting in Rita's room on the chair. In front of me were two relatively decent officers on arrest duty. They'd been at the apartment for three days, waiting—that's how long I'd been away—and had used the apartment as a mouse trap. They asked me who I was. I said, "I'm Gertrud Richter." I took out my ID, the factory ID, "And I wanted to pay a visit to my former classmate here." "Is that so, Lotte Paech? You want to tell *us* that story?" They showed me a photo and slapped me across the face. Not yet too bad. "You're coming along now with us; we've already got the others." But what marks the contradictory character of these people in uniform: Rita had pears in the apartment—actually also illegal. Then they said, "Well, now stuff your pockets full of 'em. You won't be getting much more from now." I didn't want to, but they stuffed my handbag full of pears.

I didn't know what was going to transpire. And I thought to myself, "Now I'll just try to put an end to my life." I had my small vial with me. And when they wanted to leave with me, I said, "Hey, wait a second, I have to use the toilet." They accompanied me down the half stairway to the toilet. And they took my purse away from me. I told them to please let me have the bag back, because a woman needs it when she goes to the toilet. In front of the toilet one officer said, "OK, first let me check what you've got inside." And he found the small vial immediately. That's when I got my second slap in the face. My vial was gone. What was I to do? I had to go on living. To try to hang myself there and then, that didn't even enter my mind. In addition, I had something else in my purse that I shouldn't have had, namely a photo of Richard, and also some documents of Gertrud Richter that she'd given me together with the factory ID. They then took me to the station, it was just kitty-corner across the street, underneath which was the entrance to the subway. That building is no longer there. Today it's Heinrich Heine Strasse, not on the corner of Köpenicker Strasse, but rather diagonally across the street.

They put me on a chair in the police station that was wedged in between two shelves of files. They phoned police HQ at Alex and returned my handbag. According to police custom the handbag belonged to me, it only had to be handed over when I was behind bars in prison. Sitting there, I managed to shove some stuff behind the shelves holding the files: Gertrud Richter's documents, except for her factory ID, which they had taken from me, and Richard's photo. I figured that they wouldn't be doing a lot of intensive cleaning. And if they did, then it would be sometime much later. I had to act fast and try my luck!

A very short time thereafter the Gestapo car arrived, a black civilian limousine, with my inspector, the one I always had later on, Herr Fischer, an official who stemmed from Vienna. He brought me to Alexanderplatz police presidium jail. During the trip over there he was friendly to me. That was always very odd, sometimes this way, sometimes that. At Alexanderplatz he escorted me into a large waiting room, where there was a big cage. Inside this wire metal cage was a bench. On the bench a woman was sitting. I was pushed in there and it was locked up. Otherwise the waiting room was empty. In front was a room I'd passed through where officials were sitting.

I was wearing a dress that Sala Kochmann's parents had sent me. It had a red woven belt. When I saw the wire webbing of the cage, the thought came to me: Now I could hang myself. Because I didn't know how strong I'd be afterwards. Then I indicated to the woman next to me that she should look the other way and stay calm. At that point I didn't know her yet; she was Gretel Tillack, also a member of our cause, still alive today. Then I climbed up on the bench and tied the belt into a noose. As I stood there I thought: I have such bad diarrhea, that's terrible. But this has to be. I wasn't thinking of anything much else at that point. And then Gretel started to scream. They came in and were very rough, treated me terribly. They took everything away from me: garters and belt, hosiery. A female officer searched me, checking all body apertures. Then I was brought to be interrogated. By the time my turn came to be questioned it was 9:30 P.M.

The interrogation went on until 2 A.M. They shined a dazzling light in my eyes, there was loud music playing. A whip and brass knuckles lay on the table. I was interrogated by the inspectors Neumann and Fischer. Neumann, who did nothing but stand there and stare at me, was even more disgusting than his subordinate. Fischer stood most of the time right on top of my feet. Whenever I spoke, he kicked his boots into my shins. In the meantime, I realized that everything I had to conceal was already long since known to them. I also noted—in the course of the following three weeks I was brought almost every night to interrogation—that all my alternative quarters to hide out were on record: Fischer had been assigned to observe Rita's apartment. She was known to the Gestapo; she was after all the sister-in-law of Gerhard Meyer. And she always brought things into the jail. Rita's apartment was the only one that was shadowed. All the passageways that went out from Rita's place were known and under surveillance. In addition, it turned out that Fischer had also already been in Kummersdorf. So I had nothing more at all to conceal.

In Prison: Alex, Lehrter Strasse, Moabit, Leipzig

After this first evening of interrogations, I was taken to the prison block. The whole thing had taken place in Office IV A 1, at the corner of Dirksenstrasse, near the S-Bahn. But we were in the inner courtyard, in the building where the political prisoners were held and where down below the large halls for foreigners were located. I was shoved into a cell. The only thing I managed to do was to get a quick glance at a clock. When I was inside the cell, I felt almost content. All the commotion was over. You can't betray much anymore. Case closed, now the end will come. Finished. Something like that. Suddenly there was a knock on the wall, and someone shouted, audibly through the window, "Hey, what's the time?! You've just come in from outside." I announced the time. And because all this was unfolding at the window, a male voice from below chimed in, "Schuster, is that you?"

Beneath me in a cell was Gustav. He always called me "Schuster." Then he quickly told me about everything he had spoken about in interrogation and/or what I could avoid. Everything via the window! That wasn't so dangerous, especially not at night. Because the guard below was a regular policeman. Naturally, I only figured out later how that increased our options. Police and Gestapo were not at all the same. So you could do various things inside that'd surprise you. That's how the first night passed.

I'd read about signals and other things in prisons in the writings of a Soviet author, Larissa Reisner, and in books by Max Hoelz.[116] Nonetheless, I didn't know how to give a signal. When I was alone for the first time in the cell, it was just a knocking sound that had attracted my attention. But on this one side it was also possible to shout at the cell window to communicate. I already remarked that it was a building constructed round a central shaft. It was situated between Alexanderstrasse and Dirksenstrasse. There was one wing on each of the two streets. Our building was separate, inside in the prison courtyard. On the side toward Jannowitz Bridge, where our prison came to an end, there was a large open space. Below probably was a guarded inner courtyard. We weren't able to see that. I was located on the relatively better side. It faced south and thus got some sun; moreover, there was nothing across from it. The wing on Dirksenstrasse kitty-corner from us was a prison structure, housing prostitutes. The wing on Alexanderstrasse was where the administration was located. In front of us was quite a long stretch limited probably by factory buildings. That was the better side, because down below there were only police. Most of the time they left us in peace. If we weren't up to something, that was OK.

Everyone knows what a prison window looks like. But there are still some differences, for example with the obstruction screen out in front. I've also seen that, but not here at Alexanderplatz. That's the very worst. The cell window here was a regular prison window design and could only be reached by climbing up the wall. It was inserted

---

116 For more on Larissa Reisner and Max Hoelz, see the biographical entries in the appendix.

in a lattice and had stanchions out in front. This window couldn't be opened, on top it had only a kind of hatch or movable flap. This air flap could be manipulated by a bar. In some cells that bar was missing, that wasn't good. And in some it was fused solid with the flap. In the cells with prisoners who'd been there a long time, the window frames had been removed and just stuck on again. In addition, we repeatedly smashed the panes, even though it meant we'd be freezing afterwards. We did that in order to establish contact with our fellow prisoners. Then we shouted along these windows. We experimented and found that you had to turn your head to the left if you wanted to talk to your neighbor on the right. Then the sound carried better. In time you figured all that out. In my cell there was a flat pallet bed, with two covers, and beneath a sack of straw, no sheet. There was a toilet bowl, no seat, nothing else. Everything crawling with bedbugs. At one of the subsequent interrogations, I swiped a paper clip, bent it open, and then used it to hunt them. In order to have some respite from the bedbugs. Besides, then you had something to do inside the cell.

We were prohibited from sitting on the bed but did so anyhow. When later on it became so cold, I would take the jug into bed with me and then sit wrapped around it. If I wanted to talk, I would climb onto the edge of the bed. You could do that, especially in the evening. Then the cell was locked *and* bolted shut. Initially that feels terrible when you can't see a lock or handle on the door, just the peephole. But you get used to it. Yet when they moved the bolt it was a horrible thing, mornings and evenings. Bam! Bam! All around. Then you're locked in, double bolted. When that was finished, the officials would go and have a meal or something. Then everything was relatively unguarded. And that's when we inmates had conversations. Those who had loose window frames would manipulate and jockey over the things they wanted to pass on from one window to another. Or we'd swing things over if we had some string. And since we were in a political block of prisoners, we also maintained discipline. When one guy was speaking, the next kept silent so that you could understand one another.

I had no connection at all with my neighbor on the left. I don't know who she was. My neighbor on the right was Elisabeth Schumacher. My cell walls were beautifully covered with sayings, lines from poems.

Erika von Brockdorff had done that.[117] I relearned many poems through her. I changed cells several times and always had the good fortune of being the prisoner to follow Erika in the cell. I didn't even know her yet, so I wasn't at the time aware of who had written these lines on the wall. Initially I was there for three months. During that time, we Jews never had a free hour, never time for a walk, were never let outside. The word *Jude* was written on our cell door. We received only half the food allotment. No second helpings. These things play a big role inside. We never had any artificial lighting. When the days became shorter, we'd sit for a long time in the dark. The other side of the wing was even darker, always a kind of semi-darkness. Across lay the administration building, we could hardly talk there via the windows. That's where I later learned how to knock.

But here I always managed to get through the days pretty well. It was OK. Since we weren't let outside, we invented a clock. This clock was the shadow of a factory chimney that fell into our courtyard. We would reply to someone who couldn't see the shadow and asked what time it was, "The chimney is two windows on the right side!" We oriented ourselves to that for the time and to the food van that rattled by down below. But when it grew dark in the evening and I wasn't in interrogation, I usually couldn't manage to hold up, I'd break down and cry. Then everything came back to me, with such intensity. My anxieties about the child, about Richard... Gustav soon was transferred, sent on a transport to Brandenburg.[118]

---

117 For more on Elisabeth Schumacher and Erika von Brockdorff, see the biographical entries in the appendix.

118 Gustav Paech was transported to the Sachsenhausen concentration camp in October 1942. He was incarcerated there until his trial started. On July 16, 1943, he was convicted of aiding and abetting Jews and sentenced to two years imprisonment. The sentence was reduced by the time he had already spent behind bars after his arrest, so he served only a little over one year in Brandenburg-Görden prison. After he completed his sentence he was not released, but again transferred into *Schutzhaft* (protective custody was a Nazi euphemism for extralegal imprisonment) at Neuengamme concentration camp, where he remained until the final days of the war, when he was sent on a death march, which he also survived. During his imprisonment, he contracted tuberculosis,

Elisabeth heard my sobbing. Then she'd knock. A custom developed where we would never begin to eat the meal without knocking "Enjoy your meal!" and we would never go to sleep before knocking "Good night!" We did that with the spoon. Actually, at Alex prison, there were only bowls and no spoons. We managed slowly to get hold of some. Before that we had to slurp everything. And all we got was a watery gruel. Mornings we were given coffee, I used that to wash out my mouth, then I would spit it all out afterwards because I knew they put something in the coffee called *Hängepulver*.[119] I didn't want any, and besides, it tasted terrible. Together with that we got a dry slice of bread. For lunch there was a watery gruel, sometimes with a stump of cabbage in it. In the evening we got a jam sandwich. Sundays we had a margarine sandwich and tea. That was the food at Alex.

Elisabeth belonged to the Schulze-Boysen Group. She must have been a really wonderful person. I was then already a close friend of hers. Her husband was behind bars at the Gestapo prison on Prinz Albrecht Strasse. Since they were still considered Germans, they had permission to write to one another. But I was no longer considered a German. Elisabeth would always jockey me over the letters from her husband, using a stick. "Hey, take this, like as if they were letters from your husband. Because it's all the same." I took the letters, and it was OK. And since we had been friends in this way for quite some time, we really wanted to see each other face-to-face. Normally we couldn't see one another, because they would always close her cell door before they opened up mine. But we decided together that we would both ask to go see the doctor. That was possible. Yet you had to accept that then for one, two days, there's not gonna be any food. The doctor would say, "What, so you have trouble with digestion? You have headaches? No food! On a diet!" So we reported to see the doctor, and we left his office together. Elisabeth had often been at the prison doctor and said people could see

---

which went untreated too long. He succumbed to the illness shortly after liberation. For more on him, see the biographical entries in the appendix.

119 The term *Hängolin* was commonly and jokingly used among soldiers for an alleged substance in their rations that reduced their libido. There is no documentation about the use of any such substance on the battlefield or in prisons.

each other there and have a chance to talk. We were taken out of the cell together, and that's when I met this young, blond woman… Then they brought you to a large waiting room, everyone there altogether. All those who were never allowed to meet one another—get on in there, go on in! Then they didn't pay the slightest attention at all to whether people spoke to one another or not.

In the meantime, the late autumn had come, and I was freezing something awful. That's when Elisabeth introduced me, with a wink of an eye and a quiet nod, to Jutta Dubinsky. She's still alive, and I'd like to say something about her.[120] She was also a member of the Schulze-Boysen Group and was confined in the prostitutes' wing on Dirksenstrasse. Jutta could probably see how I looked. I was wearing a checkered blouse, printed so badly that all the squares had vanished. After all, that's what we were wearing, only that, all the time, day and night. One evening there was a kind of inmate alarm on our floor. From one to the next went the word, "Hey, pay attention! Something's on the way!" Jutta had sent something from Dirksenstrasse right around the prison building passed along by a stick. Even though she didn't know my name, she just knew I was in the cell next to Elisabeth. And tied to the stick that arrived was a jacket, woolen, with diagonal stripes, slightly brown and whitish. She had tied the sleeves closed and had stuck apples inside. After all, she was allowed to receive packages. That's what she sent me. And how great that was, so terrific, you just can't imagine!

Repeatedly there were those interrogations in between, and then once again periods of relative quiet. That was always something terrible. First, because you had to pay very careful attention to what they knew and what they didn't know. And they knew almost everything. Second, because I began to notice, as a result of being in solitary, that after the beatings during questioning I started to feel a certain hunger to be out and around other people. And you felt a contempt for yourself afterwards, see, like you had that feeling you just had to get out amongst other people. That left you totally shaken up, confused. I mean, you hated these guys, you were afraid of them.

---

120 For more on Jutta Dubinski, see the biographical entries in the appendix.

And then there was this difficulty with telling a lie. You just can't imagine how hard it is to tell lies, straight out. That's terribly difficult, because after all, you always have to keep in mind that there are so many others being interrogated and lying, and they have to more or less coincide with what you say. I mean, what you can say is something you have to feel. Sure, people tried if they had contact with others, for example, via the window, to coordinate what you would say—at least to the point that in the case of each there was a kernel of truth. And it was precisely that kernel that the Gestapo then made use of. Very few consciously betrayed anyone else. Nonetheless, they were able through all the many statements to stitch something together.

I have to talk about the physical consequences that arrest quickly led to. Among these problems is that right after my arrest, I suffered a non-cyclical menstrual bleeding. And for all those years, that was the last menstruation I had. Almost all the prisoners suffered the same thing. Then from that day on, or more precisely from the first interrogation night on, I suffered from vomiting. Despite the fact that I was very hungry, I vomited up the first prison meals one after the next. In a weakened form I had that problem throughout the entire duration of my imprisonment. And this remained the situation down to 1951. Even today, in December 1966, if I'm not at home and eat different foods from what I'm used to at home, I suffer from mild vomiting. Always undigested food, which means it's a problem with the stomach nerves. And my heart trouble—earlier on I was never very strong, yet I was healthy—began after two or three interrogations. I had such an attack of anxiety before the interrogation that when the cell door was opened, I would have heart spasms. That must have been the beginning of all the heart troubles I've suffered from.

However, I also did some gymnastics, even if it just amounted to a couple of breathing exercises in the worst period, when I was too weak to even move. I always did something, I pulled myself together in a disciplined manner. After I'd seen that I could no longer prevent anything, that I could no longer betray some secret, I said to myself, "I'm not going to relieve you of your work! I'm gonna stay alive. If you don't chop off my head or hang me—I'll stay alive!" That became for me a form of resistance.

I'd like to add a small point regarding how Jews recognize each other. That also has a material basis that springs from the special fate of Jews vis-à-vis their non-Jewish environment. Because they were isolated and ghettoized over the centuries, their integration into the surrounding environment has been relatively limited. Marriages took place within a small circle. So that earlier, when there were more Jews, people said, "When two Jews come together, they're related." People always found some element of kinship with the other. And only naturally, there are always features of a big family present—the concept is not fully correct here—that deviate from the rest of the environment. That has nothing to do with race. But the mixing first started during the nineteenth century, at a very slow pace. And if you were in Italy or Hungary, it wasn't even very noticeable, because the indigenous population had similar characteristics.

So there are not just the features of individual fates but also certain collective features of a shared collective fate. That extends to the point where even some specific illnesses, such as diabetes and certain psychological disorders, afflict Jews more readily and generally than the others.

Ghettoization led to a reticulated mesh of kinship relations. As I see it, when the ghetto opened up, the contents burst out as if from an overfilled bottle. That's how people ended up in all kinds of countries. Since departure from one's homeland, no matter how bad and narrow it was, and gaining a foothold in a new country was difficult, every person naturally fell back on his or her own family, which in the meantime had some offshoot everywhere. Naturally, that had some influence on the Jews here during fascism. If I had relatives in Argentina, I would prefer to go there rather than to Uruguay.

In my case the situation was different. I wouldn't have left. I felt I had a double task: to be there for the patients and to remain here in the workers' movement, which is my home. And here I have to defend myself. While I did this I sometimes felt very bad, because of the child.

Naturally, one also had to deal with personal attacks because of that. People understood me better when I told them: one doesn't leave one's patients. But there, too, some said, "Charity begins at home." That is a bourgeois attitude. Naturally, you can say, for me emigration was more difficult. I had no money and had nothing outside the country. Yes, and to take money out when emigrating was no longer possible for the Jews. The Nazis undertook a huge bloodletting of the Jews. We had almost nothing left. But I did have some possibilities to leave, had I wanted to. I spoke earlier about Dr. Eichelbaum. Yes, and in 1933, I wanted at one point to leave. For the Soviet Union. But they soon pulled that tooth of mine.

Naturally, Germany was my home. As it was for all the other Jews who'd grown up here. But a portion of the Jews embraced Zionism. Not us. I joined the German–Jewish youth movement and the name already sums it up well… But I have to admit that I also had an ambivalent sense of home and country. Despite the fact that I said this is where I belong, I was never completely at home here. I wasn't really anchored here until I joined the workers' movement. Is it clear what I mean by that? I wasn't necessarily connected with being Jewish, but I felt not completely accepted here. I was close to nature, the landscape, German art, but not 100 percent to the people. And this sense of home and country, that feeling of home and homeland, became stronger during the Nazi period—on account of our resistance.

Nowadays, and from among those I found again in Israel or came to know in England, they are *all* homesick for this country and feel anxious on account of that. There are in fact many who didn't even want to speak the German language anymore. In my eyes those are the consequences of the very deep injury that they suffered. They're afraid to touch these scars.

Actually, there was only the *one* alternative: You grow stronger, or you break. Whoever succeeded without this alternative is really an "accidental child." I survived, mainly accidentally. Not everything was left to chance, though. While the external circumstances were often accidental, I knew how to make use of them and my attitude in that respect was by no means accidental.

Yet in general they were able to destroy human beings before they crushed them physically. People soon no longer had the will to resist, no morality of their own, nothing but the will to survive. Sometimes no longer even that, all inhibitions gone. The Jewish informers, what was that about? Those were human beings who'd been destroyed. After all, most were intelligent, otherwise the Gestapo would not have made them informers. But their humanity had been shattered, destroyed. And others too were broken, they just let themselves go, in every respect.

There were a few girls like that [who worked as informers] whom we knew. Just a small number. And they were almost all between sixteen and nineteen years old. This is a susceptible age for that. Already earlier on, when they were still living in legality or were doing forced labor—or in the short span before their arrest when they'd gone illegal—they had managed by means of their body. It was evident however that this way of managing to stay alive was extremely demoralizing. My experience is that when a person draws benefit from their body, it's not just a matter of emergency, of someone in distress, but requires a certain predisposition, what I always refer to as a "sociable lower abdomen." And also a certain weakness in personal morality. Otherwise they wouldn't do that. That's one group. Then there was a small group that never stuck it out as informers. That was a group where people acted out of fear. Out of concern for their family, in order to protect it, or because of an existential anxiety, pure and simple. They accepted the obligation to inform and then maybe "brought in" one person at the most, and then they simply could no longer continue—because their sense of morality was too strong. They weren't able to fight back and let themselves be taken away. Sometimes they said something, sometimes they simply didn't accomplish anything, and were then sent away.

And then there were just a small number of highly intellectual persons, very few, who found a certain pleasure in that "game." Of being an informer. I knew a guy, a lawyer, named Neuweck.[121] He got involved in our group, was arrested, went illegal with his young wife, who wasn't a Jew from birth. Either she'd converted to Judaism or was still a Catholic, I can't recall. Initially he probably agreed to inform because he feared for his wife's safety. She was a very young, very small and sweet, rather stupid woman, and in mortal fear he'd agreed to work as an informer. But then he noticed that he had a

121 For more on Fritz Neuweck, see the biographical entries in the appendix.

certain talent or gift for "bringing in" people. And he connected up with the informer couple Stella Kübler[122] and Isaaksohn (I'll say more about them later), and the Gestapo put him in charge of them. They had to bring in Jews while he instructed and guided them, pulled the strings. But this man came to a difficult end. The Gestapo had given him a gun and in 1945, he shot himself and his wife dead. A very intelligent and educated person, but also a brutal guy. I once talked about the blond woman whose nose had been cut off. Yes, that was the way it went.

Let me maybe return to those girls with their "sociable lower abdomen…" I have nothing against girls who earn their living this way. They're likeable because in most cases they are very sensitive and very companionable, comradely, and very sharing. I've sat together with these girls and also had contact with them from the early days (I'll mention later why). And we were talking about attempts to escape. You always get around sometime to talking about escaping if you're in jail, but especially when you're sent on a transport. And I met these girls when I was on transports. And they always said to me, "You have to make use of your body because you have no money." Later in my story I'll mention that in Leipzig I had an opportunity to flee. And I decided not to make use of that. Because I said to myself, "I'll only survive then if I use my body." And I didn't want to do that. It seemed to me that my staying alive wasn't worth it. In practical terms, maybe I would have dared to do it, but no way, no…

Complicated situations of that kind had already arisen before. When I was illegal, I stayed with married couples several times. And because people were living in such distressful, constrained circumstances, I slept with them in the same bed. And repeatedly it transpired that the husbands wanted to… I didn't allow it and then no longer used these alternative places to stay, for that reason. I never held it against a man because I could imagine that he probably hadn't been acting in a fully aware way. It was a terrible situation for me, being in a bed right next to the man's wife, who had accepted me into the house as a guest. All I could do was to try to make sure the wife didn't

---

122 For more on Stella Kübler, see the biographical entries in the appendix.

notice anything by pushing the guy away. Of course I probably would have had things easier if I had agreed. There, too, are also distinctions. You can really sleep around like some slut. But you can also look for a "protector." A lot of girls looked for some guy to protect them and gave something physical in return. I could more readily have imagined that as a possible option in my own case. Because that fits in with what I mentioned before—namely that I'd gradually begun to find it rude, in a sense indecent, to be very close with a man and then not give him what he wanted. That is nasty. It's like hanging a piece of pork in front of a hungry man and then not allowing him to have it.

Closer to the end, around 1940, the hospital was not yet a Gestapo hospital, i.e. not yet a prison, we took in a very little girl of about eighteen months or two years old. Her dad was a journalist. He had two older children. The mother had had some visitors over and had left the child—no, it must have been just a year old—in its buggy alone in the room. She'd set the table for tea, and when the doorbell rang, she left the room, and the child reached out and pulled on the tablecloth. There was a teapot on it and a small hotplate. And the child spilt the boiling water all over itself. The child was so badly injured that it was assigned a private nurse, namely me. Oh, what I had to do to take care of that baby! I wrapped the child in bandages, carried it around with me… The means weren't available then that there are today. This child belongs to my story because it was sent together with its parents and other siblings to Theresienstadt. And the mother came back with her children. The father had been murdered. But it was so rare for almost an entire family to survive. However, after the war, all four had TB. I can only remember one other family that managed to survive, also sent to Theresienstadt— that too was an interesting case. Let me think, their name will come to me... Yes, Dr. Fabian. In Theresienstadt the family belonged to the so-called *Schutzjuden* (protected Jews), and the father was transported back to the transit camp on Hamburger Strasse. That's where I met him. And they'd done that because the Gestapo needed his services—he was a lawyer—to handle the property affairs of the Jews. Naturally, for the benefit of the Gestapo! As a result, the entire family survived.

I was still imprisoned in the jail at Alexanderplatz at that time. I have to tell you something about the wing of the building from where we were able to catch sight of the chimney sundial. By the way, they virtually killed us with the carillon. I think it was from the Parochial Church and it repeatedly played "Always be faithful and true!"[123] And twice a week a police choir used to practice in the private apartments or the workshops right across from us: All the darn time, they rehearsed Tannhäuser,[124] with trumpets! I almost died, mainly because I was so furious.

I had, as mentioned, interrogations almost every evening. That was really rough. The Gestapo tried to confuse me about Richard. They told me he'd already been arrested or that he was dead. Then they said that they hadn't found him yet. Didn't know his whereabouts. And at that point they literally drained me of all the strength I had left. They knew he'd gone to Hungary. The inspector told me Richard had returned to get me. I couldn't believe that. But gradually I became totally confused. Because they constantly went back and forth, back and forth. Once during the interrogation, I just cracked, lost my composure, and started to scream. And I told them: If they ever asked me anything again about Richard, then I'd stop talking completely. I wouldn't open my mouth. They could do with me what they wanted. I sat there in silence, and they took me back to my cell. That's when I had the real nervous breakdown. And now I have to say again: The solidarity among prisoners there, you just can't imagine what it was. Very gently from all sides a soft tapping began on the walls. That was so beautiful. I don't know if someone who hasn't been locked up will be able to understand. From that point on they didn't ask me anymore about Richard.

But then something awful happened, where I failed to act properly. That was the whole episode with Gertrud Richter, from whom I'd received the ID. We had agreed that if I were ever taken prisoner and the ID was discovered on me, I should say I'd found it

123 The opening lines of a Prussian folk song from the eighteenth century, calling for unwavering fidelity to God, which was considered an expression of Prussian moral virtue. It came to be seen as the unofficial Prussian national anthem, but of course stood in opposition to the author's beliefs.

124 A reference to Richard Wagner's Opera, *Tannhäuser und der Sängerkrieg auf Wartburg* (Tannhäuser and the Singers contest at the Wartburg).

on the street. And that's what I indeed told them. That is also what was written down in the record, which I signed. But the situation was that what you said was not always transcribed exactly, word for word, but just summarized. And it was certainly not always summarized correctly. Nor did they give it to you to read. And they didn't read it out loud back to you. They just said, "OK, now sign this." You had to put your signature. At that point, it felt like it was all the same anyhow. I'd already signed my red concentration camp certificate. Every prisoner had to sign that, every Jewish one. It said there—I read through it quickly—that because of communist activities (it didn't matter whether you were a communist or not), I had been stripped of my German citizenship, that all my possessions were to be confiscated, and that I was going to be taken into protective custody. This was outside the realms of the juridical system. That was the way with all matters for Jews who were in prison: On the one hand, in part via the justice system (at that point it was still like that)—and on the other, over to the Gestapo. So that even if the justice system had acquitted you, you landed up "legally" in the hands of the Gestapo.

The Gestapo probably calculated precisely when they had worn me down to breaking point. They had experts there in human psychology. That had already been the case with the story about Richard. And at this point in time the following occurred: One day around noon I was sitting with my bowl and trying to sip my soup without a spoon. I heard something outside. You know, you lived there with your ears extra alert. I was forbidden to read, forbidden to write, forbidden to have any work activity. I was never allowed to go down for a walk. It was very difficult.

Maybe this helps to explain what I said. Namely that you almost get to a point where you are actually waiting for an interrogation. It was an interruption in the loneliness, some kind of a "connection" to "human beings." Yeah, they weren't regarded as human beings, but nonetheless they were. Outside the door, I heard this extremely loud banging and the voice of "my" Gestapo officer—I knew his voice precisely, and he was pushing some woman out in front of him. He used the formal German "you" and mentioned her name. Only in the case of

Jews were people addressed with the informal "you" and by first name,[125] and Jewish women were always addressed as Sarah.[126]

I understood that Gertrud Richter had been admitted as a prisoner. And she was placed in a nearby cell. Immediately thereafter I was taken and locked out. No, no, hold on, wait a second. It was like this: He unlocked my cell and pushed her inside, then he nabbed me by the collar and bellowed, "You're gonna be sorry if you look!" And he shoved me into the neighboring cell. So I was in no doubt that Gertrud had been arrested. That's what happened. I was placed in another cell with a Communist comrade, for two or three days, an Austrian communist woman named Heli.[127]

About two hours after this transfer to her cell I was dragged to interrogation. And Fischer said to me, "You lied to us." I replied, "No, I didn't." He again, "You're a liar. Gertrud told us everything about what happened. Don't lie!" And he pressured me, "Richter told us she gave you her ID." And I repeatedly said, "No, not true." Until I thought to myself: if they arrested her and she admitted that, then it becomes very improbable that I just found this identification card, specifically this one. I replied that I couldn't understand why she had been so stupid as to tell such a tale and to accuse herself in such a way and get dragged into this whole thing. But I said, "Yes, right, it's true, I lied. In fact, I stole her ID." Then I was taken back to the cell and some time passed.

Only later in the camp in Fehrbellin did I meet up with Gertrud Richter again. But she wouldn't even look at me. That was terrible. And

---

125 In German language, there are two kinds of "you": The *Sie* used for formally addressing strangers, and the *Du*, which is the informal form reserved for friends and family. Using the informal form to address an adult stranger is generally understood as showing a certain level of disrespect.

126 The *Zweite Verordnung zur Durchführung des Gesetzes über die Änderung von Familiennamen und Vornamen* (Second Regulation for the Implementation of the Law Regarding the Change of Family Names and First Names) made it mandatory for all German Jews whose first name was not defined as typically Jewish by the Nazi administration to add another first name: Sarah for women and Israel for men.

127 Heli's full name was Dr. Helene Schlesinger. For more on her, see the biographical entries.

then through some other comrades there, I had them ask her what the matter was. She answered, "You created a big problem for me! Why did you tell them that I gave you the ID?" Using the same indirect way of communicating with her, I answered, "Listen, you came at noon and were interrogated, after that they came and took me, and I was interrogated. And they told me you had said this and that, and then it was clear to me." "No," she responded, "They showed me the statement you'd signed." So finally, I understood there was a time problem. And I asked her, "So when did they interrogate you?" I know that I myself was taken at 7 P.M. and only returned from interrogation in the late evening. She answered, "I was taken from the cell to be interrogated around 11:30 P.M." I realized I'd fallen for their ruse.

But I fell once more for a ruse of theirs in connection with something that was much, much worse. That was also during the three days that I was together with Heli. Probably the only explanation for that was psychological. While I'd been really tough as nails up until that point, she softened me up. She said to me, "Look, why don't you make it easier for yourself? C'mon. Don't be that way. Make your life easier with the Gestapo." At that point they were interrogating me about the people I'd gotten the ration coupons from. I'd told them, "I don't know, I have no idea, I can't tell you who they were. I met this guy in a café, I can't even remember where." Then they told me that they were going to take me outside, out of the prison. The way they'd also taken Herbert out, wearing handcuffs behind his back, a coat on to conceal them, and taken him to the S-Bahn elevated station Siemensstadt. But Herbert had understood wonderfully how to warn anybody off and get rid of them.

I was also supposed to go outside with the Gestapo for them to hunt for the guy who'd given me the coupons. Heli encouraged me a lot, "Just do it! You'll get out of here!" Until I finally said, "OK, I'll go." Then Fischer came, wanted to take me. But I refused. I told him, "You can finish me off here or send me to a camp! Yes, I said I'd go but I can't. I'm not going." But one thing I did reveal: That the man's illegal name was Murks. That wasn't his name. But I said already that it was hard to lie. His name was Marksthaler. I had to say something. And that was my second mistake! They picked up the guy! Whether they had some other relevant information, whether others had said something, I just don't know…

Those were the two matters for which later on I had to take responsibility and answer for before the Party. And that was almost as bad as to acknowledge to yourself the mistakes you'd made. Believe you me.

I was then removed from Heli's cell. I was in solitary confinement before and put back into solitary again. I really think they did that intentionally. It was based on calculation, a tactic. Heli was genuine. I saw her again a year later, she looked like a concentration camp walking ghost, a *Muselmann* as they termed it;[128] probably back then at Alex she was also an emaciated inmate. She'd been through a helluva lot, had the long stretch from Vienna to Berlin behind her, and had been behind bars much longer than me.

I met Liane in this wing of the prison. She was pregnant. She'd been a member of the Schulze-Boysen Group.[129] At the time I'd heard about a prisoner, Elfriede Paul[130]—who is a professor today—and that she was regularly receiving books. So I "phoned her up," asking her to send me something, and I got something sent secretly. Two months passed, and it was getting ever colder. I changed cells two more times. And I was always placed in the cell Erika von Brockdorff had just been in. That was very nice because of all the poems written on the wall. But then suddenly I was moved to the other wing, and that for me brought a

---

128 The term *Muselmann* was used for prisoners in the camps whose bodies were maximally undernourished and who often staggered around in the vicinity of the barracks, moving back and forth very slowly and in an uncoordinated way. It is not completely clear how the term was coined. Some explanations do cite the depiction of the *Muselmann* in Carl Gottlieb Hering's song C-A-F-F-E-E, which most German guards would have been familiar with at the time. In it, the *Muselmann* is described as having "weakened nerves" and being "sick and pale." Other explanations claim that the swaying of the bodies of weakened prisoners might have been reminiscent of Muslims at prayer and that this might have been the reason for the name.

129 This refers to Liane Berkowitz. For more on her, see the biographical entries in the appendix.

130 For more on Elfriede Paul, see the biographical entries in the appendix.

colossal intensifying of the conditions of imprisonment. There were no more interrogations which made a change, but the other building was located over the courtyard, with other buildings across from it, so it was dark. It was colder because it was facing north.

Outside it was getting colder. The jug of water stood longer and longer outside the cell door before they gave it to us. In addition, I had no connection by knocking. I would often hear a hesitant knock on the wall, but I didn't understand what it meant. It was Ursula Götze from the Schulze-Boysen Group.[131] A student, a very tender and fine girl. I had seen her. So that the food could be distributed more quickly when the "trustees" brought it, the guards in this wing would open several cells at the same time. Ursula and I knew each other by sight, but initially were unable to communicate aside from scratching with our spoon (that in the meantime we'd been given), "Enjoy the meal!" or "Good night!" Only gradually did we work out a sophisticated "knocking code" system: a = . , b = . . , c = . . ., etc. We always had to count the knocks. If we counted wrong, we deleted by scratching. Between the words was a long dash. In this way we finally managed to have a conversation, although it was very burdensome. Ursel was much more insecure than I was. And she was also very afraid of dying. I actually never had any fears of that sort. I thought, "Play the cards you're dealt. Sometime it'll all be over anyhow, right?"

Then I also met Erika, who in the meanwhile was in a cell on this wing, a woman full of life, blond, with very long hair. It really had a nice shine! She brought some order into the whole wing. She was able to because she could whistle so beautifully. She gave entire concerts, beginning with *Eine kleine Nachtmusik*. She didn't let them stop her from doing that, whatever else they might do with her. She became known for that and managed, as a result, to lift our spirits. At that time, I was also lucky enough to have a shower, my first in months. That was a huge privilege for a Jew! They chased you already naked down the corridor, with half a towel. We didn't have any soap, no toilet paper either, and no other paper.

---

131 For more on Ursula Götze, see the biographical entries in the appendix.

When I was first admitted to the prison, I had my period once. I flicked the buzzer, a small contraption which you pressed on, and the guard knew you wanted something. I told her I'd like something for my period. And she said, "Use your hand!" That was how things were. I was driven down the corridor, and there were shower stalls on the same floor, naturally without any curtain. It seemed like you were entering hell because there was this steam everywhere. You couldn't see a thing. Then I was shoved underneath a shower, and another woman was also inside! Then I looked and looked, and she said, "What, you're in here too?" It was one of our nurses from the hospital. She'd been arrested on the Swiss border. She said she was to blame for getting caught. Things had been so frantic that up there on the border she'd just sat down on a bench to rest. She couldn't go any further. And the Gestapo grabbed her.

Christmas 1942 was getting nearer. December 16 was the date for the Schulze-Boysen Group. All except Erika von Brockdorff and Mildred von Harnack[132] were sentenced to death. In the following January, Hitler himself intervened, Erika and Mildred received death sentences as well and were executed in February. Exactly at noon, when the cell was opened for a meal, Erika passed by, returning from the trial. That's something I'll really never forget: this girl, torn between her desire for life and the thought, "Oh my God, everyone's to die, everyone! But not me together with them!" I myself later experienced that same emotion. That moment was just terrible, as she walked past us. After all, she herself didn't know how and what... How she could deal with that, for herself, and before the others. In the evening, at the cell windows, when we'd spoken nonetheless with all the others who had been condemned to death, we had to console her that she wasn't to be executed along with them. Afterwards that wasn't the case any longer anyhow. You can't imagine what all that was like.

Except for Erika and Mildred, the entire group was executed on December 23. That affected us all in a terrible way. I of course knew that our group had already been executed (the first group), but this was something that we all experienced together on the inside.

132 For more on Mildred von Harnack, see the biographical entries in the appendix.

But you should just have seen these guards, the way they came in and behaved with us, "Well, have ya heard? Then we'll tell you guys what happens there! It'll be your turn soon too. You just wait, kid, when they cut your hair in the back and place a paper collar around your neck..." They enjoyed doing that, telling you all the details. At this point, Christmas 1942, there was a lack of staff in the Fehrbellin camp. There was a factory there for hemp and flax. The material was employed partly for later making margarine and then prepared for rope manufacture.

Let me add one small point here. Despite all the lice, bedbugs, and other hassles, the Alexanderplatz facility was still an orderly prison, which means to say, it was in the hands of the justice system. In such a prison, you were given back your own possessions whenever you were transferred to another jail or released (which in our case never happened!). These things had been registered in a storeroom while you were an inmate. In the next prison we were placed in, everything was taken away again. When I was arrested, I had some stuff that was clearly my own. Including my purse and also a nail clipper. Now in the course of incarceration you learn over time what kind of "rights" you have as a prisoner, even though as a Jew you hardly ever make mention of them anyhow. One day I said I wanted to see my possessions. You could do that after a certain amount of time inside. I used some excuse, like that I wanted to get a handkerchief or something. No, it wasn't that. I demanded to see Fischer. That was arranged. And then I told him I wished after so many long months to get a book and pencil from my handbag. I'd been arrested with a copy of Freud's *Psychoanalysis*. So they let me go to where my things were stored, I took a book and pencil out, and then also swiped my own scissors as well. These scissors went with me everywhere after that, they survived every body search (hidden by the way outside the grating) and also my escape. So I had my scissors. It was very good to have something like that. And I had my volume of Freud, which I read from front to back and back to front. It also proved a great help to me.

In Fehrbellin, they needed more staff. After we'd experienced how on the 23rd, they rounded up those sentenced to death, they were shouting, "Everyone out, with all your stuff!" You never knew what was going to happen. I came down into the prison courtyard. And parked there was a large truck, packed full of women. Now just imagine: I'd been in solitary confinement, except for three days, and now this. That was a pleasure! All were singing and making merry. The truck drove out into the street and went right across Berlin. I was sitting in the last row. In front of us naturally were guards with guns. Despite that, it was a pleasure to be on the outside. There was a whole row of French women all wearing straw hats. They were singing *J'attend toujour...* A bunch of us were also in there. I made a connection with them. They were saying what now would happen. In the middle of the journey this huge truck stopped, and the guards provided each of us with a piece of plum cake. We started to wonder, "What's going on here?"

There were also many prostitutes in the truck, and they in any case were always very cheery and jovial. As a result, the guards were also in a merry mood. They told us we were being sent to a labor camp. Good! Then we arrived in Fehrbellin. When I entered the camp I thought, wow, it's like being outside in freedom. There was a camp street with barracks, you could move around fairly well. Of course, once through the gate, you had to first surrender all your possessions. They were put in a sack, and you had to wait totally naked in the courtyard for the delousing. It was December. Then you were put through the steam cloud, then back again into the courtyard, and you had to wait once more. Then you came to the Gestapo. All the women. Then, just as we were, we had to stand in formation and listen. And some guy gave us a lecture. Now that I've read all the material, I think that it was standard practice, and then the lecture, "Here you are in our hands. Here you can do what you like, rather—here we can do with you what we want. You can scream as much as you like, no one will hear you..."

Each of us got a dress, rather a kind of shirt the color of the garbage collectors, with a number on the back and front, and a brown kerchief. Those who were lucky got wooden shoes. I had no luck and remained barefoot. Then we were taken to a Jews' barracks. There I got together with Dorle Bahnmüller, I've mentioned her before. We shared the same pallet to sleep, it was quite large! The day began at 4 A.M., roll call at attention in formation, and the course of the day was actually just like in a concentration camp. The difference between the labor camp and the concentration camp was only that here you could be worked to death and in the concentration camp you were sent to the gas. This wasn't an extermination camp. We were guarded by female guards with dogs. The Germans, to whom as a Jew I no longer belonged, worked inside the factory. We had to load hemp and flax from rail carriages. Hemp by the way is heavier than flax. We had to stack up the bundles and were under extreme pressure to work fast. We had to shunt and maneuver the carriages, using our own physical strength. There was nothing else. It was terribly hard. So hard that I probably wouldn't have survived if I'd stayed there.

I owe a lot to the Soviet and Polish women who were there, who always said, "Listen, you go on over there in the back!" Because further in back the carriages were always loaded more flatly, and they were lighter. I had never before used a pitchfork. I couldn't handle it, and my hands quickly swelled up badly. Everything totally open and exposed. Secretly I snuck into the factory. Jews weren't allowed inside. First, I found myself a sack I could wrap around my legs, so that in winter I didn't have to go barefoot.

The latrines—that was also something special: They were long outhouses containing a channel, with diagonally placed boxes above, full of holes. You had to do what you came for in the shortest amount of time. We wore a belt around our uniform, and according to regulations the food pot had to hang at the back from the belt. The whole thing was a kind of overalls, which then had to be taken off completely. Underneath you had just a shirt. We had that shit all the time, all of us. How often it happened that someone's food pot just fell into the toilet. But then you had quite a problem! You could wait and wait, and not get any food. There was chow time only twice a day in any case. At 4 A.M., we got a piece of bread and coffee, in the evening something warm to eat. When we were then marched back—singing as we went—we had to go to the shower, there was even warm water. But be quick, very quick about it. There was no soap. Then put on your wet clothes and go and stand waiting for dinner. Jews in any case never got a full portion. Nonetheless, in the evening you could go out into the camp street. That was a kind of freedom. After all, you could see the sky.

That's where I met Cilly Bode. She was the life companion of a very well-known Communist, Beppo Römer.[133] She did a lot for us in the Jewish block. She was the one who arranged for me to be called to the clothing storeroom, because I was so thin and was constantly freezing; she gave me a pair of soldier's riding knee breeches, a very small size... Dorle Bahnmüller and I took turns wearing that under our overalls. After all, we couldn't be seen wearing those breeches. But already in mid-January, I was brought back again to Berlin, and that was my good luck, because I wouldn't have been able to hold out and survive the situation in the camp. I was taken back in a truck and sent to Lehrter Strasse. And I was told immediately that I had been mistakenly transferred out, due to the lack of workers. But my pretrial investigation had not yet been concluded.

In the prison on Lehrter Strasse I was placed in the cell for Jews. It was not as bad as one might assume. Since the jail was overcrowded, this cell was a large office room that had been cleared, and so it had large windows. Naturally with bars on the outside, but there was a water tap in the room. To describe the room's size: Imagine this—an entrance door, and on one side a double-deck plank bed, a small hallway, then the bucket. It was two-and-a-half or three meters in length. On the other side, in the actual room, there were two double-deck plank beds, in front of that diagonally was a single pallet, and there were two more between the windows, very close to the others. There were ten pallet beds in all, and we were forty women inside. At times forty-five women. There wasn't any light either. But to balance that, the prison had some other advantages as well. It had a relatively large courtyard planted with trees. The guards, they were soldiers, allowed us to walk in the courtyard in pairs. That was very nice. Although the male and female prisoners took walks separately, we were able to see one another through the windows. There was a possibility to slip something underneath a stone or plant. So you had a connection, and that was great.

---

133 For more on Cäcilie "Cilly" Bode and Joseph "Beppo" Römer, see the biographical entries in the appendix.

We had our difficulties with the non-communist, bourgeois Jewish women. After all, they weren't accustomed to being in jail, and everything for them was just unimaginable. The Gestapo itself helped arrange for people to cross over into Switzerland. They were pocketing foreign exchange for that. But then they arrested some people before they left Berlin, others they caught at the border, and locked them up charged with foreign currency monetary offences. Such prisoners then went through various prisons, and once they had been sufficiently squeezed dry, they were sent to the transit camps and on to Auschwitz. We two, three veteran "jail sisters" tried to teach the newcomers how to make their lives bearable. That included the need to wash daily from head to toe. We even forced them to do that. We knew: If a person lets herself go, then she's finished. In any case we were crawling with vermin. You can't even imagine the invasion of bedbugs we had! And by the way, we had a bed that was especially infested. We put a woman in there that the bedbugs wouldn't touch. Yes, such things exist! And then every evening, once it grew dark, we organized a kind of cabaret. Each person had to recite something, one after the next. That was simply obligatory for all. Whether a children's song or a saying or something a person made up! In that way we managed to keep up our spirits.

Then a tragic-comic event came to pass. One day the cell door was opened and a woman was pushed inside. She'd apparently been living in freedom and had just been arrested. She probably still had relatives on the outside and was totally bewildered. It was pretty dark in our room there, and it looked a lot like a scene from hell with so many women packed in, and you could hardly crawl or stand. When she was shoved into our midst, the first thing she said was, "Where c-c-can I m-m-ake a-a t-t-telephone call h-here?" Naturally, we all broke out in loud laughter. But deep down we felt really sorry for her.

Apart from my time in Fehrbellin, this was the first time I was sharing a toilet with so many women. We were sleeping four and sometimes five on a single pallet. And then something very peculiar happened to me. I knew about the execution of our first group. And I also knew that we others were likewise doomed to die. Now it was so awfully crowded on the pallet, you could only lie on one side of your body. So there would be a bit more room, I always used to lie down and position myself a bit higher up, so that I ended up lying with my head on the iron edge of the pallet. This then gave me terrible dreams about being executed. I had a real physical, bodily fear of this, and it was very upsetting. And right up to the present, here on this side of my head I still have nerve irritation... In the meantime, it's become chronic. The pain from back then, I still have it more or less today.

In our cell we had a singer, she sang so wonderfully. She didn't make it; I can't even recall her name. But she was also a burden for us in one respect—she was so terribly heavy and also had diabetes. She took up an entire pallet when she lay down. Although there was great fluctuation in the cell, some persons did remain because the Gestapo wasn't done with them yet. And so you had "old regulars" on the pallet. One was Alice. She was about my age. Her husband had arranged an escape to the Tyrol. For himself, his wife, her mother, and the child. They all reached the Tyrol border. But then they were arrested. The husband was separated from the others. Alice was locked up with her mother and child in a very small room in the school of the border village. During the night, the mother committed suicide in their presence and with the agreement of her daughter. She had some poison with her and drank it. And Alice repeatedly told the story of how frightful it had been to let her mother slip in her sleep toward death, and not to scream. And to think as she was dying, "Good, Mom, it's OK, good!" After all, it forces a person to cry out. She had experienced that horrible thing. Then she was sent on a transport, and later they took away her child. Alice had become very serious and calm, very quiet. One day she received a secret message that her husband and child were alive. This woman had never participated in our cabaret evenings. But on that evening! She didn't know how to best express her feelings. She then sang so magnificently, it was so splendid, you just can't imagine! I know that the child was later sent on a transport to Auschwitz and probably also perished, as did the father, and Alice herself as well.

We had in the Lehrter Strasse prison very different female prison officers, some very bad, others less so. There was one whom we never really figured out. She was a nimble, dark woman, medium in height. She used to address us only as "goddamn Jewish trash." But sometimes she would open the cell door and shove an empty food bucket inside that we could scratch clean. For us that was already a really great thing. The external guard force consisted of three guard details that used to alternate. The prisoners passed on the experiences they'd had with these individual guard units.

In our cell were also some inmates who had been there a very long time. We called one detail "the tigers," another "the idiots," and the third one "the good guys." That probably characterized them adequately enough. Now since prisoners were placed in our prison who had just been arrested and were coming directly from a life in freedom—some of whom still had relatives on the outside or others who had financial help out there—some possibilities existed for gaining a bit of relief on the inside. When the "good guys" were on guard duty we were able to swing down letters through our large windows, specifying that they should go to relatives or friends. They then gave the guards some money, and they brought food in or hosiery. That then was hoisted up at night in a small basket. The female guards were bribed with the hosiery. We naturally consumed the food immediately. That was the relief organized among inmates at the Lehrter Strasse prison.

Because we were able to establish contacts out in the courtyard, I met several people again from the Schulze-Boysen Group. They in any case belonged to the wider circle. I also had contact with several Soviet Communist women whom I didn't know. That was arranged via "female trustees," who were able to move around on the outside. I knew what was awaiting me because the first part of our group was already dead. Despite that I decided to make use of the time and learn some Russian. I sent a message to that effect to them and received the alphabet and vocabulary—sent in part hidden under stones or similar ways. That was also an act of solidarity, because in this way you kept up your morale.

Just awful at Lehrter Strasse were the terrible screams of the male prisoners you could hear at night, who were getting their "treatment" in the prison cellar. Except for withdrawal of food we women were not subjected to maltreatment.

Since I commented on the men screaming, I have to return to the prison at Alexanderplatz. I experienced there how the Gypsies were taken into custody. While they were still living in freedom, the Gypsies had been herded up and crowded together just like the Jews. But if the Jews were placed as an entire family living in each room in a Jews' house, the Gypsies were crammed into basements and old store apartments behind Elsässer Strasse. And then they were all brought during the night to the prison at Alexanderplatz. Their screaming at night, I can't get that out of my mind. The babies, the children, the elderly... I was for a time with a Gypsy woman together in a cell, I'll tell you about that later on. They after all had it much harder than we did, I mean the overwhelming psychological stress it caused them given their mentality.

But now I want to add something about the guard details at the Lehrter Strasse prison and what it was possible to do as a result. All my teeth were smashed by the Gestapo. That was very painful the whole time, but I never had any dental treatment. And then I heard from our *Zimmerälteste* (cell eldest) that you could report at the Lehrter Strasse prison for dental treatment in the police hospital. And if you got an appointment, the Lehrter Strasse guard details would bring you over to that hospital. You only had to make sure that the right guard detail escorted you over. Then you could, people said, if you had some money, buy something, or eat some potato salad in the hospital canteen.

I also learned from the cell eldest how it was handled at Lehrter Strasse. Every prison in the justice system had its own methods and did not let the Gestapo interfere too much and tell it what to do. Here, for example, you were allowed to receive a postal package with clean linen. Only your letters came in via the Gestapo. Now through Richard I was familiar with a communist, Ernst Jegelka. And I knew he'd also served time at the Lehrter Strasse prison and thus had to know all that. People told me, "OK, you've gotta register for a dental checkup today. In three days the 'good guys' are going to be on guard duty and maybe you'll be taken over to the hospital. We'll provide you with some money, and in return you can bring a few small things for us." The money, of course, was illegal, it was hoisted up by the guard detail or smuggled in through other new channels. I'd gotten an overcoat from the girls; we were all wearing a strange mix of clothes. We'd open up the seam down below where it connects with that from above, and sewed money inside. It was at least fifteen Marks. The cell eldest advised me, "Listen, they're so decent you can also smuggle out a letter if you want!" So I wrote to Jegelka on a small scrap of packing paper that I'd found somewhere, I simply folded the packing paper into an envelope and addressed it. That was all a gamble, you were taking a risk, but there was almost no other way, and you also became a bit callous, hardened over time behind bars. That was not at all conspicuous as a packing paper envelope, because the foreign workers also had no stationery for letters. I had stored a suitcase with my things at Ernst Jegelka's place. So I wrote to him that I was staying at the hotel he had once frequented... And so on in that tone. And I asked him to please send me some fresh linen and also wrote I'd really like some bread if he could manage.

When I left the prison, they searched me but didn't discover the money or letter. So I walked away with two of the "good guys." And since the two of them were also not particularly interested in going off with one woman, and then to boot such a tough and withered woman, one guy went over to a bar or who knows where and stayed back there. The second guard said, "If you try to run away, you'll get a bullet up your ass!" That's how he went off with me. I was on the lookout for a mailbox and when I passed one, I said, "Oh, please go a little away from me, I've got to put on my garter." He probably knew exactly what I wanted to do. But now the letter was on its way. Wait a second, I recall the following: I had been arrested in summertime. I wasn't wearing stockings or anything else, just my shoes. When I wanted to leave the place, my comrades in the cell said, "Listen, kid, it's too cold outside, you'd better put on stockings." And they gave me some stockings and also a garter belt. And when I was about to put the garter belt on, I noticed it was full of lice. But everything had to be done quickly, and so I simply left with my stockings hanging way down. Naturally, the people on the street looked—such an unkempt woman walking with a police officer...

Now he brought me to the police hospital. It wasn't very far, it stood where the hospital of the Volkspolizei[134] is today. I was taken

---

134 The Deutsche Volkspolizei (German People's Police), often referred to by the abbreviation VoPo, was the regular police force in the GDR.

up to a dentist, a staff doctor, and he was very, very nice to me. He removed the stumps of some of the broken teeth. And because I was bleeding so badly, he put special cotton wool and small rolls of wadding in my mouth to absorb all the blood. I wasn't feeling well at all, I couldn't tolerate such things. Prior to the treatment, I pleaded with him to call me in for a second appointment as well. I'd spoken earlier with the "good guy" who accompanied me. He said he wanted to go to the canteen. When I left with my mouth full of absorbent cotton and wadding and blood, the doctors' breakfasts were standing in the anterooms. Seldom had I ever had to control myself so strongly so as not to reach out and take something. Because the food at Alexanderplatz was very poor. In the Lehrter Strasse prison we got our meals sent over by car from Alexanderplatz. That was also what we called the "water wagon." The food from Alex was what we called "baptized many times over."

I entered the canteen with the guard, he sat me down in a corner and said, "Here's a portion of potato salad." I already knew that was the usual food available. Since I was famished, I took the bloody wadding out of my mouth and devoured what was on the plate. I even asked him for a second portion, which I received wrapped in paper. I stuck it in my pocket for my comrades. And I had a few more wishes for them too, I can still remember what they asked for very precisely: a pencil, a few matches, some skin cream, and a little powder. That's what they wanted me to bring back. It was for sale there. But the guard warned me, "Look, *I* didn't do anything. But *you'd* better be darn careful when they search you!" I'd hidden everything in my underarms. They found it all. First, they slapped me in the face a few times, and gave me a penalty of three days with no food, and no food for the whole cell. And I wasn't allowed to go to the dentist again. And while we political prisoners and also some of the non-political Jewish women generally bore up well under such collective penalties, nonetheless several others began to complain and curse me terribly because they now had to go hungry. We had to make it clear to them then that we'd done this for them. Later when we were punished for trying to escape—I have to tell you about that—I was always very proud we'd attempted that. You had to be glad if someone had managed to escape and had gotten a certain new lease of life. Of course, that was double-edged: If a prisoner was recaptured, he was certain to die.

Meanwhile, February had come. There was a new wave of arrests of those who had helped our group. In part that had already been known to the Gestapo, in part they only discovered this very slowly, and then they took care of it in one fell swoop. And now all of us still alive had to go to the interrogations. Confrontations, comparisons, corrections of reports and statements... I was after all now in a community and no longer had that pathological longing to have some human contact, even with the Gestapo. And actually, "longing" was at that point the wrong expression!

I was repeatedly taken from Lehrter Strasse to the Alex. And despite all the strain on my nerves, it nonetheless was a certain kind of relief. They took me there by paddy wagon, where you're always sitting with someone else to talk to. But in the Alexanderplatz building they took you into a so-called transport hall. That was located along Dirksenstrasse. It was a warm place. Women stood there crowded tightly together. They were inside "due to de job," they said in a heavy Berlin accent, meaning that they'd skipped from work, and there were an awful lot of prostitutes. They were never very hungry and used to give others their food. I then totally set aside my earlier inhibitions regarding hygiene. There never were any spoons. When we stood there and were kept standing for ages, and someone had not emptied their pot, then I of course drank the rest. One time they sent a Gestapo officer to transfer me to the Alex, a young guy, who during the trip over did not speak much with me. But somehow, he was probably touched emotionally. You noticed things like that. He didn't lock me in the hall to wait but rather in a cell. Then he came back, with a plate of food, and said, "OK, just eat this first. You don't need to go to the interrogation yet." When I finished, he brought me a second plate, "Just eat your fill!" And that seemed so kind and so-o-o very human. Then he brought me to my inspectors. With that it was finished. Once I saw him again in the hall in the prison on Hamburger Strasse. What he was really thinking, I don't know. I only want to stress how something like that sticks in your mind long after. Sometimes they naturally did things like that, in order to get something in return. But I definitely think he was sorry and just wanted to help.

I remained at the prison on Lehrter Strasse until March 3, 1943. That day they bellowed, "Outside with all your things!" I was placed on a transport to Alexanderplatz. There I was taken to the discharge room. Standing there was the group of comrades I'd been arrested with: Martin Kochmann, Felix Heymann, "Butz,"... They lined us up, separated one from another, our faces to the wall. Then we were taken all together to the paddy wagon. Also together with those who'd been arrested in February. Thus, with all the group members who'd done something good, including some we didn't know at all. If some person had provided a place for Felix to stay illegally, then naturally *I* didn't know him, or only from police lineups and interrogations. Now in the paddy wagon we had a good chance to talk openly. In doing so it was possible to compare statements and to determine how some things could have come about where before people had been wondering, "How in the heck could they have actually known that?"

In the reception area of Moabit prison, we were immediately and strictly separated again. That's the way it was in general in the justice system. The standing rule was: accomplices mustn't be allowed to come together. But in connection with transport, that played no role whatsoever. We were informed that once again we were now in the hands of the justice system—and that court proceedings against us would now be opened.

The prisons were terribly overcrowded. Of the roughly 400 women in Moabit, about 100 had been sentenced to death or soon would be. There was no room for me upstairs, so I was put in the basement, in a detention cell. There was no pallet bed, only a kind of stone sarcophagus. There was just one blanket on the hard bed. Inset in the wall was a ring. They didn't chain you to it, but everything else was difficult enough. There was no toilet, just a bucket, and no table or chair, such as I'd been accustomed to in Alexanderplatz prison. The window was inbuilt as a normal basement window, except that outside it was covered with a metal grid, and in addition had an external metal sheet that blocked visibility. I was unable to see the courtyard.

Initially, I didn't have any work. Later on, I was assigned a job gluing together cardboard boxes for children's toys (for Woolworth). Even this cell had some good points, though. First, there was no vermin; second, someone before me had scooped out some of the floor under the door so that you could grab the bread ends that the prison laundry crew—which passed through several times a day—would shove through. They were mostly Jehovah's Witnesses.[135] During the three weeks I was there I got no permission to go for a walk [in the yard]. I felt really rotten. Confined down there I started to develop a vitamin deficiency. My skin cracked open all over, and I had a rash everywhere. I felt disgusted by my own body.

A female officer who had glimpsed my condition probably felt sorry for me. She had me transferred upstairs, and I was placed in the infirmary, i.e. on the sickbay floor. I was given a single room and I felt like I was in a sanatorium. The bed had fresh linen, though in plaid pattern. There was a pallet that you could fold up against the wall. During the day the blanket had to be arranged in a special orderly way on the bed, but somehow, I liked that. Then there was a small wall cabinet, a brush hung outside, a metal bowl that we had to keep shiny (some sort of copper material), with a towel inside. Then there was a bench and table, in the form of a board you could fold up against the wall. And a toilet! It was *utter* luxury. The room was bright and clean and even freshly painted, with a bit of green in the lime. I felt very happy.

Quite soon I heard a signal, some knocking on the wall from next door—a Polish woman. Then I was granted permission for a walk. If I recall rightly, we had fifteen minutes—although it was a solitary walk, and despite the strict rules, the guards couldn't stop us from speaking very briefly with one another in the stairwell. This is how I learned that Mariechen was in a cell three doors from mine. Later, after we went underground, she aided our group. A female guard told me, "You know of course that you're here for the Volksgericht (People's Court),[136] and

---

135 Jehovah's Witnesses, at the time also referred to as *Bibelforscher*—bible researchers—is a Christian denomination, which had between 25,000 and 30,000 members in Germany during the Nazi period, who—based on their faith—refused to participate in politics, carry arms, or serve in the army. The group was persecuted, and many members were imprisoned or taken to concentration camps. Nearly 1,500 were murdered.

136 The Volksgerichtshof (People's Court) was a Nazi special court designed to operate outside of universally accepted, basic principles of law and justice. It was

you'll be sentenced to death. But you can work for the Wehrmacht."
Then slides were brought into my cell, with illustrations of various
models of airplanes. They had to be glued inside frames. I had caught
a few lice during the trip on the paddy wagon. It gave me great joy to
place a louse now and then between the two glasses and to imagine
what it would look like when the Nazis projected the "new airplane
model" on the screen. When one was finished and a whole box was full,
one had to use the door signal. The carton then stood for a few seconds
in front of the door. I quickly took a look to see how many Mariechen
had managed to finish. The enthusiasm for my work made me tingle
inside. It's wonderful to work, even though I actually did not want to.
Now I had work, and a connection with someone next door.

And then, one day I discovered that if I put my ear up against
the drainage pipe on the toilet, I could hear sounds of knocking from
other cells. As I was listening, I suddenly heard a strange cough
coming from upstairs. Hey, I know that cough! I thought long about
that and finally made a "telephone call" upstairs to inquire who was
there, we must in fact know each other, "Renate, is that you?" It was
Renate Moratz, about whom I've already spoken. She had her cough
left over from a bout with TB. We shared many night shifts [at the
hospital]. She also was arrested because of us. Renate later died of
dysentery in Auschwitz. I then went together with her to the prison
reception doctor. There was still such a professional there on staff.
It was nice: we were able to communicate, and during the evening
we occasionally managed to speak to one another via the window.
You had the feeling that there was a friend, a human being, a friend
there for you. Her job was to sort the bloody rags for the Wehrmacht.
Her entire cell was full of clothing from the dead. She slept there in
its midst.

founded in 1934 after a regular court had acquitted several accused communists
in the Reichstag Fire Trial for lack of evidence, and was designed to try those in
opposition to the regime. The group of its victims, most of whom were sentenced
to death and executed shortly after, was diverse. It ranged from simple people
accused of listening to—and telling others about—allied newscasts to members
of resistance groups. All members of the Schulze-Boysen Group and the Gruppe
Baum were tried in front of the Volksgerichtshof.

The Pole next to my cell had already been sentenced to death. They notified her she'd be taken to be executed. That's when I experienced for the first time how the entire floor stayed up the whole last night before. And we all were knocking to give her courage. The next day you just sat there eating when the meal came and felt upset with yourself while you ate...

Meanwhile, I was summoned before the examining judge. He informed me that I would be tried in a Sondergericht (special court) for wartime economic crimes and would also be tried in the Volksgerichtshof (People's Court) for high treason; the detention order would be maintained and the justice system would continue to process me. I also learned there that the second group had been executed on March 5, 1943. And because the second was gone, it was the next group's turn.

I stayed at the infirmary until April, under relatively good conditions. I was some three weeks in the basement and about four weeks upstairs.

At the end of April, I was taken out one day and brought to the special court. I didn't receive an indictment and had no defense attorney. I was then charged for being in possession of the stash of ration coupons, because the Gestapo man had stolen the coupons for bread I'd been given. I was sentenced to eighteen months behind bars. Sentences of up to a year were served at the prison on Barnimstrasse. Everyone sentenced to prison and for not too long, but more than a year, was sent to Leipzig-Kleinmeusdorf. I hardly recall much about the trial. I was alone in the dock. "My" inspector was there as a witness. And the guy I'd obtained the coupons from was also under arrest; he received an equally ridiculous sentence. I also learned that I was considered a first offender, because the month I'd been sentenced to for the abortion had in the meantime been deemed non-valid, because it had been the abortion of a Jewish fetus, a so-called "worthless life."

Immediately after the trial, I was placed in a transport cell, also in solitary. I was prepared for transport in that everything I'd come to possess in the meantime was taken away, except for a minimum of clothing. I was searched from head to toe, and all my orifices, too.

Then, I had to wait until a transport left for Kleinmeusdorf. It took four or five days.

Then I was summoned to the superintendent of the women's prison at Moabit. She was an old social-democratic social worker who had been transferred for disciplinary reasons to her post at the prison. Several of the female prison officers were in that category. She told me—addressing me respectfully using the formal "you," I still remember that well—that I actually was behind bars waiting to be tried for treason before the People's Court, and that I really should not be sent to the prison in Kleinmeusdorf, because the exact time for that trial had not yet been decided upon. But the transport documents had been issued and signed, and so the following day I was to be transported, come what may. She said she had added a note to my papers specifying that I had to be sent back again with the very next transport. She told me all that.

And then something happened which again is incredible. That night, an officer was on duty whom we all liked a lot. We called her *Dackelbein* (Dachshund leg)—we weren't allowed to know the names of any of the guards. She was a woman who'd been drafted into service, and she did what she could for us. She entered my cell. We were alone. And then I told her that I knew that Jutta Dubinsky, the woman who had given me my jacket, was imprisoned there as well. I said I was as good as sentenced to death and that Jutta probably wouldn't be. She had done me a good deed and I had the desire to tell her a few words. I would also have a small request for her to carry out for the time when I'd no longer be alive. The guard said, "OK, I'll go and get Jutta for you!" She brought Jutta from her solitary cell, and then locked her inside with me in the transport cell, and we stayed together that night. I told Jutta how she could inquire about little Eva in order to locate her. She promised me that if she stayed alive, she'd take responsibility for Eva, and that she would look for her. That was a very big deal for me.

The next morning, I was taken out of the cell, they took me to the storeroom, and all my possessions were handed over to me. Then I was chained to a policeman and brought downstairs. There stood a truck full of people, we were all crammed in and taken the short distance to the Lehrter railway station. Then the long line of prisoners was taken from the truck out into the station, one by one, each escorted by a policeman.

I was the only woman there. The people around naturally all looked at me. I held my head high... I felt a certain pride.

I was placed in a prisoner transport car. I'd never seen anything like that before. It was a rail car and inside it was like a jail: a long corridor connecting a large number of small cells you were then locked up inside. In the jail we'd been given a chunk of bread as food for the trip. Then the train departed, headed for Leipzig. We traveled for about twelve hours. Probably the car was repeatedly uncoupled and coupled to another train somewhere. In Brandenburg and elsewhere, more prisoners were taken on. There were after all a huge number of jails. Ever more prisoners were shoved inside; it got more and more crowded. In Magdeburg—we went the long way round—they gave us a jug of water and a cup. It was passed from one prisoner to the next. I received it too and must have infected myself when I drank. Because before I'd been in solitary.

When we were taken off in Leipzig, I was part of a small group of female prisoners. That same evening we were taken to Kleinmeusdorf, in a paddy wagon a bit different from that in Berlin. The prison there was once probably a castle, today it's a detention hospital. While we were walking over it looked great, like a sanatorium. But it proved very inhospitable. It had already become totally "Aryan" and no longer admitted any Jews. For that reason, they locked me up in the basement until I was sent elsewhere. Since I was again covered with lice from the transport and dirty, and they had given me a jug of water—I was completely alone—I took off all my clothes and washed them in this jug. Then, like a good prisoner, I lay down under my blanket, totally naked, and waited. Toward morning, a female guard came by, took away all my things, stuck them wet in a bag and said, "Over here, you will receive a prison uniform." You were given a shirt, and the so-called "Aunt Ida pants," which are not much trouble if you have to go to the toilet, you can just fold them down, a strange kind of bra, and a prisoner's dress. Then I was taken back down into the basement.

The next day I had to undergo a prison reception exam. The first thing the doctor did was to rip off the bra and tell me correspondingly that a "Jewish broad" didn't need one. "We're pure Aryan here, see to it that you are moved elsewhere." Now and then he asked me terribly nasty questions. You know, I'm a nurse, I'm well accustomed to all forms of human behavior. But *this* was something I don't even want to recount. He probably took some sexual pleasure in all that. Then he stated, "She can't stay here another minute, she has to be sent on." My prison clothing was kept right there. The prison trustee had to bring my bag with all the wet clothes inside, and I had to put them on. I was not taken back down into the basement.

Two female officers escorted me and one of them took me on a journey through all the prisons in Leipzig. None of them would accept me because they all had become strictly Aryan. But the prison trustee, who could move around freely, had in the meantime run and brought me a net bag full of potatoes. They'd been cooked inside the net bag in their skins so that the portions were all equal. That was such a good deed. I was famished! All prisons had the same procedure: the newly admitted, were provided no food for at least twenty-four hours. One had to be punished for being transferred to a new prison! I was shivering in my wet clothes as we walked, but I stuffed myself with the unpeeled potatoes.

Because they probably had no paddy wagon for me, I walked under guard from Kleinmeusdorf all the way to the *Völkerschlachtdenkmal*.[137] I was feeling more and more miserable. But I still caught sight of the great monument. The lessons I received from my prostitute comrades back behind bars about the way to freedom went through my head, "What if I made a run for it?" But then I thought, "No, I don't want that. Why? Your comrades are dead, what's the point? Whether Eva is alive or not, you don't know." Moreover, I was probably also weakened by fever.

At the Monument to the Battle of the Nations, one of the officers took off and disappeared, she probably went home, and the other got on the streetcar together with me. I felt so sad at that point. I was dressed in shabby clothing and suffering from a fever, but I nevertheless got a taste of freedom. I saw the people around me as if through a veil. They were looking at me, and at that broad next to me.

---

137 Completed in 1913, the *Völkerschlachtdenkmal*, a monument for the 1813 Battle of the Nations, is an important landmark in Leipzig.

After inquiring at a number of jails that refused to accept me, I finally was "accommodated" in one that still had one Jewish woman among its inmates. She had a non-Jewish partner and was awaiting trial for *Rassenschande*.[138] I was placed in the cell with that Jewish woman and five Polish women. The Jewish woman was the "senior inmate" of the cell and as a result enjoyed the privilege of the pallet. We others slept diagonally on the floor. The cell now was full. I had been admitted in the evening.

The next morning, I joined them and went down to report for work. This prison was also one of those structures built "all around" a central shaft. We went along our corridor and at the narrowest point, we climbed down a spiral staircase. We then had to cross a long corridor and went on through the men's prison. We reached another wing of the prison, structured just like ours. But this wing was outfitted down below as a workshop. There were tables in two long rows facing the window. People sat there working at a job that to my mind was terrible: small threads had to be attached to small price labels for some kind of item.

There were guards observing the inmates, since conversation between prisoners was strictly prohibited and you were not allowed to let your eyes stray from the job. In addition, there were quotas: it was required that you complete a substantial number of labels in a specified time. I knew that I was going to be sent back to Berlin. But then I thought, "If this goes on here much longer, I might have 'good' prospects." I found that terrible. Several times the trustees transporting food came through from the men's wing. The female officer sat there on a raised stool. When the doors were opened to allow the men through, she called out in the most beautiful Saxon dialect, "Hey, gaels, toern

---

138 The crime of *Rassenschande* (racial defilement) was introduced in 1935 alongside the Nuremberg Laws. It prohibited marriage—and extramarital sexual relations—between people categorized by the Nazi system as Aryan, and Jews or other people categorized as of lower racial status. Initially, the accused would often face public humiliation at the hands of the stormtroopers and—if tried and convicted—prison. Women were usually not tried for *Rassenschande*, but often sent to a concentration camp and/or tried for giving false testimony when they tried to protect their partner. *Rassenschande* and similar forms of criminal persecution led to further isolation of the Jews on German-controlled territory.

aeroend, aeh maen's coeming!" Because the men were not supposed to see us. That was common practice in all the prisons—you had to stand facing the wall, and continue to stand there, on and on...

I did endure that for just one day, though. In the evening we were returned to the cell. Already that night I noticed I had a fever and sore throat, and felt really horrible. The next morning, I couldn't get up. And I knew I must be very sick, because I don't tend to develop a fever. I told my cellmate. She said, "Just stay lying down, you can rest on my pallet." She didn't even know yet what I had contracted. At night we'd talked a lot to one another. She told me this was a proper prison. The prison management took care of censoring the mail, it didn't go through the hands of the Gestapo. She also told me there was a social worker working at this prison, who probably was a Social Democrat and someone you could trust. I also had the right to an admission letter.

And precisely because it was a proper and orderly prison, she went in the morning and reported that I was sick. One of the female officers came and looked at me. I already had a rash and realized myself that I was probably coming down with scarlet fever. She called a doctor who served in the prison. He didn't enter the cell. Rather, it was opened up and I had to get down from the pallet bed to report just like any other prisoner: prisoner number so-and-so, cell number so-and-so... He told me to pull down my shirt. I stood there below the window, totally naked, and he stood in the doorway. He took one look at me and said, "scarlet fever," gave a nod, and then the cell door was closed shut. The consequence was that although I received no treatment, I was put in quarantine for six weeks. The others were transferred out of the cell. I remained all by myself. I heard from the prison trustees that the others, when they got scarlet fever, were likely sent to a hospital. Naturally, the same was not true for a Jewish woman: she stayed in the cell.

I was quite ill and felt terrible. Due to the danger of infection the cell door was opened only once a day. That's when I received some food and water. And that was all.

There was an old toilet system there. They didn't provide a bucket, there was a real toilet. But since you weren't allowed to get rid of anything, everything you excreted was collected on a flap. It remained there the whole day and created an awful stench. You should keep in mind that all prisoners always suffered from diarrhea. Once a day the flap was opened, and water was flushed on through. But sometimes they forgot to open the flap before they flushed. Then the cell was flooded. You had to mop that up yourself, whether you were sick or not, and they also didn't care what you used to do that. I had to do it several times.

While I did that, despite my illness, I discovered something very important and beautiful. In a crack in the floorboard I found a sewing needle—probably left by one of my predecessors. That was a great thing to have. When I started to feel a bit better, I tore off a piece of cloth from my prison shirt and made a small handkerchief from it. That was in June 1943. I hoped that I could then smuggle that out somehow for August, for my daughter who had her birthday then. Although I had no idea where Eva was!

At that point, a stump of one of the broken teeth in my mouth began to come loose and started to hurt me terribly. Via the trustee, who came by once a day, I requested that they should please help extract the tooth. I knew I couldn't go out. And I understood that nobody could enter. I asked whether they might give me some instrument, which likewise was not possible. And after a whole lot of pain I finally tore the tooth out with my own fingernails.

But it was nonetheless a decent prison. One week after I'd begun to feel better, the social worker came by, the guy about whom I heard. And because I still had the prison admission letter with me, and also assumed that this might well be done without any problem, I told him I didn't have any more relatives in Germany, but rather only in Hungary. And asked him whether he'd be willing to send the admission letter document to Hungary. He said no, he couldn't do that. Hungary after all was not yet under German occupation. But after I beseeched him, saying please oh please, he declared he was after all ready to help and to send a notification to my "relatives" in Hungary that I was sick. I knew that Richard's relatives lived in Budapest at Szabor utca 3. I thought, "If they and Richard are still alive, then they could learn from this bit of news that I too was still among the living." I was also fairly certain I wouldn't be causing some disaster because the mail did not pass through the hands of the Gestapo. The social worker ensured me he would pass on the news. And that he did. In my later narrative you'll note that this news evoked some response. When I felt better he also brought me something to read.

In the meantime, we'd reached the end of June.[139] I repeatedly heard that I was being summoned. When one sits isolated and without an occupation in a cell, one can only participate by listening. And thus, I also overheard that "this one" was supposed to be sent to Berlin to go on trial. They didn't make the effort of trying to find out the cell number of the prisoner whose name was called out, they just shouted along the corridor. Then you had to trigger the cell signal to inform the officers where you were. Repeatedly, I also heard that "this one" is in quarantine.

Since July 1, 1943, a new directive was in force:[140] Jews were no longer under the German justice system but rather an exclusive matter of the Gestapo. At that point, however, that hardly changed the situation for the worse anymore. The justice system routinely sentenced all political prisoners and Jews to death as well. You had to die in either case. However, at this juncture, to die at the hands of the justice system meant execution by the guillotine, and you knew that beforehand they wouldn't be subjecting you to any extra torture. In the case of the Gestapo you just never knew. Not all deaths are created equal... In that respect, the situation had worsened significantly! At this point in time I knew nothing about that directive. The People's Court in Berlin meanwhile had its own ambitions and still wanted to do away with us. To that end they also needed me. When they received notification from Leipzig that I was sick and in quarantine, the trial date was set for June 29. My case was thus tried in absentia.

---

139 Charlotte Holzer mistakenly spoke of the end of May, which is impossible, since her 6-week isolation ended on July 16, so by the end of May, she was not even in quarantine yet. Charlotte's trial and her death sentence was on June 29, which also indicates that she dated this wrong. Since it is an obvious mistake, it has been corrected here.

140 This is a reference to the Thirteenth Regulation under the Reich Citizenship Law. It states in Article 1 that "Criminal actions committed by Jews shall be punished by the police." Charlotte Holzer dated this wrongly as June 1. This mistake has been corrected here as well.

The fever slowly passed, the rash subsided, and I had taken care of my dental problem myself. The quarantine came to an end on July 16. That day I was let out of the cell again for the first time. I was taken to the doctor who had once come to see me outside my cell. He sat at his desk, I was brought in and reported to him. He said, "Turn your hands!" I showed my palms, then the soles of my feet. Then he said, "Is fit for transport." He saw my skin was no longer scaling. That was all that interested him.

I was again taken in the paddy wagon to the train station, this time without the chains. The railroad prison carriage was less crowded, and things also went faster than on the trip to Leipzig. I was brought again to Moabit, only briefly processed in the admission, and was subsequently placed in the women's wing. When you've been somewhere before, you're welcomed better than when you're a first arrival. "Oh, hey, you're back again…!" It almost felt like returning home.

I was immediately taken to the head officer who was on night duty. "Oh, that's the one from Kleinmeusdorf! So you're the one charged with high treason…" Then she leafed through some papers. She informed me, "In your absence you were sentenced to death. What the legal effect of that is isn't completely clear to me in this case. Probably you'll be called again before the People's Court."

Because it was standard practice that all women sentenced to death were held in group detention together, while the men, by contrast, were immediately placed in solitary after the death sentence, I was brought that same night to Hall 11. This was a large room, with a sign posted outside: Poles, Russians, Jews, Gypsies. This order also more or less reflected the Nazi hierarchy. However, at that point most of the inmates in the cell were Jewish women. Like at Lehrter Strasse, crammed into this not very big cell were thirty-five to forty women. Before the prison had become overcrowded, prisoners had slept in one room and worked in another. This had formerly been a work room. At this point we slept and worked in the same room. Our work comprised of packing bird food. We slept on the sacks with birdseed. There were four or five sacks of straw in the cell. In such a shared cell, inmates work out a hierarchy based on seniority that defines who is allowed to have access to greater comfort. This also has a certain element of justice. It isn't as hard for someone only there for a short time as for someone who has been there already six or nine months. When I entered the cell and its darkness, it felt once more like something out of Dante,[141] but I was after all now used to that. The women were lying there all the way up to the cell door, so that you couldn't walk in any further; I had to scavenge a spot to lie down up front near the door.

In the morning when it got light, I saw my comrades. There was also a senior prisoner in this cell, she'd been there for more than six months, an older Jewish Pole, a very nice woman. She helped arrange the work a bit. Two sawhorses were set up as a trestle, and a board was placed on top. Then we pulled over sacks to sit on. We filled the bird food into small bags. The woman at the end of the table then used a special machine to close the bags. We were all famished, but me especially after that long infectious illness. The birdseed was a very good side dish for us, even though it was very hard to chew, and despite our observation that the Nazis were providing food of ever poorer quality for the birds as well. But the open areas on my skin that had developed due to vitamin deficiency closed up again.

Three times a day we were taken out to the three toilets in the lavatory diagonally across from the cell. We had some female guards who took pleasure in letting us sit there only for a few seconds and then to repeatedly chase us out. They shouted, "You damn Jews! We'll give you less to eat, then you won't need so long to take a shit!"

In the room itself we had an open bucket, with a tripod and a rim to sit on, a lid on top. But the strong stench penetrated to the outside nonetheless. We all tried very hard not to make use of that during the daytime. On the wall was a rack with a food bowl for each person. In the evening we had to line up at the cell door and then hold out our bowl. We received water; it was also our water for the next morning. And since for us forty women we had only three washing pots, which all leaked, we also had to wash ourselves using our food bowls. Nonetheless, the three washing pots had to be clean and shiny like a mirror every morning. They apparently were made of copper.

---

141 A reference to writer and poet Dante Alighieri (1265–1321), and the concentric
    circles of hell described in his *Divine Comedy*.

We also had to wash our food bowls in those pots. But we were given nothing for cleaning. So we scratched out a little mortar from the wall and used that for washing and shining the pots. The French women also took some dust from bricks when they wanted to tidy themselves up a bit.

When we had to answer nature's call during the night—and given the poor quality of food it was unavoidable—we had to submit to a system in this cell that was very poor but had become customary: whoever used the bucket first had to carry it outside the next day. It couldn't be agreed upon to make it an alternating shared task. The consequence of this rule is that the women struggled not to defecate until they just couldn't hold it back any longer. The prisoner who had the worst place, right next to the bucket, got soiled alongside; the bucket ultimately overflowed, so that we had to use our eating bowls to urinate in... Otherwise things were not so bad at Moabit, but that was really awful.

When we were let out for a walk, we always passed by the large pails filled with sand to put out fires, which were standing there because of the bombing raids. We had a regulation that from a sack of bird food we had to make a specific number of bags. But since we ate so much of the birdseed ourselves, we always used to top off the bags with some sand as well. Despite the strict supervision, we also did some dealing on the sly with the bird food. Now and then we were able to exchange some birdseed for a chunk of bread. Sunday evenings we got tea. And then we took turns with the tea for washing our hair. I'd arrived full of lice from the transport and my hair was half-shaven. They had left the hair at the front of my head but had shaved it at the back.

There was a woman named Hunni in our cell. She was a great burden both to herself and to us. This Gypsy girl was maybe in her mid-twenties. To be a prisoner was much harder for her than for us. She was dead set against working, while we always were really eager for work. But Hunni had a special talent: she carefully searched for and removed lice. She freed me from vermin, and one was very grateful for such things.

When we had no birdseed to pack, we were given some medicine to put in packages. I no longer recall what it was for, but it was called Urizidin.[142] We always used to set some aside because we'd discovered that it was very good mixed with tea for using on our hair as a lotion. In addition, we used to put small slips of paper in the medicine boxes with slogans against the war. They were just small notes. Bird food was packed only by our cell. But when Urizidin was packed, the whole prison was involved. Therefore, it was impossible to find out who added the notes to the packages. After Stalingrad fell, Italy left the Axis within the same year. The female officers became very calm and quiet, withdrawn into themselves, some even asked if we'd vouch for them later on! But that changed again very rapidly in the days that followed.

I was arrested in the summer of 1942. I was imprisoned at Alexanderplatz. At that point, fall had come. Winter arrived, at Alex, in the camp, and at Lehrter Strasse. In March 1943, our second group was executed. I was sent to Moabit, then to Leipzig, and again back to Moabit, and I knew already 100 percent that I wouldn't live, that every day was a gift. You can understand that Moabit was a very orderly prison from the fact that I really had the opportunity every day to walk outside, leastwise from the time I was transferred out of the basement to the first floor. Every day we were let out into "our courtyard" for a quarter of an hour.

The Moabit prison consisted of a star-shaped panopticon building for the male prisoners, facing toward Alt-Moabit street. Parallel with that was the court. Between the two a diagonal building was the women's prison. Toward the star-shaped building lay the courtyard of the women's prison. It was oblong, with a grass strip in the middle. We were allowed to take a walk on the paved pathway around that. And at the end facing west there was a nut tree.[143] I want to mention that because it really moved me to see this nut tree in bloom! After all, to see the buds sprout, never knowing—is this the last time I'll ever see

---

142 Urizidin was used at the time to treat gout.

143 It is rather unusual for nut trees to bloom in late July or during August. It is likely that Charlotte Holzer misidentified the genus. On the other hand, during very hot summers—and the summer of 1943 did see very high temperatures in Germany—some trees react to the stress by blooming a second time against their natural schedule.

that? From the other side of our Hall 11, you had a view of the prison courtyards. The vans bringing prisoners to court drove in there.

There were some women prisoners—one lived very much by the ears and overheard things—who didn't want to go out for a walk. We naturally were extremely eager for the chance to have a walk. It was nice for many reasons: the air, the tree, encounters, possible contact, exchange of birdseed for something, to get some news, and above all—to see who was still there! Some of the female officers in Moabit were very decent, and you often heard them shouting, "What do you mean, you don't wanna go downstairs? Just look at those women there sentenced to death! They're happy for a little air." You could hear that. It wasn't black-and-white. That doesn't exist, not in prison either.

In our Hall 11 the majority were Jewish women. Mainly, as also at Lehrter Strasse, women who had been accused of so-called foreign exchange crimes, because they wanted to get across the border and had somehow arranged to obtain foreign currency. Our senior inmate was an older woman named Rosenberg. She had been a prisoner for a long time and had a wonderful air of calmness about her. Her nationality had yet to be determined. An extradition order had been filed, to Switzerland or the U.S. Then there was the Gypsy girl and a French woman, a very amusing woman, but with something unfathomable about her. She told us she'd been engaged in espionage during the First World War for both Germany and France. Which indicated that she wasn't a young woman. Then we had Polish women in the cell, some of whom were antisemites, so-called "nationalist Poles." But they had been in the resistance and were torn this way and that in their sentiments, especially when it came to the small number of us political prisoners. I mean those of us who had joined the resistance not only because of our fate as Jews.

Several of the Poles had already been sentenced to death. I participated there in two "last nights." The women were all between twenty and thirty years old. Then I saw how much easier dying was for them because of their Catholic faith. It was poignant, the certainty with which they spoke about seeing their relatives again. At times you could almost feel a bit envious. But as a result, you yourself were motivated to think again about your own position regarding these issues. Then you saw clearly that this consolation was not available to you, that you must have other forms of consolation, namely that things will really change, that there was meaning to what you did. Unfortunately, it was so little. You felt that again and again. Unfortunately, so little.

We had a Belgian woman in Hall 11, who I will mention later. And then Frau Rosenberg was released. Where she went, I don't know. I became senior inmate. That provided me with some advantages since I was provided with a sewing machine. No longer was I packing birdseed. Now I mended stuff for the entire men's prison, especially the underwear and the blankets. That was very nice. Because we used to cut off a small piece from every blanket I was given to repair, we sewed shoes for ourselves, like slippers, from the pieces. We had no possessions left after all. Twice a week the linen trustee used to come to the cell with a basket of new linen and picked up the old one. They were *Bibelforscher* (Jehovah's Witnesses). Naturally, one would receive news from them, and they always stuck a chunk from a loaf of bread underneath the linen. We took turns, each time someone else got it. I actually had it much better than the others; apart from the time after I had scarlet fever, I never felt great hunger. And I also never smoked. Our Hunni always took some straw from the straw sacks, and then she rolled her own using the birdseed bags. Then she still had to find a match... In addition, I probably also had a bit of a talent to take things as they were. You learn so much inside a prison. I'd learned nothing is worse than when people have trouble dealing with their fate. That becomes such a burden for the others. You cannot allow that to happen... That helped me a lot.

Now the directive was already in force that Jews had to be handed back over to the Gestapo. Why was I still in prison here, the last Jew after Frau Rosenberg? They were conducting the so-called supplementary trials, first for our "Aryan keepers," as they used to call those where we stayed in hiding, and second for all those who'd had anything to do with us. And they needed witnesses for that. So as long as these trials were underway, we—including also the three others who'd been sentenced—remained alive. And available to the court for the trials against the so-called Aryans. These trials were a colossal burden for me. I didn't know all the members of this illegal group and most certainly not those who had offered places to stay. But I was alive, and so I was summoned to testify.

The good thing—yes, that may hardly seem conceivable—was that one received double the amount to eat. One would receive a meal at the court, and then the food in the cell. It just stood there; the other prisoners didn't touch it. So that was quite something. The other was that possibly you'd see some comrade. Third, most of the time the guard we nicknamed "Dachshund leg" would escort us over to the court. And when she accompanied us there through the subterranean passages, she would open her heart to us. Then she told us, even if just through hints, that she'd been drafted into service as a guard, and how terrible that was for her. And then we had to console her. Although it's wrong for me to say "we." Here I was still very much alone.

Later on, I was once taken over to the court with Rita, now Rita Zocher. They locked us up in horrible holding cells. They were very similar to the sluice rooms that we have in the polyclinics. I don't know if there was any source of fresh air. Actually, I only remember a bench in the back and the cell door in front of me, waiting. Everything was painted black, and there was hardly ever any light. Naturally, one would knock. But down there the guards were very decent, they always took good care of us.

When one day I was taken over together with Rita, they locked Rita up in the cell next to me. Probably they drew a star on our cell doors with chalk. Me they already knew. And when somebody was sentenced to death—and I was considered such a prisoner—then they viewed the person either as some kind of attraction, or were somewhat compassionate. You know, I don't like to deny that people also had these attributes. I was always privileged, treated a bit "special." They opened the cell door. Before that I'd heard them at Rita's cell, "She gets nothing! She's a Jew." But for me the guy brought a meal. I refused and thus achieved that Rita got a meal as well. It was potato soup, such a big bowl! In my experience, even terrible Gestapo officers were impressed if one was assertive and able to push through ones demands. They opened the cell door again and asked if I wanted seconds. My response, "Yes, if my comrade also gets the same!" So we got our potato soup.

You waited there half a day, or the whole day, depending on whether you were needed, or sometimes maybe not. When we came back down—I didn't know the accused at all—the guard asked us again, "Well folks, you want some more potato soup?" We were so excited we couldn't eat anything more. But Rita is a great organizer. She said, "Yes, we do want some more. But we want to take it with us!" He paused for a moment, then he went out back, took some old files, and folded them into cones. The soup had in the meantime turned cold and thick, so he could put a portion inside of those. He cautioned us, "Look, be careful, don't let them catch you with this. And it wasn't me who gave it to you!" We hid the soup under our arms, hidden under the jacket. And we were lucky, we weren't searched. Our cell benefitted from that. Rita and I both survived, and the memory of that potato soup binds us together, along with various other things. The soup was a kind of social cement between us.

I was also summoned to the trial against Gustav, my first husband. I tried to say something, keep him out of it a bit. He had been arrested for aiding and abetting a Jew, because he took in his child and facilitated my escape. I did what I could. His sentence was three years, six months behind bars—unfortunately such a short penalty! Yes, had it been longer, he probably would have survived. But as it was, he was soon sent to Neuengamme concentration camp and perished later.

One day I was brought down again into the black cell, and I saw Martin being brought in, and confined in the cell next to me. I tried to signal him by knocking but was unable to make contact. The same old guy was still there, locking the cells. He was kind. When he opened my cell door, I reminded him that I was sentenced to death. And told him that the man in the next cell was my old buddy, also condemned to death. I said I wanted to talk to him once more if I could. He allowed us to do that. He opened the cell door for both of us. At the end, when Martin and I were about to be taken away, we were allowed to meet in the corridor.

Martin was wearing a black prisoner uniform with yellow stripes. He placed his handcuffed hands around me and told me about the trial. He also told me then that Richard had probably been arrested and was no longer alive. He said that had been pretty clear from the trial proceedings. That was so terrible in addition. But at that moment I still hadn't really taken it in; our shared fate was still the central thing. We then agreed that we both wanted to request to be permitted to go together to the execution, side by side, like the first and probably also the second group. Then Martin took his hands off me and I watched as he walked on and disappeared down the corridor. I still had to stay... Then I was brought back to prison. At that point I realized for the first time: the two groups are dead, Richard is no more, and we soon will...

At that point it seemed pretty much like the end. For some eight days I retreated, hiding under the table in the cell. And all my comrades there respected that. We were still packing bird food at that time. I didn't wish to see anyone at all. I knew I couldn't help it and had to cry. I didn't wish to be a burden to anyone. So I just stayed there under the table. And at mealtimes, they transferred my food to there.

That period, however, passed. And now the craziest thing happened. Shortly after, the cell door was opened and a shout rang out "Pech!" (my actual family name is Paech) "Over here! You have mail." Mail? I once received a postcard from my mother, but that was long ago. And at this point, my mother was already dead.[144] I received a postcard, from Hungary! From Hungary, a postcard! It was written in pencil in disguised handwriting, without any sender, without anything, but with Hungarian stamps. "Everything's OK. Richard is waiting very much for you to come!" That was the gist of the message. Now that was even more terrible because I did not know what to believe anymore. For this reason, I was always swaying back and forth, uncertain—is he alive, isn't he alive? Maybe that's from the Gestapo? Have they dreamed up a new way to torture me? And after all, I still didn't have any idea what the situation was with Eva. That was the time when I had an intense desire to die soon. I didn't want to live anymore, didn't know whether to go on or not. However, I did recover in the end.

---

144 Charlotte's mother, Margarete Abraham, was deported from Berlin to Auschwitz on March 12, 1943, and perished in Auschwitz on an unknown date. See *Gedenkbuch Berlins: Der jüdischen Opfer des Nationalsozialismus* (Berlin: Edition Hentrich, 1995), record 477. For more on Margarete Abraham, see the biographical entries in the appendix.

Initially during my first period in Hall 11 we were allowed to go to religious services. We took advantage of that. The chaplains were permitted to walk freely among the cells. The pastor of Moabit had contact with the Confessing Church and was very courageous; I went up there three times altogether. First of all, you came out of the cell, you had contact with others. And then—I don't know if you can understand this—it was an experience. A few candles and some words the pastor said to you, kind human words. But then a directive was issued and Jews were banned from participating. Prior to that, the pastor had been in our cell, and I had asked him to please send my regards to Fräulein von Harnack, who I knew personally. A little after that she sent me a message, "All is OK." From that I understood that Eva was alive.

The summer arrived, and she would be celebrating her tenth birthday. I mentioned that I'd stitched a handkerchief for her. Now the bird food bags had to be packed together using paper stripping. I opened up the stripping and from the glue used to seal the bags and the stripping, I crafted a small animal. It was supposed to be a deer, maybe it looked like a dog, anyhow it was an animal. When we were let out one day and guard "Dachshund leg" was on duty, I remained the last one in line. She was wearing a black smock with large pockets. I stuck the stitched handkerchief, the small animal, and a letter to Fräulein von Harnack in her pocket. And I told her that if she wanted, she could report me. But that I didn't think she would. I told her my daughter was going on ten years old and believed these things would reach her. She didn't reply but she passed on these small things. Only Eva didn't receive them. At that time Eva was with her grandmother, the woman had kept her alive but otherwise had not done very much for her. She took these things away from her. Maybe she'd meant well, she didn't want Eva to be reminded of me, have memories awakened.

That was pretty much the most difficult time, because it was the most uncertain. When our cell was dissolved, I was placed in a cell with four other women, we were all sentenced to death: three Poles, the Belgian Jew, and me. The Belgian Jew, Rita Arnould, was a Communist comrade, she had gone through the horrible Breendonk camp and had been sent to Berlin to appear before the People's Court.[145] Of the Polish women, two were nationalist Poles, no special prominence, nice girls. The third was a more exceptional woman, Wanda Wengerska. Until today I don't know whether she was a nationalist Pole. She was a very smart woman. She was still incarcerated even after all the others from her trial had long since been executed. She didn't know why. One day when we were all together in the cell, she was taken away, sent to Poland for the burial of her father, who had been murdered. Probably she was sent as bait. She came back, totally devastated, and was then executed. After she had been taken away for execution, an officer came back and gave us Wanda's bobby pins; she had requested they be given to us, we could use them. It was a present. Just so terrible. I also watched Rita Arnould go to her death; then just three of us were left. The two girls only spoke Polish. Wanda knew Polish and French, and I'd been able to communicate with everyone via Rita and Wanda. When someone went off to their death, the guards afterwards used to tell us about everything, all the details. You started to feel you would have preferred to die with them or in their stead... And the worst thing was, the day after you nonetheless were sitting there eating again, laughing again, talking once more about recipes.

I was then transferred from this cell to a work cell. There was another Jewish woman in that cell, Grete, and we got along well. She had to wait until the sentencing of her husband for "racial defilement." Then French and Belgian women were placed with us, crammed into the tiny cell. Again, it was only as long as two pallets, and not very wide. But there was a wall between the toilet and the rest of the cell! Most of the Belgians were prostitutes who'd been brought here to work. I learned a lot from them. Also in those matters. They said, "If we get bombed, you'll be free. And then *that* is all you've got." They described stuff to me that, heaven knows, you sure don't learn as a nurse. They provided me with very precise instructions about the peculiarities of the human being. But I mean in such detail that I always thought, "If I ever get out of *here* again, I mean, then *that*'s not what I want. More trouble than it's worth."

---

145 For more on Rita Arnould, see the biographical entries in the appendix.

I had a special protégé there, a particularly unhappy Belgian girl. Very dear girl, about the age of eighteen. "I'm a whore," that's what she kept saying about herself, "My mom was also one. She turned honest. Now she has a brothel with five girls..." This kid had recently become infected, had oral syphilis, early stage, and was suffering terribly. She was a decent person and was afraid she might infect us. There was no treatment for her. The others felt disgusted by her. I didn't and tried to protect her a bit. One day another girl was put in the cell, Jacqueline Minière.

We were crammed in this cell, squeezed together, you couldn't fit more inside. What work we had I can't recall. I think I was also mending stuff. Anyhow, one day there was a pretty big fuss outside our cell. And I heard a voice I recognized, Rita Zocher's voice, "You can't do that to me, no. You can't stick me in with the Germans! They don't want to have any Jewish women around! Aren't there still any Jewish women around here somewhere? I'm scared of the Germans. You can't do that either. You'll get into some trouble if you do..." And our cell was opened up. Another addition! How was I going to deal with that? If it was a Jewish woman, then we had to accept her into the Jew cell. I didn't want to disclose at that point that I already knew who she was. Rita was shoved in. I said, "Careful there, don't trip, come on over here."

I was sleeping together with the Belgian girl on a pallet, two women were sleeping on the second pallet, and the others were sleeping on the floor. The Belgian girl said, "Wait, I'll make some room." She moved down below, and Rita came to lie together with me on the pallet. She was also taken for interrogations. Naturally, we talked the whole night. In order to help exonerate several women, I mean politically, she had told some story about Section 218.[146] But in doing so she'd implicated them, was sentenced

---

146 Article 218 of the *Strafgesetzbuch* (German Criminal Code) forbade abortion, under punishment of imprisonment. Under Nazi rule, defendants who had performed several abortions could face the death penalty. By "lifesaver" the author means that it saved her from deportation to the East—just like what happened to the author herself.

herself to imprisonment and sent to Cottbus. Her intermediate penalty, however, turned out to be her lifesaver.[147]

In the Camps Grosse Hamburger Strasse and Jewish Hospital

The Zajdmanns. Mr. Zajdmann was considered illiterate because he only knew Hebrew.[148] But his special gift lay in the realm of business. His wife was the soul of the business, hardworking, but also very kind and human. The children, Moische and Esther, were highly gifted. They probably had a lot of money, they dealt in diamonds. Their father had connections to someone in Switzerland, had obtained passports. They'd been pursued by the Gestapo, had fled once already to the Swiss embassy at Pariser Platz. But then the entire family was arrested nonetheless and thrown in jail. There was supposed to have been a trial for some foreign exchange violation. But then the directive was already in force; only Gestapo, no trial.

Which other prisons the father and son had gone through, I don't know. Esther and her daughter were incarcerated here in Berlin in an emergency barracks prison; there were 400–500 women imprisoned there. This prison burned down. Most of the women perished along with it. They didn't unlock the cells! I saw when they came to Moabit, into our prison, dressed in rags, wrapped in a blanket, everything singed from the fire.

Stella Kübler had also been confined in that prison. She later became *the* informer for the Gestapo. A seventeen-year-old, gorgeous, blond Jewish girl from Poland. The child of good parents. Her father was a quite well-known composer, his name was Goldschlag.[149] Stella was

---

147 Following this paragraph, the original German manuscript has a gap of a total of fourteen pages. According to a letter sent by Dieter Heimlich to Margot Pikarski in 1983, he had given these pages to Charlotte Holzer for review, but never received them back. Despite all efforts, the missing pages could not be retrieved.

148 This is probably a mistake. The Zajdmanns likely spoke Yiddish, not Hebrew.

149 For more on Gerhard Goldschlag, the father of Stella, see the biographical entries in the appendix.

married to a pious young man named Kübler, also an Eastern European Jew. Stella likewise gained her freedom through that fire, along with her mom. Stella obeyed a call by the Gestapo and turned herself in. And they gave her some assignments.

Zajdmann—father and son—had also been in that prison. The Zajdmann family now went into hiding. Immensely musical themselves, they couldn't refrain—during their second stint in illegality, in which they were far more at risk than the first time—from attending the opera. Esther, Herr Zajdmann, and Moische went to the State Opera House. At the time, Stella went into the bars and cinemas. Cinemas were a popular place for Jews in illegality because it was dark inside. The Zajdmanns were arrested as they emerged from the opera, after Stella had reported them. Then Esther, Papa Zajdmann, and his son Mohrchen, as we called him, were imprisoned, sent to the camp on Hamburger Strasse.

Esther was an exceptional girl, we were friends. She was smart, decent, open for anything people might say to her, and steadfast all the way. They beat her terribly! First because of her mother. She said, "My mother burned to death." You can't imagine what that means for a pious girl. Her mother was on the outside. We had an orderly we called "short Goldstein." We had two orderlies, one short, one tall, same name. Short Goldstein was arrested after 1945, mistaken for tall Goldstein, who was a bad guy, and killed.[150] The short one smuggled secret messages for Esther to her mother. That was significant to me, because afterwards I knew him as trustworthy, I mean for the connections I had to establish.

So the Zajdmanns wanted to escape. And short Goldstein smuggled in a saw, sent by the mother. In the cell where Esther was confined, they later sawed through the bars. Two bars. Five prisoners escaped and Esther stayed inside. The five men who escaped were all captured. All the men were killed except for Papa Zajdmann and Moische, because Switzerland intervened. But Esther suffered a terrible ordeal. One of the guards came during the escape. She no longer could make it out. She was beaten terribly—with a whip, by the guard whose

---

150 For more on Bruno Goldstein ("the tall Goldstein"), see the biographical entries in the appendix.

nose had been cut off. I'd never seen a Jew suffer like that before. They forced her to stand for two days and three nights, with no food. Naturally, we passed something on to her when we could... When it was over, she collapsed into my arms, totally drained, exhausted. And I took care of her down there. And Esther survived. Afterwards they walled up our windows, but only afterwards!

The escape attempt had not occurred during a bombardment. We had an orderly who was the most decent I knew. His name was Friede. He was dark blond, a huge guy with a beard, loved books, always immersed in his thoughts. He was on duty on the outside in the old cemetery, and the five men who had escaped had made use of that. They had calculated that he was the slowest to come or go. Friede was then placed in the standing cell. He cried terribly. Because of his family, and because he was destined to die. I tried to buoy him up, "Look, maybe you don't have to. And if you do, then keep in mind—five made it to the outside." And really, after five weeks they took him out of there, extremely ill. They put him to work at the cemetery. Then they murdered him, the Gestapo men. His non-Jewish family immigrated after 1945 to Israel.

So the five men were captured and brought back. The Zajdmanns continued to stew and rot in the cell, but Mama Zajdmann never came back again. They kept it mum that she was on the outside. That the three others stayed among the living was due to the story with Switzerland. They weren't set free or extradited though. They just sat there and stewed. In 1945 they were set free, and when they came out, they were still wealthy. They didn't feel any responsibility toward the "Germans" nor toward their laws. They lived in Charlottenburg, traded on the black market, and supported us all as much as was possible for them. Whatever was impossible to find but badly needed, the Zajdmanns procured. Pieps, who during the final weeks down in the bunker in the prison had met a small Hungarian girl, a violinist who'd come back from Auschwitz, married her. That was the first Jewish wedding after the war. Zajdmann organized everything, so in our eyes it was like a royal wedding. That's where I also met Zajdmann's wife. Among the company at the wedding was also a child. When she saw Mama Zajdmann, her eyes sparkled like in a fairy tale and she asked,

"Is that the Queen Mother?" Our Mama Zajdmann, who couldn't even speak correct German, just imagine!

The days in the bunker were slowly drawing to an end. When "my people"—Konrad and buddies—fled, I told Konrad I didn't know what I would do out there, that I had nobody. And he replied, "I don't know how I can help you get out of here, but one thing I will do. I'll prepare something for you. You'll get a message." And he kept his word.

In the meantime ever more prisoners sick with spotted fever arrived, and all of Hamburger Strasse was vacated of Jews. Among the recent transports we'd gotten a young Dutch Jew who had already been through a whole series of camps and was on the way to Auschwitz. He was no longer thinking clearly. In his confused mental state, he was telling everyone the truth, including the Gestapo. He blurted out everything. He just kept shouting. And he was a very handsome young man, no matter how emaciated. He was good at gymnastics. Aside from that he couldn't talk normally to anyone. And everyone in the bunker spurned him because they couldn't stand his shouting. There was one more thing about him: whenever he saw women, he exposed himself. But I liked the guy nevertheless. It was as if I could see his inner core, and it was so clean, so orderly. He was beaten again and again by the Gestapo, but also by that blond guard. I decided to go on a hunger strike. And I was quite well respected. I said, "You can do to me what you like. I won't eat again as long as you're beating him." And that helped. They left the boy in peace. But afterwards, he was sent on to Auschwitz. Then I caught sight of a young man passing through; he was *my* infant from the nursery. You see, we had *our* children. I recognized him by name—it was a Dutch name, Manfred de Vries. How terrible that was for me, you can't imagine. I held this one as a baby in my arms, and now I witnessed him go to his death!

In Hamburger Strasse, I was then sent upstairs for a few days to a larger room, containing maybe twenty-five to thirty women. When they entered, I had to search them for medicines. Yes, and then you ended up finding something on someone to enable them to commit suicide. That was a very difficult decision: Should I try to convince them not to, or should I just turn a blind eye? For us as well it was also always a double-edged decision. If there was a suicide, then the transport "vacancy" was filled by taking another. We had two girls there, sisters. When they were supposed to come down for *Schleusen* [processing before the transport], as we called it, they were lying upstairs in a deep sleep, in a tight embrace.

We had a Jewish doctor named Stern. He survived the war but passed away long ago. He was another one of those who did anything the Gestapo told him. He brought the girls down and began to pump out their stomachs. Then he called for me to help. I told him, "I won't do a thing. What the heck do you want? Just let them die in their sleep!" He didn't do that. Both were carried out alive on stretchers. We managed to achieve that so that two others wouldn't be taken. When they were sent off, they counted as alive. One of them woke up on the train and went berserk; they killed her immediately. The other went to Auschwitz and was pushed into the electric fence.

Then I met a girl the Gestapo had captured in a public pool. They immediately abused her and then let her go free but as a "catcher" to hunt down Jews in hiding. She brought in her aunt and then fled herself. She survived. Afterwards there was a trial at a court of honor. We let her live and said she would have to come to terms with what she did herself. She was pregnant at the time and had found her boyfriend again who had provided a hiding place for her. One cannot know if in different circumstances, she would have become a bad person.

One day two guys were brought into our room and things were kept strictly secret. But then it seeped through that they were mixed of the first degree whose mother was housed among the Jews on the lower floors. They had joined the Wehrmacht in order to protect their mother. And someone somehow blackmailed them upstairs. Their name was Hochhaus. Why they actually were in prison I don't know. In any case, sons were constantly being played off against their mothers, and mothers against their sons.

A man was there who claimed he was absolutely not a Jew. He was a parachutist and had been taken into custody and imprisoned, suspected of being Jewish. He was a disgusting dog who later on served the Gestapo. That was mid-1944, one of the dregs washing in toward the end. That was not a typical case!

Then there was a woman named Edda. She's still alive. She was probably a Viennese Jew who had married a non-Jew. She had told the Gestapo so many lies about her origin that in the end she herself no longer knew exactly what was what. She'd gotten so caught up in her role that we always used to laugh about her stories. A short, very blond woman, who survived, she managed to stay on in the camp telling her false tales. She probably was not sent on anywhere because no one could figure out what the actual truth about her was.

At Hamburger Strasse prison I found another man I knew from earlier. His name was Berger. In order to save his wife, he agreed to bring in someone to the Gestapo. He managed to save himself twice from being sent on a transport by pledging to bring someone in, a counterfeiter, someone important. After two transports, he acknowledged that it had all been just a lie, and he was then added to a transport.

We also had a non-Jew who'd hidden a Jewish woman at his place. When the Gestapo came to take her, he stabbed the Jewish informer, who was with the Gestapo, in his chest. He now was imprisoned and wrestled with his actions. He said that if he'd known it was a Jew, he wouldn't have stabbed him. For us this was also a contentious issue. I knew that the informer had been brought to the hospital, and I had to take care of something there, always under guard. The informer asked, "Well, how about it, would you raise your hand against me or not?" I replied, "You're so rotten it would really be very difficult for me to do that. Please don't ask me, I don't know what I would do to you."

There was a man there named Neuweck, he was a lawyer, married to a Roman Catholic, a woman of small stature. He also had agreed to work as a Jewish informer. And by dint of his intellect he played an exceptionally pernicious role. He shot himself later on.

Another man there was a Jewish proletarian, a plumber or something like that. He was in hiding, illegal for over a year. Then he could no longer stand it. He went down to Sonnenallee, where the Jewish employment office used to be.[151] He reported there and told

---

151 It is unclear what Charlotte Holzer referred to here. The available records for Sonnenallee, which had been renamed Braunauer Strasse (after Braunau am Inn,

them he could no longer stand living that way, he wanted to have a well-ordered situation. And they said, "OK man, we'll get you orderly circumstances alright." They called the Gestapo and he was taken away. He was placed in a camp, but not deported onwards, they kept him there. Somehow his behavior impressed them. He became a kind of trustee for all kinds of matters. And since he was (and is) a very decent person, and just a little stupid, I also "made use" of him a bit.

We still had a small number of Jewish doctors in the hospital. Most of them were protected by their mixed marriage. There was only one still there without such a marriage: Dr. Cohen. I think he remained there right to the end. He was seriously disabled, could hardly walk. A good internist, he was even consulted now and then by the Gestapo. He also saved a few people from being shipped off on a transport. Not many, but nonetheless some.[152]

Another was Dr. Helischkowski.[153] He was a gynecologist and his nickname among us in the hospital was Father Stork. He had to accompany the transports to Grunewald train station. The Gestapo had commanded him to. Depending on their mood at the time, sometimes they simply took a physician along. It didn't mean anything. Helischkowski was a very courageous man, outspoken, always saying what he thought. He criticized it when people were being crammed together or were maltreated. The consequence: Although they didn't come and take him into custody, they often took him along to the train station, where they ordered him to do knee bends while the people were loaded onto the train. Heli died about eight years ago, and that harassment was probably one reason for his death. It upset him a lot, but he was always courageous and decent. Sometimes he would slip me a sandwich or bring me a bit of news.

the birthplace of Hitler) at the time, do not show any employment offices specific to Jews, only several sites where forced labor was employed. However, there was a regular employment office in Sonnenallee, and the special employment office for Jews was nearby, at Fontanepromenade 15.

152 Dr. Cohen's given name was Helmut. For more on him, see the biographical entries in the appendix.

153 His full name was Dr. Siegmund Helischkowski. See the biographical entries in the appendix.

I've already mentioned that my uncle, the youngest brother of my mom, was working in the administration at the hospital, assigned there by the Gestapo. He never gave me anything. I had my birthday and Heli, who knew that, suggested to my uncle that he might at least send me a couple of sandwiches as a present. But he said, no he wouldn't, it was forbidden, and he wouldn't do that. After 1945, he told me, "You see how good that was, that I didn't do it, I might have been put on a transport otherwise!"

The dentist Dr. Ehrlich was also in the hospital camp. At that point he no longer had permission to treat people inside the camp. But twice a week they allowed him to go over to the hospital, where he had to take care of dental treatment and look after the Gestapo. Now I have to backpedal and say something about Ursula Reuber.[154] She herself, not an entirely pure Aryan, had spent six weeks behind bars because of Konrad Latte.[155] Then she managed to score a coup: She went to the camp commander, Dobberke,[156] and told him she had unfinished dental work, treatment begun during her time in the camp. And she requested that Dr. Ehrlich now finish the dental work. And when people came directly to Dobberke, that impressed him, and so he gave his permission. Ursel came to Dr. Ehrlich—and I was given a telephone number on the sly. Ehrlich told me, "Listen carefully! You can't be helped to get out of here, but here's a telephone number. Maybe some time you can use it... But don't say anything about me..." I knew then that something existed. It was my first reference point to the outside.

Meanwhile Iwan Katz had arrived in the bunker below. He started to do great political work with the prisoners down there. He gave them political education sessions and did gymnastics with them every day. He himself was no longer a young man. But he energized and pepped everybody up. He received support from several Czech Jews who had once been imprisoned in the fortress in Theresienstadt and

---

154 For more on Ursula Reubner, see the biographical entries in the appendix.
155 For more on Konrad Latte, see the biographical entries in the appendix.
156 A reference to *Kriminalobersekretär* Walter Dobberke. For more on him, see the biographical entries in the appendix.

had escaped from there. They now joined our bunker (i.e. under the authority of the RSHA)[157] and had the same status as me. All Jews who entered there were registered and given an "Ost-number," that meant Auschwitz, or a "Th-number," i.e. Theresienstadt; and we, the Czechs and I, were classified as "NR," not registered, meaning that we were not to go on a transport but were at the disposal of the RSHA there. So they were doing the political work together with Iwan down in the bunker. I went down once a day to distribute medicines, and in this way, I also had contact.

We not only had orderlies from a mixed marriage, we also had mixed marriage prisoners. Among others, Hopp, who had been recaptured, and a smaller older guy whose name I have forgotten. The two played at being glaziers. And then there was Hänschen Rosenthal,[158] whom the Gestapo had arrested in his delivery truck, which they confiscated. It was arranged that after every air-raid alarm—and there was one every night—the three had to make the rounds of the building with their truck and replace any broken windows in the Gestapo offices. Hänschen was responsible for the two and vice versa. That was one thing. Then I had "short Goldstein," who went to little Eva on my behalf, pretending to be a Gestapo man.

At that time, I was quite happy because the situation around me had become more relaxed. In addition, the war was nearing its end. That was evident. Once I asked, "Hey guys, if the building collapses, and I'm here without a roof over my head, where should I go?" They said, "Don't worry, we'll arrange something for you." In the meantime, they also got a horse cart. One day they came back and told me, "We've got something for you, where you can stay and hide out!" And they gave me an address, on Grunewaldstrasse.

---

157 Founded in 1939, the Reichssicherheitshauptamt (RSHA—Reich Security Main Office) was the central administrative body that bundled together all security police forces (criminal police and Gestapo) with the Sicherheitsdienst of the SS (SD—security service). Headed by Reinhard Heydrich until his death in 1942 (and later by Ernst Kaltenbrunner), it was the central institution for the persecution of all groups the Nazis considered enemies and one of the key organizations in the perpetration of the Holocaust.

158 For more on Hans Rosenthal, see the biographical entries in the appendix.

I had worked in this hospital for fifteen years and I was familiar with the whole basement area and all the underground passageways. I imagined that I could use it to escape at some point. A second possibility also came to mind. We were upstairs at that time and when an air-raid alarm sounded, we all descended into the basement together. Once down there we were covered with debris. That was pretty unpleasant. Seventeen bombs had fallen on the hospital grounds. They hadn't hit

The Jewish Hospital's inner courtyard, ca. 1935, Herbert Sonnenfeld
Collection of the Jewish Museum Berlin,
Yad Vashem Photo Archives, FA5409/2685.

the hospital, but the shockwaves had left us standing up to our hips in debris and mortar. The Gestapo left me only for a short time in the main basement before bringing me to their basement. They had their own basement area; it was specially fortified and bomb resistant. They gave me a first aid kit and took me in so I could be of help to them. Moreover, I was an "NR" case, not registered, and they had a special responsibility for me.

There was the main basement, then the gateway, then the small Gestapo building, and underneath that the Gestapo basement. Those separate parts weren't fully interconnected underground. I had to cross the entrance hallway to get to the small basement. They escorted me there. But they let me walk back by myself. And while doing so I noticed that during an air raid no guards remained outside. They were also not in a hurry to return. In addition, the gates were not closed. I always went as far as the gate, looked out, and then came back. I did that repeatedly for weeks on end—quite intentionally! If, I thought to myself, then only when I am sure about the Gestapo. After all, they are not going to disappear!

One small episode from earlier. In the prison on Hamburger Strasse, we were never let outside. No chance to take a walk. We were constantly in that basement, without windows, without anything. You really became just like an isopod. Over here, we weren't let outside initially, but later an area inside was fenced off where we could take a walk. But well before that, one day we were taken out of the cell. We were ordered to form a row, and coal and wood for the Gestapo was unloaded. We had to transport that over. I was happy: finally some fresh air and manual labor. And the guards were all Jewish, so we could work slowly. I was driven by a desire to work. It was so nice. But then Dobberke appeared, that disgusting guy, and said, "Just look, our Charlotte! How diligently she's working!" That set my teeth on edge. Dammit! How could I have behaved so wrongly? To a degree where they actually started praising me?! That for me was a slap in the face. It seemed as if I'd forgotten who I was. Naturally I stopped immediately and also passed on the message, "Hey guys, continue to work, very, very slowly!"

Whenever I read or hear about the fates of various people, despite all the differences, I notice how similar many things are. The dreams are alike, and so are the experiences. Especially penned up in prison, we mostly dreamed about eating and recipes. Given my mentality, which I cannot help, I had it easier than many others. Among those dreaming, I was one of the few who actually ate during a dream. In the morning we used to exchange tales about the dreams we had. And most explained that they'd seen a magnificent hunk of ham or a butter sandwich, and the very second they'd wanted to take a bite, it was gone. Either the dream was interrupted, or a hand had taken the food away from them. But I ate while dreaming and woke up satisfied from the experience of eating. I had erotic dreams only at the beginning, and those were always dreams of hindrance, frustration. Later on I had no such dreams at all. I dreamt about Richard many times. But I was no longer able to reconstruct his face completely. Oddly enough, I always dreamt of his shoulder blades and the soles of his feet. But actually, it was not odd at all. Before I was arrested, I had loved to sleep close up against his back. Richard was after all always very reserved and shy in his tenderness. But that he liked. And for me it was pleasant. That way, I always felt the sensation of the soles of his feet and his shoulder blades. And those were the things I dreamed of. Those sensations stayed in my mind, and also the longing for them. Very, very often I dreamt about my child, mainly as a baby. I did not have any dreams of a sexual nature anymore, but some about a failed delivery, dreams of births where nothing came out. I don't know at all how to analyze that. Maybe it was connected with the abortions. Each time I felt like I was losing a piece of me, a bit of tenderness toward the not-yet living creature within. It can probably be explained in that way.

I've, however, forgotten to tell you about the following from the prison in Moabit: The female officers had cats upstairs. There were two. And when we were allowed out for a walk, we saw their food bowls standing there. And that left us terribly embittered—those bowls of milk. Sometimes there were pieces of leftover meat in the bowls. Then you just had to tell yourself, "You can't be furious with these animals. It's not their fault." Thus, you always had to be in control of your feelings. But probably everyone felt the same way.

That's also why I can narrate my story so openly. Because I know that I don't need to be ashamed of my own feelings and reactions. They only varied slightly and in terms of their degree of intensity from person to person. That's also why I think that such private experience has general validity. From that springs my view that I have the right to pass on my experiences to others.

But since we were talking about animals: My lasting fear of dogs is something that comes from my childhood. I don't think I was born with that; on the contrary, children usually have a good relationship with animals. I assume it was my mother's doing. We kids, the five grandchildren of my grandparents, enjoyed answering nature's call next to a tree on Roscherstrasse. Aunt Bertel, Mom's sister, was my type; my mother was more like my sister–more elegant. I'll never become refined and elegant. And Aunt Bertel enjoyed arranging us five little brats one next to the other, each at a tree. But that was always terribly embarrassing for my mom. Since I was the "dirty little Lotte" and in some ways very natural, Mom especially wanted to break that habit of mine. So she said, "Watch out, the dog will come and bite you in the behind!" That may be the origin of my fear of dogs. That was still a more or less normal fear that I had. In the Fehrbellin camp, however, we we were always accompanied by dogs, in the early morning, roughly from 3 or 3:30 A.M. to about 5 A.M., as we were being brought to our place of work. And they also set the dogs on us. I felt very miserable there. And then I'd seen the dog bites, the scabs from Esterwegen. That intensified my fear. And whenever Dobberke came down into our bunker, he had a big wolfhound with him... After the war all that intensified. When I became familiar with heart attacks and seizures and knew that fear can trigger such an attack or seizure, I was afraid of that fear. And since in addition I never knew how far the consequences could extend in such an attack, I gradually developed a fear of even the smallest dog. Especially if I encounter a dog alone on the street, I turn back. I have learned that the animals notice my fear immediately. In a very busy street I'm not so fearful, but I'm especially afraid of dogs in our neighborhood.

But let me go on regarding the situation at Schulstrasse.[159] An addition: The young guy who wanted to have a well-ordered situation was Rehfeld;[160] the guy who accompanied Stella Kübler was Rolf Isaaksohn. Then there was a man with us named Bolz, I think Kurt Bolz. He picked people up, maybe he was also a minor informer. He most certainly did bad things, though I can't prove anything against

159 This is a reference to the Jewish Hospital, which was situated in Schulstrasse and was used as a prison and assembly camp from March 1944, when the central assembly site at the Jewish nursing home in Grosse Hamburger Strasse was closed down.

160 His full name was Berthold Rehfeldt. See the biographical entries in the appendix for more on him and the others mentioned here.

him. In character he was a vile little dog. Sorry, he seemed very un-Jewish in his behavior. He was one of those brutal types, very non-intellectual. Frequently he also went with Kübler and Isaaksohn, so he was a "catcher" as well. He was sharing a cell with Rehfeld. Rehfeld was an exceptionally ugly-looking person. I mean, I didn't think that way at all about him. He looked like a good dog, a bit of a mongrel. Bolz promised the women they could avoid placement on a transport if… So they were standing in line for Bolz as well. And Rehfeld was allowed to watch. So that also took place. Rehfeld probably never had a woman, or almost never.

I mentioned earlier that we had people inside boxes intended for animals. One day a woman was caught whose child was still on the outside, in hiding. That was already at a time when there were no longer any free Jews outside. Her first name was also Lotte. She had brought her child in, based on promises the Gestapo had made. First, she couldn't see any pathway forward for the child, a twelve-year-old. Second, they probably promised her something. But now they were scheduled for transport. She wished to stay alive, with her child. So she agreed to work as a "catcher," betraying Jews in hiding. And she told the Gestapo a story that she knew people who were making counterfeit documents. She was a clever woman, about thirty, thirty-five years old. She'd said she could bring in the guy, a non-Jew, who was taking care of the Jews' documentation. Over in the area of Grünau. And that there was a colony there, which sheltered mostly Jews living in hiding. But she knew absolutely nothing. Yet she continued with that story, and, in that way, avoided two or three transports. Then the Gestapo discovered that she actually knew nothing, everything was just made up. And I saw directly how Dobberke beat this woman. You just can't imagine. She was lying there and couldn't live or die. Then he dragged her by her hair. I saw it all, they threw her in this box for animals. She lay inside until taken away for transport. Then she was sent off, together with her young daughter. I'm telling you this because sometimes people say, "Oh, the transit camps were nothing at all, just transit camps."

In addition, there was a small concentration camp for children. Actually, it was once the hospital's children's ward. When the hospital became the property of the Gestapo, they collected the children there.

Children whose parents had already been arrested, kids who were in hiding and had been found. Children who had been taken away from people in mixed marriages who had divorced, or those like the child of Alice, who was sent on a transport. Among them was a child I knew very well. Her name was Sylvia and she was the daughter of a Jewish performing artist, a Polish dancer, who in Paris had married a German stage artist. According to Nazi law, it was an illegal marriage. Her husband was arrested when Paris was occupied, transferred to Germany, and charged with "race defilement." The mother was sent away with her child, then eighteen months old, on a transport. She stayed together with the child until they came to the Rhineland. Then the child was taken from her. She was sent to Auschwitz and her daughter was placed in Berlin in the children's concentration camp.

Sylvia had become a very sweet little girl, was already able to walk, had begun to talk, and was naturally a bit behind in her development, like all the camp children. But since she could hardly speak, she walked all over the hospital carrying a small spoon. And everyone gave her something. All were starving, but everyone gave her a little something. My uncle, who was in the administration there, saw this little girl, and succeeded in displacing Sylvia's papers. Thus, the child remained alive. After 1945, he took her to his place. He took care of the girl until 1947. Then *both* her parents contacted him. And as difficult as that was for my uncle and aunt, they returned the child to her parents. But with other children it was different. At that point, after all, there were only "catchers" left, the "collectors" no longer had anything to do. When the catchers had not brought in enough and the number of Jews scheduled to be sent on a transport was insufficient, they simply took some babies, small children and bigger children from the children's concentration camp, and hauled them over to us. They were all packed into the small delivery truck, the trailer of the furniture truck. That's how they were sent off on a transport.

In the hospital we had a very famous head doctor as internist, *Geheimrat*[161] Hermann Strauss. He had introduced numerous medical

---

161 *Geheimrat*—literally, secret councilor. In modern times it was an honorary title given by the state in various parts of the former Holy Roman Empire to people who achieved prominence in their profession.

innovations, had developed a special diet for stomach ulcers, and a new treatment for kidney disease. He was an internationally prominent physician. For that reason, he belonged to the so-called protected Jews. They were a very small number of Jews whom the Gestapo preserved as an example to foreign countries. *Geheimrat* Strauss at that time was around seventy years old and was no longer working. But he was still free and lived somewhere in the west, outside of Berlin. However, now and then he used to work with us at the Jewish Hospital. As a result, he had a special ticket and could travel on the subway. At Gleisdreieck station he wanted to change trains. And there an SS man stuck out his leg to trip the old patriarchal doctor. He stumbled and was arrested, the SS man claiming Strauss had intentionally bumped into him. He died in Theresienstadt.

Our head doctor in surgery was Professor Rosenstein, who later immigrated to Argentina and died there some time ago.[162] Then we had a communist professor who later also left, I know nothing more about his fate. After he left Walter Lustig was taken on as a surgeon.[163] He was Jewish with a non-Jewish wife. He was chief medical counselor in the civil service, a well-known physician, and a specialist in medical administration. He had been employed with the municipality and had administered the state examination for candidates in the hospitals. I too had taken the state examination with him presiding and signing the paperwork. Dr. Lustig was now appointed surgeon, but had no experience or training as a surgeon, and he revealed himself to be a very bad person. He was more or less protected, but he started to work together with the Gestapo. He didn't just tell them what they wanted to hear. I have proof of his criminal behavior in at least one case.

Our nurses, those still on the job, were actually decent and courageous individuals. The Jewish Hospital was at that point a

---

162 A reference to Professor Paul Rosenstein. See the biographical entries in the appendix for more on him.

163 Walter Lustig (1891–1945), was the head of the Rest-Reichsvereinigung (the remnant of the Reich Association of German Jews, an organization responsible for the coordination of Jewish self-help activities during the Nazi era) and the Jewish compound in the Jewish Hospital. For more on him, see the introduction and the biographical entries.

reservoir for the Gestapo. And I have already mentioned that once Jews were inside, they seldom came out again. They also took some of the "mixed Jews"—I have to repeatedly stress that I am intentionally using Gestapo expressions—in order to fill up the transports to the specified quota. It also happened that a "full Jew" who'd been arrested fell ill and was placed in the hospital in order to recover so he could be sent on a transport to be gassed. Our nurses took great pains to prevent that. In the typhus ward, when a patient was sick with typhoid fever, they distributed his excrement to all patients, so that their samples looked bad as well. They also had a method—I know how they did it—to produce an artificial fever and rash in a patient. In this way they kept people from being sent off on transports. Every person saved from being transported meant a step closer to peace! In my eyes that was a form of resistance struggle!

The nurses were risking their lives in doing that. In formal medical terms it was of course not correct. And it also involved a certain danger. This way of creating an artificial fever could lead to kidney damage or harm the eyes. They were aware of that and so were the patients who let them do the procedure. One of our nurses was Ilona. She was largely in charge of this activity. One day, two were scheduled to be sent on a transport and during the night, she made both of them sick. The next day Lustig discovered who was behind the ruse and he himself took Ilona over to the Gestapo prison. I was a witness to that. My comrades handed Dr. Lustig over to the Soviets in 1945 (I had already fled), and he was shot. Justifiably so. There were degrees of wrongdoing and culpability: If a Lotte deceived the Gestapo or a Berger agreed to bring in some people and later said he couldn't do it…or if someone brought in a person at a time of mortal fear, or if such a person was shot dead or punished in another way, or what not, what do I know…I cannot excuse Lustig's actions, but the blame is still with the Gestapo in the end.

We had another physician, our eye doctor. He was a good surgeon whom I had often worked with before. Afterwards this man also cooperated with the Gestapo. He used to drink with them and play cards. Through this relationship it would have been possible for him to secretly remove a specific family from the card catalog or to ask that they be released from there—there were such instances now and then—and he actually did that several times. In order to gain a few good character witness testimonies. But he did that in exchange for a large amount of money. And he abandoned the people if he learned that they had no money, and subsequently reported them to the Gestapo. My comrades also turned him over after the war. He was behind bars for a few years and was then released.

In the hospital we had a head nurse who gave the impression of being a kind of somewhat ossified virgin. She was a bit older than me and may then have been in her late thirties. For years, she was the mistress of Dr. Lustig. Dobberke took her over. She was sleeping with the Gestapo. In this way she avoided being put on a transport and deported. We did nothing to her after 1945. We held her at arm's length and pushed her to emigrate. After 1945, that was all in the hands of us prisoners. The percentage of those who were bad might seem substantial, in reality, however, it was very small. And I constantly have to repeat that those who knew how to jostle and use their elbows to get ahead certainly survived the longest. These people alone were not the guilty ones. Our comrades who were on the inside balanced accounts, so to speak. They passed on all those who had dirt on their hands for a reckoning. Or if it involved small guys, then they decided on some reckoning themselves. I reproach others for not having done that. Those were also my reservations against a large segment of the population after the war. What did you do with your Nazis, the ones you knew?

Inge Jakobi was in our cell. She owned a gorgeous nightgown made of voile. Inge slept between us. We knew what was going on with her. The Gestapo had probably thought, "She's a little informer, in addition she can do small things for us inside the cell." And since we knew that, we used to shower her with chocolate, and we always told her our opinion. But one day Inge Jakobi went outside and disappeared. And I quickly made short order of that nightgown of hers. I told the others, "OK, guys, give me that nightdress! After all, I don't know how long I have to live. And it's so beautiful. It just feels so beautiful and soft on my body!" And I ran off with the nightgown underneath my prison clothes. I managed to carry that through, and I think the tattered remains of that nightdress are still lying somewhere at home. I was so in love with that gown, despite my distress and sorrow.

I was asked once by our orderlies, by the way, if I had some special wish. And I told them, "a portion of semolina pudding." My stomach was in such bad shape, and I suffered from constant diarrhea. And they actually brought me some cooked semolina pudding. That was such a delight!

When they placed me on a transport from Moabit to Leipzig, they decided "everything has to go"—and returned all my personal possessions to me. And in Leipzig they were immediately taken away from me again. Then I was sent back to Berlin on a night transport. And because the storeroom was closed at the time, I was given nothing. So I lost all those belongings. That was in June 1943. A year went by. I think it was in April 1944 when I was summoned by the Gestapo. And they handed me back all my belongings!! It had taken almost a year for them to send those things from Leipzig. Among them was a watch my mother had once bought me, a pocket watch. In a small leather case, with a small leather cord, because at that time, we nurses were not allowed to wear wristwatches, and rightly so.

One of the women in our camp was Inge von Krenczewski. She is still alive. She was a working-class half-Jew, despite her aristocratic family name. Her mother was a street-market trader, I don't know what her father did. But this girl was very much a Berliner! I liked Inge a lot. She had gone through a very serious brain operation, which had inhibited her development to a degree. She also had a fistula of the ear. I was the only one who helped her to keep that clean, the others all shied away from her. She was very grateful to me for that. As a result of her "mixed race," Inge remained alive in the camp. She served in the clothing storeroom, didn't do anything bad, but worked for one of the bad women there (I'll come back to that). Inge had a wish, "Lotti, may you live. But if something ever happens to you, then I'd like to have your watch." And one day, I put the watch down on her pallet bed, as a gift. That was before I escaped. I ran into her again, in 1955, at the Jewish cemetery. The first thing she said to me was "Lotti, your watch, it survived alongside me."

Back at the prison on Hamburger Strasse someone had slipped me a watch once—that naturally was all illegal, we weren't allowed to have anything of that kind—it was a wristwatch, given to me on the sly by a woman who was going to be searched before being sent on a transport. She told me, "Wear it for as long as you live and then pass it on!" Later, I took the watch along when I escaped. I'm a person who becomes a bit attached to such objects; my daughter Eva once kind of criticized me for that. They have to stay with me. Today that watch can no longer be fixed, as it's a very cheap little watch, but it remains with me.

Inge von Krenczewski worked in the clothing storeroom under a woman named Tamara. She was inscrutable. Tamara claimed she wasn't at all Jewish, but Latvian. And I think that might have been the truth. She didn't look Latvian, and I didn't know her family name. After 1945, I first saw her again working for the Soviets as an interpreter, and later working for the British. She was involved with small informer tasks inside the camp. And she made use of the clothing storeroom as she pleased. That Inge was her favorite helper didn't bother me, and it was in fact fine with me, but Tamara also worked with a very different set of people. Moreover, she took everything away from others. That was really terrible. Aside from the psychological loss, every little possession one kept hold of could be used to buy something small, being it bread or some facilitation. It meant that you could purchase a little piece of life.

I wanted to tell that story about my watch in order to show how Prussian the way things were managed was. After all, the goods belonging to someone else are not to be retained. Even if it takes a year from Leipzig to Berlin. It all arrives!! And if the person to whom it belonged has long since been gassed, no matter. The main thing was that protocol was followed.

At that time, the conditions of my confinement were loosened a bit. To the extent possible, I worked as a nurse inside the camp. I helped a guy relocate to somewhat better conditions, to another I gave a helping hand. I also distributed medications that I had access to in the camp. One day I was summoned to the Gestapo, and an inspector was waiting for me whom I didn't know. He started to interrogate me. Since I was already very accustomed to such procedures, I responded, "I know nothing, I did nothing, I'm a blank sheet, I'm here completely without justification…" The Gestapo man replied, "Don't try to pretend with me, we've known everything for a long time." So I said, "Well, so if you know everything, you don't need to question me." Yes, I was certainly pretty cocky. "OK then, this and that was established, signature here, finished." I never saw him again around the camp. Probably he'd been sent over from another office, and his name—I accidentally overheard it—was Gogoll.[164] I remembered that name because it was the same as that of the writer.[165] It played a role after 1945.

A short time later I was called again to the Gestapo office, and Gogoll was lying there on the couch, writhing in pain, with renal colic. Want me to do something? OK. I phoned Heli, and he said he wasn't coming over but would send me an injection. Because Heli no longer came to the Gestapo. He sent me morphine and I was sitting there wondering what I should do. Finally I told myself I don't really have much of a choice, so I'll give him the shot. After all, I know how painful renal colic is. Then I stayed with him, and when he was better, I said, "Inspector, you know that I'm sentenced to death. I've helped you, what will you do for me?" I would never have been able to say that in earlier years. But I was a senior prisoner by then. Moreover, I had nothing to lose. And he replied, "Well, listen up. Over there at Kurfürstenstrasse, there's a pile of files. If yours is at the bottom of the pile, it's at the bottom. If it's at the top of the pile, your time's soon up." That was what he told me. I replied, "Inspector, please, if you will, please tell me when my turn is coming." Silence. He said nothing more, and I was led off.

From that point on my detention conditions were exacerbated. I was locked down in the bunker, I wasn't allowed out with the others for a walk, and I wasn't allowed to do my service as a nurse anymore. The situation was dire.

Naturally I thought of trying to escape. But I saw no possibility. Time passed; I was summoned once again to the Gestapo. There was only a secretary. She asked, "You're sentenced to death?" I replied, "Yes…"

---

164 For more on Fritz Gogoll, see the biographical entries in the appendix.
165 Nikolai Vasilyevich Gogol (1809–1852), was an important and influential Russian novelist and playwright.

I must add something: When I was still young, long before I was arrested, I read Vera Figner's *Nacht über Russland*,[166] so I knew something about life inside prisons. Later I realized that you have to experience everything yourself in order to correctly understand it. I also read Max Hoelz, writing about his time in prison. He spoke quite a lot, at least as I recall, about sexual matters. He gave a set of instructions for people who find themselves in jail. Certainly with intent, because proletarians always ended up in prison when they were doing political work. He mentioned that you had to satisfy yourself as often as possible in order to maintain your capabilities. When I read that I was probably still a virgin. It seemed awful to me then, but I made a note of it. And I know that in the long days of solitary confinement I sometimes thought of that. It always seemed so ridiculous to me then. I sometimes thought, what nonsense! Aside from the fact that I did not expect to live much longer. But even when you've got that, what's the point? That would be pure and simple theater. You would have to provoke something that doesn't exist. So I never tried it. And I didn't miss it.

But I did have something else to consider. In the long days and nights of solitary confinement I had a very strong need for physical contact. The cells after all were only opened to shove in some food. And a constant thought of mine was, "If I could only reach out and shake the hand of the trustee sometime." That was impossible. But I knew that in the prison on Prinz Albrecht Strasse,[167] the prisoners were located in the basement and their cell door was never opened. Rather, they had a small window that could be opened from the outside, through which some food was shoved in. I constantly thought of those poor people. I at least could see the trustees, yet they could see nothing at all. While we sat mostly in darkness, they always

---

166 Vera Figner (1852–1943), a Russian revolutionary socialist and leader of an organization which aimed to overthrow the monarchy through terrorism. For more on her, see the biographical entries.

167 A reference to the *Hausgefängnis* (in-house prison) of the Gestapo at its headquarters in Prinz-Albrecht-Strasse 8. It was also used as a temporary holding facility for those prisoners that the Gestapo wanted to interrogate. The interrogations conducted in the prison routinely employed physical abuse and torture.

had artificial light. My distress though extended to the point where sometimes I would consciously touch my own arm. Only to feel some skin.

One more addition: His Excellency Schiffer[168] was one of the protected Jews, a very well-known personality. He was a lawyer and a Jew, one who could allow himself to be addressed as His Excellency. And that was very rare. He was already very old. The Nazis had interned him in the Jewish Hospital, on a ward. And he remained there. His daughter was with us, in the prison on the back side. She was sent to Theresienstadt. I carried secret messages for her. At that time, I was still able to enter the hospital to pick up medicines, even though under guard. His Excellency Schiffer survived and after 1945 was in the magistrate of Greater Berlin.

I have to correct something: Ursula Reuber didn't bring me a phone number. Rather she arranged to have someone tell me that I could reach Konrad Latte at a certain place; he was outside the city. That already was also quite a lot, because in so doing she had placed Konrad's fate in the hands of Dr. Ehrlich, who gave me that information orally. And now comes a totally unreal thing: Aside from me there were several other nonregistered Jews, people with an unresolved "question of race" or something similar. And if they had been in the camp a long time, then they got a kind of leave—for a few hours, to visit their families, if they could give a significantly good reason for doing that. And always under the pressure of the threat: If you don't return, your whole family will be imprisoned. For me that was actually impossible. Yet the Gestapo knew quite well that I had a daughter on the outside.

Something else: We had a "catcher" there named Abrahamson, a peculiar young man, an intellectual, who probably still had no specific profession.[169] It was likely he also fooled the Gestapo. He didn't bring anyone in, yet he managed to remain in the hospital camp the entire time. I found this guy, who was initially living down

---

168 A reference to Eugen Schiffer. For more on him, see the biographical entries in the appendix.

169 Likely a reference to Günther Abrahamson. For more on him, see the biographical entries in the appendix.

below in the bunker, and then up above, interesting. Once I gained more freedom to roam around in the camp, I talked with him. Often. Through these conversations I acquired a pretty good knowledge regarding the individual members of the Gestapo there. Thus I learned that one of them, who either had the near future in mind or who was "soft" in the Nazi sense, was a person you could start something with. And when he was on duty, I requested an afternoon leave to see my daughter. How I justified that I can't recall. In any case I asked to see my daughter, whose whereabouts were known at the time. She had a pending application for "declaration as a *Mischling*."

Anyhow, I was granted leave and they assigned me a Jewish guard who was responsible for me. They probably even knew that I would have never escaped, if it meant incriminating someone else. But it was important for me to contact Konrad. To achieve that, I had to have an orderly who was so much under my spell that he'd let me take off without coming along; and second, it was important that he shouldn't think too much about it. But he had to have a high degree of trust in me, that I would come back. That orderly was Rehfeld, who in the meantime had advanced with the Gestapo to caretaker for the rabbits, as well as a gofer and orderly. Rehfeld adored me, I knew that from the way he looked at me. He was also stupid, and decent. So he had all the prerequisites, he fit the bill perfectly.

I was able to work things out so that Rehfeld accompanied me. And as soon as we came to Badstrasse, I told him, "OK, now you go to the movies, and we'll meet later." Rehfeld, "But th-th-that's not r-right, no!" It was awful. Finally, I said to the guy, "Now look, maybe I want to have an experience some time? I mean, I've been in detention so long and…" So, the upshot was that Rehfeld, with his tail between his legs, went to the movies. And by the way, the Gestapo used to let us all, all the prisoners, go out without wearing a yellow star. Because officially there weren't any Jews left. Another small addition: My uncle, who was required to make Jewish stars, had to make a whole bunch for the Gestapo. Just as a precaution if the tide turned and… I'd already escaped, he told me that later, it was the end of 1944.

So then I went to Konrad's place, to the address I had been given. Without knowing whether he was there or not, nothing. And that was on Klosterstrasse, on the corner of Rathausstrasse. There's a bank there. The first house there has a gateway. Over the arch of the gate is a small gatekeeper's window. A small narrow window. But it goes down right to the ground. In that small room lived Konrad, a Jew in hiding, illegal. In the middle of Berlin. He'd been taken on by the air-raid warden as an assistant air-raid warden, arranged by the canteen owner in the Moabit prison. He had already been doing illegal jobs for a long time, even if perhaps not always for the most noble motives, though I'm not sure.

Konrad naturally was there because he never went anywhere. The air-raid warden had hired him illegally, because actually he wasn't allowed to have a stand-in. But now at night at least he could get away now and then. So I got the telephone number from Konrad that put me in touch with Ursula Reuber and/or people from the Confessing Church. I didn't know myself where this number led to. But for me, it was an extremely important matter. And besides, it hugely strengthened my will to try to escape. Because you can't imagine what a huge effort it was, what strength and energy it required to prepare an escape. Yes, to get yourself, in pure psychological terms, out of this rut. The fear of death, the fear of implementation of the sentence is almost not as great as the fear of life, but above all, the fear of being recaptured. Then I left Konrad's place.

When Konrad and I saw each other, first we both broke down in tears. But the whole thing went very fast. He told me the number. I also had a terrible fear of implicating him, making a problem for him too, by visiting someone living illegally. He also told me then that he'd seen Ursel again, but only for a short while. They'd been forced to break off their meetings. He told me his parents were gone and are likely not alive anymore. Then I left and walked from Klosterstrasse to Gesundbrunnen. First, because I had no money, and second, because it was always dangerous to use public transport—for illegals in any case, and for me especially so. And I would have made terrible trouble for Rehfeld to boot. At Gesundbrunnen Rehfeld was standing there, very pale, trembling. He said, "Lotte, thank God you're back! I thought I'd made a colossal blunder." I tried to calm him down, "When I say I'm gonna come back at this or that time, I will. How could you think that way about me?" We went back to the camp at the hospital, and everything was OK. That was still at a time when things were going relatively well for me. Otherwise I'd never have managed that.

One more addendum: Right on Schulstrasse, I realized for the first time that I could still have the feelings of a woman. That was in connection with something very strange. I was after all relatively free to move around in the camp. The new arrivals had to be examined, also officially in medical terms. I did that. Then the Hochhaus brothers were brought in. Both had been in the Wehrmacht and their mother was inside, down below. One of the two was married. And when his personal data were being taken down, I heard that he had a wife and twins. And strangely enough, when I heard that he had twins, I felt something rush through my body, "Oh, my God. How? You still notice that?" In retrospective, I reconstructed my reaction as a comment to myself, "That's a guy who begot twins!" I knew of course that he couldn't have had any influence on that. But every time I saw him again, I had to think of how at our first encounter I'd had that odd feeling rushing through me. But I had no other interest in those guys than the interest I had for many others and their fates. The fact that I was capable of that feeling at that precise moment, I attributed at that time to the easing of my circumstances in detention.

However, the time that I'm going to continue with now in my story was shaped by the conversation with the Gestapo secretary. She summoned me and informed me that my file had arrived and that I should expect that the sentence would soon be carried out. I still recall exactly how that was. Very calmly, I asked her how long that would probably take and when it would likely be. Down below, Iwan Katz and the others were out for their walk, and the orderly who escorted me brought me back precisely during yard time. I was trembling like a leaf. The bunker people surrounded me immediately—they told me later about it—and supported me so I wouldn't fall; they immediately knew what the matter was. They told me that I looked pale as a corpse, as if it had already happened. And it became so extremely and bitterly hard for me. Because I'd seen the child, because I'd tasted freedom, because I could see that the war was nearing its end, and also because now I was alone, because all of my comrades were already dead. I found it far, far harder to deal with than it had been at first. I didn't say much. It was the last walk I was taking. It was spring. At the corner of the hospital administration building there was a large elderberry bush. And it was in blossom...

So now I was not allowed out of the bunker at all anymore except for the air-raid alarms. But there were alarms already day and night.

Escape and Hiding in Potsdam and Anklam

Events came to a head. The name Müller plays a role. He was the commander at Kurfürstenstrasse[170] and came for inspection in our prison. He criticized that there wasn't additional fencing around the barbed wire, toward the hospital area. Naturally that had to be taken care of. But since everything was being done by prisoners, it wasn't known how, when, and what. In about eight days, this new second barbed wire fence had to be ready, I knew that. Pieps had been one of the men working on it.

I noticed in the meantime that no matter how much I went to the gate, it would have been impossible for me to escape there. I wouldn't have gotten far enough. The whole area was too open and visible. I no longer dared to attempt it on this side, because I needed to gain a certain head start. Immediately after that announcement I didn't think much more about the possibility. But then within eight days, seventeen bombs fell on our hospital. We were half-buried down in the basement. We felt physical fear, not very pleasant at all. We helped dig each other out of the debris. But I knew about the seventeen bombs and wanted somehow to get out through the grounds before the barbed wire was put up and closed tight. I wasn't completely clear about the *how* of it. I interviewed anyone I could about the grounds. And about how things look in the hospital. I was told the maternity ward had almost been obliterated and

---

170 This is likely a reference to *Kriminalrat* Erich Möller, who served as the last head of the Jewish Department of the Berlin Gestapo. In this function, he was responsible for overseeing both the manhunt for hidden Jews and for the assembly camp in Schulstrasse. For more on him, see the biographical entries.

that the nurses' home, serving at that time as a military hospital, was pretty badly damaged and there were holes in the wall.

Then something occurred again that was quite unreal. On that night of the seventeen bombs, the phone rang at the Gestapo with a message that there were two attempted suicides on Hamburger Strasse, and that they absolutely had to be kept alive. They shouted that Hänschen Rosenthal should go and get them and that Sieke Hopp should go there with Hänschen's delivery truck. I was still in the gateway, overheard that, and said he should let me go along. They were attempted suicides, maybe I could do something. The guy looked at the two of us and said, "That girl, bring her back here, or your number's up." I told the boys immediately they had nothing to worry about. I wouldn't try anything. I just wanted to get some fresh air, see the area, and really help, because there was after all something for me to do.

We drove with our delivery truck through the burning night to Hamburger Strasse. Picked up the two, half dead, whom I took care of, and then we pulled up in front of the hospital. I told the boys they did that. Now that they had indeed brought me back, I was beginning to consider my options for an escape. Then we drove in up to the hospital and the boys hauled the two upstairs. I said, "Listen, I'll go alone back to the prison, I just can't continue anymore." And they saw that I couldn't go on. Because such things upset me a lot and it showed.

Then I went very slowly through the hospital garden. The sun was rising. It was magnificent. I looked at everything and discovered that the wall over toward Schulstrasse had been smashed in. And just as I was about to go over there, an orderly appeared, one of the "bad ones." He approached me and asked, "Hey, so what the hell are you doing here?" I thought lightning fast, "Now you can't run, you have to make him feel secure." He'd addressed me as if he'd noticed that I wanted to get out of there. I said, "I want to go to the other side, to sleep." "And where are the two others?" I replied, "They're still busy out front, they will return when they finish." The orderly brought me across. What you feel in such a situation is hardly describable.

So I was inside the prison again. That was on Friday. I knew that on Monday, Müller would return and by then the new fence had to be finished. I had learned about the duty hours of the Gestapo, from Abrahamson. On Saturday "my" Gestapo man was to be on duty, I think his name was Tietze. They were on duty from Saturday noon to Sunday noon. Then Sunday afternoon there were only orderlies inside, outside the Security Service, no Gestapo. They didn't come on duty again until seven in the evening. And I wanted to take advantage of that.

So early on Sunday morning—it was after all the last Sunday when a possibility still existed, and psychologically it probably was also necessary, otherwise I wouldn't have been able to give myself the kick in the behind I needed—Blond was on duty inside, he was responsible for the camp. In his case I wasn't worried at all that I might damage his position. So early on I indicated that I wanted to go to the Gestapo. There was a regulation in the camp that when a prisoner reported to go to the Gestapo, he also had to be brought over there. They thought, "If someone voluntarily reports to the Gestapo then he must have something to reveal." For that reason, there was the directive for the orderlies—they *had to* bring us over. I told them—I was locked in the cell—that Blond should come over. He came and I demanded to be taken to the Gestapo. He asked me why. I said I would tell that to the Gestapo. So he took me over. There was this guy, Tietze. "Why, what do I want?" I said I had a request to make. "A request?" I had never requested anything there, aside from that temporary leave once. "So what do you want?" I said I wanted to take a walk once outside the fence. "Are you crazy? How did you get that idea?" I replied, "Inspector, you know that I'm sentenced to death and that now it's time. I'd simply like to be outside the fence for a while one last time. Is that so hard to understand?" That impressed the man. So he told me he'd pick me up at noon for a walk outside the fence. Well, that wasn't exactly what I'd had in mind, but I had to accept it. I don't know what I might have done if he had actually picked me up. Then probably I wouldn't have escaped. But to my good fortune he forgot me. And in the afternoon, about 4:30 P.M., there was nobody around from the Gestapo. Blond was on duty. And the bunker had time scheduled for a walk at 5 P.M. So I literally pretended I was going crazy. I asked for Blond to come over and told him I wanted to take a walk outside the fence. I reminded him that he was present when I received permission for that. He said that was out of the question, that guy was off duty already, and so on. I told him no, it wasn't out of the question. And I screamed and shouted and behaved in such a way that finally he said, "Well, OK then, Lotte will go out."

Now the situation looked like this: The building was here, here was the courtyard for the bunker prisoners' walk, inside and outside guarded by orderlies. I walked on the outside, next to the orderlies. Since I'd once told my bunker comrades that I was totally without a place to stay if the prison should ever be destroyed during a bombing, they had not only found me an address but had also collected some illegal money for me, which was now in my pocket. When the comrades caught sight of me outside the fence, they knew immediately what was happening. And there's hardly ever been such a funny, merry stroll as this one was. They started acting up like crazy. They flocked together, joked with the orderlies, made noise, and ran around—frolicking in a humorous way! And I walked back and forth, back and forth. I said a word or two and then walked on. A few steps into the hospital grounds and then back again. A bit to the other side and then back again. Past my elderberry bush and then back again.

I did that for about ten minutes. And then when I saw that they'd gathered together very nicely, I went into the administration building of the hospital. There, I immediately descended into the basement system that I knew so well. I passed through it. I returned to the surface in the ruins of the former ward for infectious diseases. Then onwards into the ruins of the maternity ward. And there I stayed for about an hour. And I couldn't decide: what now? Fear overcame me. Later I learned that they had started to search for me very early on. What happened was actually what I had expected. Our Jewish orderlies never called the Gestapo. For one thing to give the person escaping some breathing space, but also for themselves. They told themselves, "Why tell the Gestapo if we might still manage to find the person." That wasn't spoken about, but it was obvious for them all.

The customs officer, the uncle of Herbert Baum, told them, "Charlotte once told me that she does not want the Gestapo to end her, so she likely committed suicide, she must be hanging somewhere in one of the attics." He told them that deliberately therefore knew

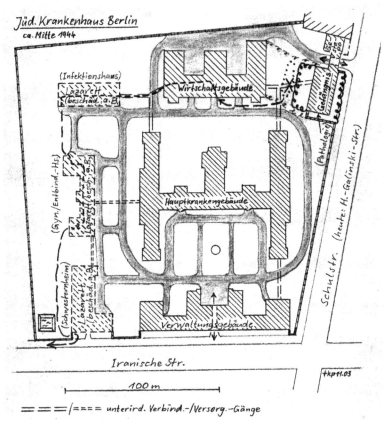

Sketch of the Jewish Hospital with Charlotte's escape path. Map created by Klaus Pistor based on Charlotte's testimony, her sketch of the hospital grounds, data gathered from the archives of the Berlin construction supervision department, and a tour of the underground tunnel system under the hospital.

how familiar I was with the basement of the complex, and therefore suspected it to be my escape route. So initially, they searched all the attics. I meanwhile ventured a bit forward toward the nurses' home. That's where the wall was. Across from that was the Jewish retirement home, which had become the dormitory of the Nazi BDM girls. It was already 6:30 P.M., and the girls were sitting on the small balconies—there were these continuous windows—playing guitar, and I was terribly afraid. In front of me was the wall, to the right an emergency fire pond that I'd never seen before. Then I suddenly saw that they had added another wall to separate the nurses' home from the pond, and that this wall had a hole in it, about 60 centimeters long and not very wide, a little above the ground. It went on an angle toward the hospital, and I had no line of sight toward the street. And I thought, "It doesn't matter anymore, you have to go on through here. Don't look, don't, don't. Just push your way on through." I hesitated for a second wondering, head first or feet first? How I did it I can't recall; I think feet first. And then I was on the outside.

The street was empty as far as I could make out. It wasn't a busy street. It was Sunday evening. Without running, I walked quickly in the direction of Seestrasse, then the whole of Seestrasse via Moabit on to Grunewaldstrasse. I had my place to stay there, the hideout they'd arranged for me. I had the money, but I wore a strange mix of clothing. That wouldn't have even been unusual among foreign workers, but informers roamed the subway and other places. I was much too afraid. I had the name and address. And went on upstairs. They had told me he would take me in. I just had to get out of the prison on my own. I couldn't notify him. I went on up and had no idea who I would meet. I knocked and a very good-looking, middle-aged man opened the door, a Belarusian. He lived with a female dancer. He welcomed me and immediately understood the situation. I remained in the room only until I had briefly outlined who I was, and he had done the same. During my entire illegality I had never left anyone in the dark about my situation and the possible danger for others that it entailed when a person consciously took me into hiding.

He stemmed from prominent, ennobled officer family in Petrograd who later joined the Red Army; was then shunned and immigrated to Germany. He was also an engineer and had sold a locomotive patent to the Germans. Therefore, he enjoyed a special position in the country, but had to report regularly to the Gestapo. I found him strange. I noticed that he had a large collection of Marxist literature sitting openly on the shelves of his cabinet. He said just as candidly that he was helping to hide Jews and traded diamonds in order to make a living. After he'd told me all this, which wasn't to my liking at all, he led me through the kitchen and up a ladder to a tiny servant's cubbyhole. I remained there for several days. This stay was in every respect very burdensome and worrying for me. After all, this hiding place had a connection; if they'd done some investigating, they would have discovered the people who must have known about it. Hopp and Rothschild knew. But as much as I trusted them, I also knew the methods of the Gestapo.

Moreover: As wonderful as it was to speak once again with an intellectual, and he was so nice to me, he nonetheless remained quite inscrutable. And something else: it was on the fourth floor. And the bombs kept falling. Everyone went down to the basement, but I was upstairs, locked in. Then he had also told me that he couldn't keep me there very long. I wasn't planning to burden him for long, either. And then I had to take a dangerous risk—I had to take similar risks several times later on—and give him the telephone number I'd received from Konrad. I had no choice. He didn't let me get near the phone downstairs and thus had forced me into this situation. I hoped that this was a cover number operated by someone else, but there was nothing I could do about it.

He then made a telephone call and informed me that I was to have a meeting that night. At the subway station Bayerischer Platz. I went there extremely frightened, and standing there was my friend Ursula Reuber. She said, "Yes, it was a cover number. Listen, I have two addresses where I can bring you. We'll go first to one and check it out." We then walked from Grunewaldstrasse to Babelsberg. There we came to the home of a woman, Frau von X, a follower of the DNVP,[171] who received me in a very friendly manner. She also belonged to the Confessing Church. Ursel had told her she had to find a place to hide me because of the bombs. She was an extremely talkative older woman who would later, in 1949, ask me to give her a rehabilitation reference.

171 The Deutschnationale Volkspartei (German Nationalist Party) was the leading nationalist party of the Weimar Republic until the rise of the Nazi Party. It incorporated monarchist and völkisch–antisemitic ideology and initially cooperated with the NSDAP. Soon after the Nazi rise to power and the dismantling of all democratic institutions, the DNVP fell apart, with some members joining the Nazis, while others stayed neutral or joined the resistance.

She told me about her nationalist past, thus against Hitler. But she was staunchly antisemitic! She then left the room to make tea for me, saying I was probably exhausted. And while she was out in the kitchen, I told Ursel that I couldn't stay there. I said, "It's impossible. I did not run from the Gestapo, from those scoundrels, only to be in this environment. No, I just can't." Ursel said she also had a weird feeling and that we should move on. We drank the tea and left.

We took the train and traveled the short distance to Potsdam. Traveling at night, in an empty carriage, was very dangerous. There we went to Charlottenhof, to the residential area on the Havel River, on former Hermann–Göring Strasse. Ursula said, "Well, I have to leave you here. I'll bring you up to the house. The woman there is someone you will like, but I can't wait. She also knows you're coming. Once she hid Konrad's parents." Then she went with me up. After that she had to leave. She, the former student of literature at university, was in forced labor and had to be on time for work in Berlin, sweeping the street.

I want to quickly say something about Ursel. She lived on Ihnestrasse in Steglitz. They had a small house there. Ursel didn't speak very kindly about her brother. He survived. Her mother played a role with the Social Democrats after the war. All three were evacuated. Ursel, however, remained there, alone in the house, and she was continuously taking in Jewish women to hide. Right at the end—it must have been the end of 1944—she took in a Jewish girl her age. Then came an [air raid] alarm, and all that could be found of the two afterwards was some hair... I learned about that shortly after it happened. That was terrible for me.

But I now had landed at the home of Muttchen (Mama) Schneider. It was 4 A.M. when we arrived. She was in a nightgown as she opened the door and said, "Very quiet, be very quiet! Just go on into the room, lie down, blanket and pillow are there. You have a working day ahead of you, don't you? Just get a little sleep first!" Yes, naturally. She pushed me into a small room. There stood a harmonium, then a big desk, on it the portrait of a man in a black frame, a crucifix. There was also a round small couch, a tiny table in front, and above it a large picture of Bismarck. You have to imagine all that in the state of mind I was in.

But it was already all the same to me; I really had to do just one thing: lie down and rest. I lay down, maybe also dozed off. Then Muttchen Schneider came in. In the meantime, she had very quietly prepared her daughter, Christa-Maria, nicknamed "Mädi" [Girlie]. She'd already left home, was a student at university.

So Muttchen entered, brought me something to drink, and said, "Jesus has lain you at my door." She said this so kindly and beautifully that I wasn't startled. Rather I felt there was something serious in these words. She was a petite and delicate old woman, with smooth white hair, parted in the middle, the very image of a pastor's wife, which she indeed also was. I told her immediately that I I really liked the atmosphere at her home, but there was something she should know right away; I was Jewish. "I know that!" I added, "I'm also a Communist and believe in nothing." She replied, "Nonetheless. You're the child Jesus has placed at my door. I'll take care of you as long as I can."[172]

Muttchen Schneider had a two-room apartment, a large bedroom and small study. She had divided the bedroom in the middle with a large curtain. The front half was the small room of her daughter, the back half behind was her own. Her daughter's bed stood directly next to the curtain, parallel on the other side was a couch on which I slept. She had very little, and I didn't wish to cause her much extra work. But since she didn't wish for me to sleep without linen, she gave me, in mutual agreement, a bed cover. I didn't have a nightgown and was used to sleeping without. Thus I slipped every evening, just as I was, into my bed cover. Then Mädi opened the curtain with her finger and said in a whisper, "Naked woman in a bag!" We got along wonderfully. But it was very difficult because of the air-raid sirens. At first, she didn't take me downstairs. Later she took me down and said that I was staying with her because my home had been destroyed in a bombing. But I was very rarely downstairs. The new buildings swayed a lot. But that was not really the problem there. Every night I was screaming—in my sleep, there was nothing I could do about that.

---

172 Muttchen Schneider's given name was Dorothea. For more on her and her daughter Christa-Maria, see the biographical entries in the appendix.

Muttchen Schneider told me that she once had been an enthusiastic Nazi, a "*Nazisse*." She had lived with her husband and small daughter in Posen, which had become part of Poland in 1918. After her husband passed away, she "came home into the Reich." Here her eyes were opened. And this woman, who had probably never done anything bad to anyone, even when she was an enthusiastic Nazi, now felt so guilty and responsible for what had happened that she swore she would help as much as she could. Thus, she continually took Jews into hiding. Konrad's parents hadn't been the first. She also accepted my declaration that I was a Communist, just as it was. She'd never gotten money for her assistance, from anyone. She always shared her food ration coupons. That woman went hungry. After me, she also took others in to hide.

I was even in correspondence with her afterwards, in Anklam, the long way round. She wrote to me about her *Herzblättchen* (sweethearts), as she called her illegals in hiding. All that was mediated via the prison pastor Poelchau from the Confessing Church. The only condition she set, which bothered me a lot, but which I did for her sake, was: I had to attend church on Sunday. She said, "Nothing will happen to you there, the dear Lord will hold His hand over you." I, however, had my doubts about this outstretched hand. But then: I just couldn't do that to her! So I put on Mädi's BDM uniform and went with her to church. And before the service I always helped decorate the altar with Muttchen Schneider. If I say "always," maybe that was two, three times. I spent five weeks with her.

Now you may ask how I came into contact with Harald Poelchau.[173] The contact was mediated initially via Ursula Reuber, through the Confessing Church, and also via Elisabet von Harnack, who wanted to find a place for Eva to be cared for. Muttchen Schneider, whose place I was hiding at, also belonged to the Confessing Church.

I also have to tell you about the conditions that Muttchen Schneider imposed on me. As I said, I had to attend church dressed in a BDM uniform, and I also helped to adorn the church. I may say though that the religious services touched me very deeply. First, because of

---

173 For more on Harald Poelchau, see the biographical entries in the appendix.

the relatively open language of the clergy. It was a very clear language of slaves in bondage, one which paints things over a bit, but for all who wished to understand it was comprehensible. And probably the Gestapo, who knew the people it was dealing with, also understood it, and had only for this or that reason not (or not yet) taken action. Those were for me, after so many years, also very powerful artistic experiences—the music, but also the art that is in a church, the objects, statues, decorations, architecture. Yet the church music was pretty hard to endure. Nonetheless, it was bearable, because in a Protestant church, everyone joins the singing, so it's not very artistic. But once, I can recall, Muttchen Schneider took me along somewhere on the way back from her church, "compelling" me to go with her to the Russian colony. It was a gentle compulsion. You probably know where that is in Potsdam. She took me into the church. It was packed. And, as soon as I entered, I heard these deep Slavic choral pieces that are so different from here. At that point I suffered a severe nervous breakdown. Perhaps because I had been with the Polish girls the two last nights before their execution in prison. They also sang a lot… I have to jump ahead—after liberation, for several years, I couldn't listen to any music without breaking down. I also didn't like to see pictures. Back then I was afraid of everything.

Muttchen Schneider brought me back home and I didn't go with her to church after that. My stay with her lasted only five weeks. I was actually supposed to stay for two, but stayed for five because I still had no alternative. Muttchen Schneider had contacted Poelchau, who was engaged in underground activity alongside his official activities. However, since such circles make decisions based on personal impressions, he asked me to come and meet him. I didn't know him. We agreed to meet at the Charlottenhof train station.

I can't recall the secret sign for meeting that we used. I only know I was totally astonished: A comparatively young man approached me, looking a bit like someone in the youth movement, with a rucksack on his back. We exchanged a few sentences and then he gave me a blank form, a police cancellation of registration form, already officially stamped. All I had to do was fill in the personal data. He told me I had to do that. Muttchen Schneider then did it for me. But he told me I should get the personal data of someone my age, who knew nothing about all this, who had lost her home due to bomb damage several times, and who ideally also lives in an area where the local police station had been destroyed in an air raid. So that was the one thing. The other was that he gave me a name and address in Steglitz. It was a welfare worker who wanted to see me. She was representing the woman in Anklam who was willing to take me in. She had a similar background as the others, and also wanted to get a personal impression first. So I went to Berlin, full of fear, and went to Steglitz to see this intermediary. I talked with her. It was brief, but nice and friendly. And she recommended that Ursula Teichmann would take me in, in Anklam.

Now I had to locate someone who fulfilled those prerequisites for the police cancellation of registration form. Muttchen Schneider knew nobody. But then I thought: It was highly probable that Harry Cühn was still alive. He was the life companion of Edith Fraenkel and was sympathetic toward our group. A very clever guy. I knew his address and telephone number by heart. If he was still alive... I told myself if there is one guy who can help, it's Harry. From a phone booth in Potsdam I rang him up. And you should have heard that conversation. After all, I couldn't tell him who I was. But I had to tell him what the matter was. He had to find out who I was though and had to recognize that it was unlikely I was under Gestapo surveillance.

I was very lucky and reached Harry. He was still alive and lived at that same address. That was one of the many miracles. I told him that I was nurse so-and-so, and I had helped deliver his wife's baby, I asked if he remembered. I said I had traveled from my hometown to Berlin for a visit and would like to see him. And he understood immediately. I sensed directly on the telephone what a shock this was for him. He had assumed I was dead. I told him I'd really like to see him, I had such good memories of his wife and of him, I spoke as if his wife and child were still alive, and I arranged to meet him. I asked him if he had time for a short trip out of town on Sunday, that I was taking a trip to Potsdam, and that we could meet there. I can still recall the hesitation in his voice. But then he said, "OK."

I told him we could meet at a place in Charlottenhof, a park where usually many people went out for a stroll. Both of us hung up, full of fear. It was but a few short steps "back home" to Muttchen Schneider, and I waited. Sunday came. I walked back and forth over there—but no sign of Harry, no Harry. And then suddenly a heavily pregnant woman approached me. That was Djidja! Harry had done for Edith what he could. But when she was arrested, he quickly found Djidja. All that was quite peculiar. Djidja was a student of German language and literature in Poland, and had come to Germany as a forced laborer. In some kind of roundabout way, a lawyer had requested to have her employed as a maid, in order to protect her. That was probably Masur, because Harry had contacted him regarding our girls. Then Harry met her and she immediately became his companion. Since he didn't know if everything was completely genuine with my call, he went out to Charlottenhof with Djidja, and for quite some time he just checked out the scene to assess the situation. Adroitly! I didn't see him. Then he sent Djidja over to approach me. I give her credit for that, because in doing so she was once more risking her life. After all, she was already illegal, and her pregnancy wasn't legal either. Then she told me that Harry was there somewhere.

As we went past the house in question, I could see him standing in the doorway. And I knew: things were OK. I mentioned already that Harry was a strange, singular kind of guy. Very soft and sensitive and at the same time so ambiguous. But people aren't single-track, that's something I've often experienced. I'll never forget his face; it expressed so much love, joy, and fear. My eyesight then was much better than today. I explained to Djidja what I wanted. And she passed it on to Harry. She spoke such a sweet, Polish–German—and she was in general a very sweet, tender, Slavic girl. We had a second meeting after that. Outside, because that was the only way. Harry had worked in a group in Berlin, even if just sporadically, where Berta Waterstradt was a member.[174] Thus, the resistance group of Berta Waterstradt played a role in my rescue. They decided, as a group, to help me. And they got me what I needed. As a result, from then on, I was Hildelotte Lukas. They gave me the key details of Hilde Lukas's life, where she was from, where she'd once lived, etc. Then my blank form was filled out, and I could travel to Anklam.

174 For more on Berta Waterstradt, see the biographical entries in the appendix.

That was a difficult story for me. Because of the air-raid attacks, all the trains in that direction left from Oranienburg. First you had to get there. Second, there was a new directive supposed to be coming into force: Anyone who wished to leave Berlin needed to have a police permit to do so. I recall it exactly. It was a Saturday. Poelchau had contacted Mädi again, the daughter of Muttchen Schneider, and had passed on word to me that it was necessary to leave this coming Saturday. He said that was the last day you could get out of Berlin without a permit, and there would be huge numbers of people traveling. Muttchen Schneider dressed me, decking me look like a teacher. I had on a simple hat, wore glasses, which otherwise I never did, and in general she made me look very "proper." In contrast with the outfit that Rita Zocher had styled for me, in the spirit of a "chic girl," even if I wore a Salvation Army hat. "Proper" was more successful. I lamented a lot nevertheless.

The journey from Potsdam to Berlin wasn't all that bad, nor was the trip to Anklam. Naturally I was afraid of everything. But then came the Gesundbrunnen station! And there I had to change trains and get the one to Oranienburg. I knew that's where the informers were. That's where they were for sure. I can't recall whether I was talking a lot. But Muttchen Schneider said, "Wait, my little rose, I'll accompany you." And that was what she did... I mean, you can't imagine what a deed that was for a woman to take upon herself so much risk and danger. I said, "No, you mustn't!" But she took me to Gesundbrunnen and then even helped me get settled into the other train. From Oranienburg, I knew I had an immediate connection to Anklam, which was great. The train I switched to was absolutely packed.

In Anklam I was registered at the apartment of Ursula Teichmann.[175] She received me into her home, with love and kindness. She stemmed from a German–nationalist family, an officer's military family, antisemitic in their views. She herself was educated on an estate of the crown princess, and was trained as a housekeeper. Then she was probably at home for a short time, and they had a subtenant who was a Jew. Maybe I'm wrong about that... In any event she made the acquaintance of a Jewish man. Through her education on the estate

175 For more on Ursula Teichmann, see the biographical entries in the appendix.

and her relationship with a Jewish man, she gained a certain insight and understanding. In part out of opposition to her upbringing, and in part from the realization deep down that "this is a human being!" She abandoned antisemitism and distanced herself somewhat from her family. Then somehow, she became acquainted with Konrad Latte and his family. They also came from Breslau. So they knew each other already. But Ursula had married an officer who moved with her to Anklam. She had four children. In 1943/1944 both her brother's legs were shot off and her husband went missing. Her mother went insane, and she was left alone with the four children. In Anklam at this point an airport was being built or had already gone into operation. The Arado aircraft factory was situated there. Initially, bombers heading for Peenemünde always flew over Anklam without dropping their payload. I was told that the English had dropped warning leaflets stating that if the new airport and Arado didn't disappear, Anklam would be become an air-raid target. They'd even set a deadline. Naturally nothing was removed. Up until that juncture no one had ever gone into the air-raid shelter in Anklam.

Shortly before I came to stay with Ursel, the following had occurred. Ursel had a small house in the center of Anklam. In its semibasement, the protective walls had been heightened and fortified. When the bombs began to rain down, she ran with her children to that basement. As they ran, Ulrike behind her (she was eight years old), and Ursel carrying her one-year-old, with two more kids, aged four and five years old, in front of her. The bombs fell and this interior wall collapsed. Ursula was still holding onto the tiny feet of her baby, both children ahead of her were gone. She herself was buried under the rubble with Ulrike. And when she came out from the rubble, she said, she decided that from then on, she would work against Hitler. That was the reason she accepted me into her home. Her reaction probably was: Now I have to do something, otherwise I won't be able to stand it.

She had been assigned an apartment on Hermann Göring Strasse! She had the upper floor of the two-story house and lived there with Ulrike, nicknamed "Mücke" [mosquito]. She took me in like a sister, gave me clothes to wear, did everything for me. Nonetheless, it became ever more difficult for me to endure staying with her. Deep inside, she was still a German nationalist. She was a bright woman, realized that the end was near, that the Soviets would be arriving. "After all, you're our enemy, you belong to the Soviets," she said to me. "I am conflicted, what should I do? I have an enemy of Germany here in my house." I couldn't change her mind. I was unable to explain to her the difference between an enemy of Hitler and an enemy of Germany, and that I was not the latter. Likewise, I couldn't explain to her that the Soviets were not enemies of Germany.

In addition, Ursel in her distress was very religious, she was constantly praying. That wouldn't have bothered me so much, but she dragged Ulrike into it too. The child kept saying she wished to die and go to Heaven to be with her two siblings. And for an eight-year-old that is terrible. During every air-raid alarm, the two would sit and pray to die. I myself had gone through the experience of not wanting to go on living if everything one loved was gone. It became unbearable there, because that resignation was tied to this reactionary faith. I don't want to be arrogant and speak against those who are believers. I respect them. But in this case, it strongly influenced the mind of that small child. Ursel liked me, I liked her too, but politically, the gap became unbridgeable. And because she was a woman who could only think in her way, that was very difficult. Until one day I told her, "Listen carefully, Ursel. I'm not in a position to free you from my presence here, because I just don't have anywhere else to go. But it's up to you, and if you like, go to the Gestapo and report me." I simply no longer knew what to do. She, of course, didn't do that. Ursula herself was so very torn in her feelings. But then, in a way, fate intervened to assist us.

She arranged a job for me as Hilde Lukas in a rope factory, owned by a "good German" named Czechas, a rope manufacturer, who—as I always said—was "tying the noose" for Hitler. At his factory, I worked with a Soviet woman, a forced laborer, Katarina. We got along wonderfully. She also knew immediately that there was something going on with me. I didn't tell her *what*, but did confirm that there was something. When air-raid sirens sounded, we weren't allowed down into the basement shelter but had to stay by our primitive machines. Czechas exploited Katarina terribly. She worked from night to night because she also had to take care of the household. He treated me somewhat better; I was after all in his eyes still a German. But he also regarded me as somewhat odd, even more so because I got along so well with Katarina.

One day the sirens sounded again, and this time for quite a long time. You could hear the bombs raining down, and against the will of Czechas and his old lady we rushed down into the basement for sheer naked fear. You could see it unfold: First they came like a swarm of bees humming way up high. Then you saw the bombs being released. That didn't even look particularly terrible. And then these beasts plummeted down upon us. Yikes! Then everything shook all around us, and we simply decided to rush down to the basement. Czechas was as pale as a sheet, so he let us in. Then we heard terrible shouting outside, "Everyone out of the basements! The hospital is on fire!" When Charlotte hears the hospital is on fire, she forgets she's an illegal in hiding. I rushed up and out, and ran past "our (Ursel's) house." That day Ursula had gone out into the countryside with Mücke, to get some food supplies. I saw that the house was still standing, so I hurried on to the hospital. I worked like a maniac. I ended up with charred shoes because the ground was so hot.

After all the patients had been brought out of the burning inferno, I ran back to "our house." When I approached it, I realized that only the front wall was still standing! Everything behind was gone. Behind the hall was a steep staircase that went to the upper floor. The staircase was still hanging there. I climbed up because it was after all Ursel's home. A small hall had survived, the kitchen was intact, and next to the kitchen a tiny room. And on the other side a yawning empty space where the living room had once been, but the stove was still there. Ursel naturally was shocked when she returned. What should we do now? Ursel and Mücke moved, like others who'd been bombed out, to the large guesthouse on Market Square, where they stayed for a couple of days. Then she traveled on to Hiddensee. She knew some people there. But she told me immediately that it was impossible for her to take me along to Hiddensee. It was much too small a place. I said, "Look, Ursel, that's also not necessary but if you could let me stay here in the small room and the kitchen." She agreed, brought me all the food she had gathered from the countryside, and said, "If you have the courage, there's a ham inside the stove."

Well, we shall see. I decided to get myself a bombed-out certificate issued in the name of Hilde Lukas, in order to have some valid document of identification. I went to the bomb-damage office at the police station and reported that I was the victim of bombing damage. They wanted to know where I'd come from. I told them from Berlin and showed them my police cancellation of registration. Yes, they said, but the bombed-out certificate had to be from a person's home community. They said they would send the letter there, that I didn't have to do that. Well, I said, I had to write to them anyhow because my ID papers were not complete. Because when I was bombed out in Anklam, everything had been lost. But OK, I'd take care of that myself. Initially they seemed to accept that at face value. But when they realized that I was still living in the ruins of the house and not at the guesthouse, their attention began to shift toward me. I had to flee.

I had already established contacts with various people. One was with my small Soviet girlfriend in the rope factory. I mean, she came by and brought me a hunk of bread and some other stuff, and finally even a chicken she'd stolen. She also brought me some rope. I tied it around myself and then crawled around in the debris, got into the stove, and pulled out the ham. So I had enough supplies. There were, however, constant alarms. I couldn't go to "the Germans," because I was scared. I couldn't go down into any of the basement bunkers. I had stopped working at the rope factory, giving the excuse "Bombed out. I can't do it anymore." So I ran to the countryside. Over to the River Peene. Foreign workers from a whole series of countries were working at the Arado aircraft plant, Russians, Poles, Dutch, Frenchmen. They were not allowed to go down into the basement bunkers. Simply weren't allowed. They were forced out into the countryside and had taken cover along the Peene River. At that time there were already strafers in the air, low-flying aircraft. So this wasn't pleasant at all. That was already January, February 1945, or maybe two months before that... cold, dead of winter. But there were other people around. Human beings want to be with other human beings, and particularly in a case like my situation, where I'd been alone for so long. I always went to find people when I could. But now I was living alone in my ruin. In the tiny room next to the kitchen there was a folding cot, which had been lying folded up in the storeroom. The slant wall above me in the small room had a hole in it, underneath which a bowl now stood. I could reach up from the bed directly, there was a kind of hatch I could pry open. So actually, I had it pretty good.

Whenever there was an alarm and I rushed over to the Peene, I always lay down near the Frenchmen. Because I could speak a bit with them. Once this guy, another time someone else. And I was a woman, so they were always interested. Despite the fact that I looked so odd. So I had a little contact with them. And when Katarina arrived one day with the chicken, I certainly couldn't manage to eat it all alone. So I took it over to the Frenchmen, and we shared it. That improved our relationship...

Across the street from the ruin was a dairy shop. The woman in the shop there didn't know that there was something going on with me, but I must have caught her attention. Every few days she brought me a jug of buttermilk. That's how I lived—healthy; bread, buttermilk, once a chicken... In Anklam there was someone else who knew about me, knew what my story was, the Ladewig sisters. The sister of Käte Lupescu knew them well. They also belonged to the Confessing Church and were both nurses. They'd inherited this medical practice from an aunt, a "miracle doctor." They specialized in diagnoses based on the eyes and the hand. The older sister probably even believed in it, the younger one didn't. But they were able to live wonderfully well from this. At that time, everything was paid in kind. So they always had something to eat and sometimes gave me a bit of their food. It was pretty great that they knew about my situation and accepted it. Thus, we celebrated Christmas in winter 1944/1945.

A "French Woman" Among Forced Laborers

But now I was being searched for. They had already been to the ruin and had left a note that I should report to the police. In addition, the deadline had long since passed by which I had to produce my papers.

Consequently, I had to do something. One day during an alarm I told a Frenchman who seemed trustworthy that I had to discuss something with him. I told him I was an illegal and didn't know how to go on. I asked him if they could help me. I told him that they also could report me to the Gestapo and receive some perk for that. I just risked it. I trusted this group of French workers because although they were all civilian workers, they were all serving a sentence. They had been brought into Germany as an aggravation of the penalty, and that was good. After all, it disclosed a form of rebelliousness or resistance. He was angry with me for making that comment about the Gestapo. He said I should wait a while.

A little later, still during the air-raid alarm, Henri Le Doux approached me. He was the shop steward of the French workers. Henri was a small, short Breton with somewhat Slavic cheekbones, I've got a small photo of him at home, a man with beautiful sad eyes. The others didn't call him Le Doux but Le Vilain, a nickname meaning "the ugly dude."[176] And ugly he was. But everyone trusted him. That's why he was the representative of the camp and the liaison to the Germans. He looked me over, spoke with me, and I told him a great deal about myself. He thought for a while and then said, "It will work out, because at the moment, many are returning from Eastern and Western Prussia." It was horrible. At that time, there weren't yet marches, but trains that arrived. It was bitter cold, and the corpses, especially of children, were being tossed out... You know, even then, I didn't have an attitude that allowed me to say they were "just" some Germans! I felt terrible seeing how much these people suffered.

He went on, "At the same time, the foreign workers are returning as well. Because the weapons factories where they had been working are also being relocated." At that time, in February 1945, there weren't any armament factories that made weapons in their entirety anymore. This part was produced in one place and the next part in another. Things often just ended up lying around and decaying. That's at least what I observed.

---

176 An alternative meaning of "*Le Vilain*" would be "the bad boy" or "the villain."

Le Doux continued, "And when the Germans return, they have to register at the police and with the Nazi Party. But all the foreign workers who are coming through Anklam have to register solely at the Arado plant, with the shop steward of their respective country." That was what we were going to take advantage of. All the French registered with Henri Le Doux. There was an aggravating factor, though: There were very few women among them. Afterwards we were several hundred French, but only five French women, me included.

Henri said I should just wait until a new transport arrived. And transports arrived daily. He issued me a new ID from Arado, and I was now Louise Franquelin. But I had to work at Arado as a French woman. By this time, I had almost nothing more to wear. Ursula's shoes were burnt, and some of the clothes that she had given me had been lost in the bombing. I had nothing more. It was so bitterly cold. Henri immediately provided me with a pair of factory shoes. Those were clunky, large rubber shoes, the *Kindersarg* kind.[177] They were stuffed with straw for insulation. I still had an old, knitted jacket from Ursel, which I had to climb into and then button up in front. I was wearing quite long pants. I owned a shirt, a blouse too, and a jacket. Then I found a pair of black pants that had been part of Ursel's dead (or missing) husband's tuxedo. With this motley clothing, I walked toward Arado. This didn't create any further difficulties because the others looked similar.

There is a main street running through Anklam where there was probably once still a town gate, and in front of that gate lay the train station. At that time, the street bore the name Hermann-Göring Strasse. In front of the gate was a square with the guesthouse I mentioned earlier, and the street went past the square and out of town, in the direction of Berlin. Then you had to cross the train tracks. From Ursel's house the walk to the Arado plant would have been five minutes. Behind the tracks leading to Arado was the sugar factory. And it was packed full of foreign workers. Across from Arado was a camp. When it was bombed out, the Germans just left the foreign

---

177 In parts of Germany, large, oversized shoes are colloquially referred to as *Kindersärge*, literally meaning "children's coffins."

workers there. The workers then created something for themselves. The Arado plant was largely destroyed. Only a small number of us were still working directly at the factory. I worked in a small furniture factory that Arado had confiscated. It was located at the other end of town. So we had to walk across town to get there, which took forty-five minutes. For us foreign workers, our workday was from 6 A.M. to 6 P.M. That meant we left the camp at 5 A.M. and returned around 7 P.M. in the evening. There was no transportation, and in any case, we wouldn't have been allowed to use any. We also were prohibited as foreign laborers from walking on the sidewalk; the residents of Anklam didn't tolerate such behavior...

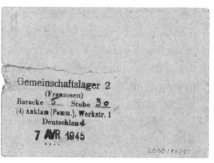

Charlotte's foreign worker's ID under her assumed name Louise Franquelin.
Jewish Museum Berlin, item no. 2009/86/1.

When I was still at the main Arado factory, I worked in checking and monitoring the varnish finish. The master artisan had looked me over and said, "You have smooth fingers, go over there!" You did that job with your fingers. The varnish was for the fighters, I think Focke-Wulf. We made the tails of these planes. In the beginning we got a so-called fighter breakfast. All weapons workers, including the foreign ones, received an additional breakfast portion. It consisted of soup and a sandwich. That was very important for us. Because the food given to the foreign workers was more than meager. After a very short time, this extra portion was cancelled for the foreign workers. What I experienced with the German workers there was exasperating. If I hadn't told myself that all those Germans working there must be very devout Nazis—because otherwise they would not have been deferred from deployment to the front—I probably would have been in deep despair. The way they treated the foreign workers! I spoke very little. My French is very poor, but I didn't speak a word of German. So the Germans didn't know that I could understand them. How they pushed the foreign workers to perform! With what language! You can't imagine. But we did some excellent sabotage. We slowed down at work, we inserted faulty rivets. I ignored that in my monitoring job. And I have to tell you—I did that with great pangs of conscience. Because I always thought, "God, what a terrible thing that is for me. Maybe I'm deciding here about a person's fate, and I don't know anything about him!" And then I told myself, "It has to be, it has to, has to. That is a conflict in which I can only stand on one side, doing my small bit."

Before Ursel Teichmann departed, she turned up once more, and brought me a keg of herring. Up until then I'd only once consciously eaten herring. One time in Moabit they gave us some kind of herring muck as soup, probably from a barrel. They had diluted it and put in a few cabbage leaves. But since I was so terribly hungry, I ate it. Closed my nose—and down the hatch it went! However, the keg of herring came in very handy for me. The news got around very quickly among the civilian workers. Thus, Polish women approached me and asked for some "*ryby*." And I gave them the fish as a present. I was already working at Arado and established contact with them as a result. These Polish women would bring me something or other occasionally that they had managed to steal, potatoes, such stuff. I, in turn, swiped some parachute silk at Arado, very hard to come by, and burlap. Using these fabrics, I sewed dresses for the girls. That's how people helped one another.

We always worked at Arado in artificial lighting. We came and left in darkness. Therefore, I was fairly secure. My shortsightedness helped me; it had started already by then. I didn't even pause to look around first, because I wouldn't have seen anything anyhow. I told myself, "Just walk straight ahead!" That made me look a lot more confident than I actually felt. At this point, I had also started to make friends.

Especially with two French boys. I only have a slight recollection of one of them, the other was from a working-class family in Paris. I took note of him because he was always singing to himself. He was younger than me, but both of them were interested in me. They found out very quickly that I wasn't completely "genuine." I think Henri also told them something. The two shielded me. They constantly demanded that I talk, talk, say something! Whether incorrect or not, talk a lot! Then a tricky situation arose. We were walking in a group of French workers through a kind of park, in the center of town. A police security sweep was in progress. All the men were being stopped by uniformed military police, so-called "chain dogs," who were on the lookout for German soldiers that did not return from furlough. And exactly when they were approaching us, I tripped. That was the worst timing because you can't control what you may shout in such a situation. But I shouted something very typically French, "Ohlala!" So this situation was also mastered without a problem.

Something else in Arado: That was the first time in my life that I entered a hangar. It was very impressive for me. And I had never worked in a factory. The entire atmosphere made a powerful impression on me. Just punching a time clock.... Then we were working nights. At midnight, soup was served. This kind of food led to many "breaking wind" terribly, flatus. I was always tired, very undernourished, so for much of the time I worked in a kind of half-dazed state. And somehow, I had this funny idea of oh how good it would be if everyone had a little purple flame burning at their behind: When the flatus came you could just get out of the way. You can get some really peculiar ideas.

At Arado the provisioning for the workers had apparently been exemplary at some point. Even at that time there was a regulation that any kind of injury had to be checked at the clinic. We were working then with duralumin and people said it was poisonous. I assume they had some test series running, because they also sent foreign workers to the clinic. I had a dental problem; my face was swollen, and I also ended up at the clinic. They in turn sent me to a private dentist in Anklam. And then something happened that bothered me a lot and nevertheless was very pleasant. The dentist discovered that I had a PDL infection in a healthy tooth—probably from the duralumin, he didn't know exactly. He made me a root resection. And during all this, I was under pressure: I am "French!" The man spoke French.

I don't know what the old doctor may have surmised. He was nice and kind to me. He didn't wonder or grow suspicious about my identity, but he took an interest in me. That tooth festered, suppurating again and again. He had to open it up at least four times. And each time he gave me a sedative agent. That was a terrible ordeal for me, because I knew that when one is sedated, one is much more likely to say something than in general anesthesia. You mustn't say anything. So beforehand you had to concentrate, so as not to say anything, not to speak! The other thing is that from the few times I had this sedation, I became addicted. It eased tension. Afterwards I really yearned for it. I couldn't care less whether I had pain or not. I accepted it. Through such abnormal situations you also develop very abnormal reactions. They probably also cause lasting psychological effects, which you only overcome slowly, if ever.

The two French workers were young and badly wanted to be with me. I refused. I neither wanted nor could. As a result, the friendship with one of them ended, the other accepted it. But one day Henri Le Doux came to me. I had more in common with him. He was a communist, a real and kind human being. And he wished for the same from me. I didn't know if Richard was still alive. And I thought, "I mustn't refuse his request." In addition, I was also curious about myself, my feelings. And then a situation arose that I'll never forget. We were in a tender embrace, but it wasn't working. That was a terrible thing for him. Less so for me. I then had to console him a lot. I told him that when all this was over, that too would come back. And that he could be tender and loving with me as often as he liked. He had to come to grips with many moral questions and decisions. Henri had been a soldier. And there had been a directive of the Germans according to which POWs could be reclassified as civilian prisoners. I think it was at the behest of his political group. But that was also considered dishonorable. And that troubled him a lot. Then he was in a terrible penal camp near Stettin for a time, and as further punishment he had been transferred here. But here he became the shop steward of his comrades. I mention this because I want to stress what difficult situations fascism placed such individuals in who nonetheless were capable of pulling themselves up out of the dirt, by their own bootstraps.

Back when I was with Teichmann, I met a somewhat colorless woman, a bit older than me, around forty. And when Ursel left she told me that woman was an illegal Jew staying somewhere in Mecklenburg with a pastor's family that had twelve or thirteen children. She said the woman was thoroughly exploited but kept alive. And recently she'd volunteered for earthwork in East Prussia, because officially she was a German housekeeper. I was never exploited by Ursel, she was like an older sister to me. But I have empathy with that woman, coming into conflict namely with the people who took her in, and with her decision. I can't reproach Ursel for her attitudes. She basically lacked political maturity. When you have no clear direction, no clear worldview, you're vulnerable to influences.

I was then relocated to the furniture factory. It was much smaller and unimaginably noisy. It was the beginning of March. At the start of April, we stopped completely, there was no more work. But then we were still making aircraft tails, and we always said, "Someday, they'd be beautiful baby bathtubs. We hope they store them in a good place." In April, when Arado was shut down, the foreign workers were locked inside their camp. Me too. My beautiful shoes were taken away from me since I was no longer working there. At the most we were allowed out of the camp once a day. And now we were dependent on finding our own food. But there was still another woman in Anklam who knew about me being illegal, Fräulein Dose. I'd met her at the Christmas party that the Ladewigs had made for me. She seemed like an old spinster to me. She was a social worker or librarian.

The fact that there was no longer any work showed us very clearly that the war was approaching its end. At that time, I had learned that Greifswald had remained totally bomb-free. The weirdest and most comical rumors were in circulation about the city. One circulating among the foreign workers was that the illegal organization of the POWs was situated in Greifswald. It had connections with the English and Americans. Whether that was correct I don't know.[178] However, there was a central office that our French workers had established contact with around this time. And there was an exact plan as to where the various groups should go once the war neared its end. We were all supposed to meet in a small village called Neuenkirchen. And indeed, later on we did that. In the meantime, we were given only one more meal in the camp. The food became less and less, the quality ever poorer. The Polish girls were taken for earthwork. Around Anklam a wall was erected. Among us foreign workers, by the way, those considered the least trustworthy were the Dutch workers. The Gestapo depended most on them. Maybe because of their language, or because the Gestapo regarded them as the most "Aryan." Henri Le Doux regularly updated me via the two French boys about who was an informer and whom I should be careful about. For reasons of security he used the boys to inform me about this. Despite our close personal contact, we did not discuss such matters directly.

Across from Arado, on the railway, there was a huge flurry of activity. Transports of food to the front came past. The front was about an hour away in Pomerania and was moving constantly in retreat westward. Sometimes I saw the Volkssturm move on past.[179] That was

178 In the case of Greifswald, a group comprised of members of the opposition and prominent citizens around deputy mayor Siegfried Remertz started making plans to surrender the city to the Soviets to avoid harm to its infrastructure and population. They managed to convince City Commandant Rudolf Petershagen of their plan. When the Red Army attacked nearby Anklam, a group of parlementaires traveled across the lines, met the Soviet commander, and managed to convince him of the veracity of their offer to surrender Greifswald. On April 30, 1945, the Red Army moved into the city. It encountered no resistance, and damage to the buildings was avoided. Many women among the population, however, were raped by Soviet soldiers. Remertz and several other members of the group were later arrested and died in Soviet custody. Petershagen, after returning from a POW camp, aligned himself with the East-German regime, which elevated him to the status of a national hero.

179 The Volkssturm was a last-ditch militia comprised of a heterogenous mix of males, often below or above regular military age, with insufficient fitness, equipment, and training. Commanded by the local party representatives, and thrown into the defensive battle in Germany, the Volkssturm had little military impact, but in some cases, fanatized units led prolonged, futile battles, participated in atrocities, or executed Germans who were accused of defeatism or cowardice.

a group of eight to ten old men, three or four young boys aged fourteen or fifteen, all with a rifle! Sometimes they also had three bazookas. One story I recall was this: The assembled Volkssturm of the neighboring localities was taken by train to the front. And the next evening they returned, in their underpants. On their train, the officers had all jumped off a station before. When they came to the front, the track was the actual front line. To the right were the Soviets, they got off the train on the left. Since they'd been given old SA pants to wear, they were afraid that they would be spotted. And since they were neither eager to fight nor properly armed, the old men simply undressed, discarding their pants, and returned just in underpants.

In Anklam freight trains arrived but got stuck in town, and couldn't go further on to the front. So naturally we provisioned ourselves with what we could find. That was after all only our right. So once we latched onto some rice. We gathered potatoes from the freight cars and placed them in the barracks under the floorboards. Soon the Anklam police became aware of this. They always let the foreign workers steal. Then they searched, confiscated the potatoes, and handed out penalties. That was a good thing for them, because they themselves could not steal from the freight cars. And they could even justifiably confiscate the stolen goods. Anklam was also already without any food supplies.

Let me skip back again: When I was still at Arado, I'd occasionally see contingents of German soldiers pass by who were incarcerated in the military prison in Anklam. They had to fix broken windowpanes and make other small repairs. And naturally they too were hungry. The population was not allowed to give them anything for their work, not a thing! And I arranged now and again something for them in the plant, which I then left underneath the long benches along the street. You see, among the oppressed there is always great solidarity. I didn't know what the soldiers had done but I saw these men as brothers. The receiver understands that too, and you feel an immediate mutuality.

So then we were just lying around, no work. And the most diverse rumors emerged about what was to happen with Anklam. One was that Anklam would be declared a free town. Though almost no one could quite imagine what that meant. Another rumor was that the SS was coming and would occupy Anklam; the town was to be defended. There was speculation back and forth. We were guarded ever more strictly. And were no longer allowed out of the camp. So we decided to abscond according to plan. We began in small groups. At the beginning of April, however, the camp administration assembled a gigantic transport, with workers from all countries. It went to Potsdam. The date of its arrival can be determined. They were all put on Zeppelinplatz. They were to be distributed to some small armament workshops. Then came the huge attack on Potsdam and many of our comrades lost their lives.

Meanwhile, I started to sew backpacks from the burlap I'd stolen. We were a group, a detachment of nine, eight males and one French female—namely me. I had trouble walking, I no longer had appropriate shoes, and I said we ought to have some kind of vehicle to take all our things along. Then I recalled that in Ursel's house, near the kitchen, there had been an old baby buggy. We stole it back. I had taken stuff from Ursel (I told her that later): a top sheet—because in the meantime I'd developed a craving for beds made up nicely—and a set of cutlery. Then we discovered that the baby buggy was quite rickety. It was announced that women and children were being evacuated. And while the eight French men went on individually through the checkpoints—we called that "making oneself scarce"—I as a German woman with a baby buggy and our packs went through the checkpoint inside a large group. Taking a huge risk, without papers, without anything. I got through because the situation was so totally chaotic. The Polish women had thrown up these barriers and a kind of tollgate had been installed. Guards were positioned there. It was announced that within a few hours all women and children had to be out of town.

I recall something else: There were always evacuation transports of German civilians arriving from Stettin. They had been ordered to evacuate their homes within ninety minutes. Several of them later returned quietly and secretly to Stettin to get something from their homes. They told us then—Stettin was occupied by German soldiers— what the Germans had done with the apartments. How they had looted them!

At the beginning of April 1945, I saw in the market square in Anklam how they had hanged three German men. Women accused of having a romantic intermezzo with a Frenchman had previously been chased through the streets with their heads shaven and signs hanging from their necks. And the local Anklam residents all came running to watch this show. Especially the local women. After all, there weren't many men around anymore. I had to pass by this spectacle of a public hanging in the square, because at that time I was still working at the furniture factory. And I made sure to get past quickly. The children were playing with the legs and shoes of the men hanging there! I had always tried to make a difference between Nazis and non-Nazis. But what they had succeeded in doing with the population was atrocious. Then you examined your own heart, since maybe you too had already been a bit corrupted. On the other hand, you had to grow a thick skin. I tried as best I could to keep myself free from that.

I recall that a delivery truck once came to the camp on Schulstrasse. A dead couple lay inside, they had committed suicide while being picked up to be taken to a transport. And the orderlies told me they had a watch and rings on their hands. And we needed illegal money for the bunker. Once the Gestapo arrived, those valuables would be removed from the bodies. The orderlies themselves didn't dare to take the things. They said, "Look, you're a nurse, go ahead!" I thought about that long and hard. Disturbance of the dead is a dumb concept. They're already dead. I would take something from the Gestapo in order to give it to the living for whom it's important. So I went in and did it. And I, who always apologized to every fly—and who, as a nurse, whenever I had to take care of the dead, always tried to comfort them with a few words—simply had to say something, to express my feelings about this. It has nothing to do with faith. I have none. I told the dead that I am doing this for the living. And in this way, I did not feel involved in this loss of life that was caused due to the actions of the fascists.

It shocked me bitterly in Anklam to see what women were capable of. I can't help myself—women after all have a greater responsibility toward life than men. They are the ones who give life. Men have been wrecked by the millennia of wars they have started.

The death penalty and what comes after dying—naturally, we political prisoners spoke about that often. And it always gave me a splitting headache. I have always been in clear opposition against the death penalty and still am today. But I had said that we can't eradicate it unless we also physically destroy the top elite—i.e. Hitler, Goebbels... There was no other way. When we spoke about the subject, there were people who'd gone through an awful lot and said, "Oh, killing is not enough, no. We must do the same to them as they did to us!" I always rejected that view. I said to myself that the elimination of the plague after the war was a necessity, but only the most influential, the most virulent of the plague. Everything else had to be resolved afterwards in some other way. How—I didn't know yet back then. But an eye for an eye, a tooth for a tooth—I've always opposed that. After all, I'm not a fascist. I mean, you make your very self evil and dirty by having a hand in that... Whom do you want to relegate that job to? After all, by acting in such a manner you attract the same kind of evil people again.

A bit before that I'd gone with my baby buggy past the Ladewig home and had scurried up inside to see them. I told the Ladewigs I was leaving because the town would probably be defended. They immediately pressed into my hand what they'd just received for their last treatment; a nice hunk of butter (in their alternative herbal medical practice, they accepted payment in kind). I put it in my buggy and off I went. You see, a gesture like that a person never forgets. Sure, for nine persons it wasn't much, yet it was such a precious treasure for me.

I got through the checkpoints. Shortly after, I met up with the boys in a small forest. Then my buggy broke. We had to tie it together with some string. Each put his bag in the buggy, and we headed off toward Neuenkirchen. That was in the direction of the front. Our plan was to reach the Soviets. We encountered a multitude of people in columns on the move, Germans, who had taken along everything with them, including chickens. For five days we stayed in the countryside outside Anklam. We lived in miserable conditions and were very strict in rationing what we had.

We saw Anklam going up in flames, blazing. And couldn't get any further, for reasons I can no longer recall. Finally, we moved on, already weakened, with nothing left. We couldn't find any onions, there were no more potatoes. The people fleeing in columns had taken everything they could find. If you came to a house and searched inside, there was nothing there, cleaned out. Two of the French workers went off searching for something edible. They came across a very, very small piglet that was alive, and a round hunk of Tilsit cheese. No salt. They killed the small animal before they brought it to us. But we couldn't use it as we had nothing for cooking. So we ate the cheese. It gave us diarrhea. Then we arrived in Neuenkirchen. On the way we'd repeatedly put our ears to the ground to hear the tanks and Katyushas. But there was nothing. We were in the village for several hours. Some small groups came in and occupied the houses. And suddenly the Soviets arrived as well.

Yet it wasn't soldiers with Katyushas, they were small wooden carts loaded with the wounded. We stopped them. They were terribly distrustful. Then came the Soviet troops, and a short time later German troops moved in. There was a terrible exchange of gunfire. A Soviet soldier came into every little hut. They told us how we should behave. We had to lie down on the ground here, then there. They really made sure that nothing happened to us. The battle lasted two hours, then the Germans were pushed out. Much of the village was ablaze. It then became apparent that on the local estate, there was still a stable with animals. And they were screaming. There was also a terrible stench. Finally, we lay down to sleep.

Then came a horrible liberation for me. My comrades were unable to protect me. I would never have believed what was happening. It was horrifying. The next day I burned all my underwear, the little I had. It was all so disgusting. I told the boys I couldn't stay any longer in that place. They understood that. And I went off by myself, crying all the time. The boys were very nice and gentle with me, they left me alone, understood. Then we found five bicycles. A part of our group could pedal on ahead and find some supplies. We found ourselves a small hay wagon, a frying pan in which we fried the little pig, and stuff like that. We didn't get very far with our bikes. Then a group of Soviet soldiers came and took the bikes away from us. Soon we all came down with diarrhea. From that time on Henri was my sergeant, my *marechal*. If I had to relieve myself, he came along, stood out in front of me and guarded me. I didn't feel any shame. He was discreet, and I had dire need for that. The fear since the experience was greater than the sense of any shame. We were repeatedly stopped by Soviet soldiers, they asked us for something to smoke. And we gave as long as we had. In the meantime, we'd stitched together a tricolor. Sewn from rags, fastened to a stick.

Liberation, Soviet Detention, and Release in Prenzlau

We then came to a place that had been occupied by the Soviets. At the entrance to the village a young soldier was standing next to a well. He shouted, "*Stoi!*" [Stop!]. He wanted something to smoke. Everyone said that they had nothing left. He started shouting terribly, cursing us. In Russian, which sounds very threatening when you don't understand a word of it. Then one of the boys pulled out a small bowl of tobacco and handed it to him. But he continued to holler and curse and barked, "*Stoi!*" He then went off. This young soldier had managed to pin down a group of nine people, even after he walked off. We were completely convinced he'd gone to get reinforcements to lock us all up. Why, was no longer at all clear. After a short time, he returned, holding—a large pot of lard! He gave it to us in exchange for the tobacco and let us go on. You see how important the knowledge of a language is! This, however, was now the last possession we had.

Then we came to another abandoned settlement, but Huguenots had once lived there. There were still French books lying about, and for the French guys that was a pleasant surprise. I still have a small volume that I took from there at home. Then we entered a house, and from the basement we heard horrible screams. I have to say, they were very shocking, loud, and penetrating, and I too felt afraid. In the kitchen was a trapdoor. Two of my comrades climbed on down. And lo and behold: it was a goose that had been forgotten and was screaming terribly. Well, we freed her from her screaming, and she helped us in return.

In the meanwhile, we came through a town that was totally flattened. The French boys said, "*Bien détruit!*" Which meant, "nicely destroyed." And actually, I was happy to see that as well. It was the town of Pasewalk. Much worse was encountering old people living rough next to the road. They were still alive and yet no longer living. To walk past these dying people was horrible and really difficult for me. But I didn't know what to do. I saw an old woman. I was very weak, yet I was simply able to lift her up, she was light as a feather. To lift her up, bed her a bit more comfortably, that was all anyone could do for these people dying along the way. After Pasewalk there were provisions to be found. Already at that time! Wehrmacht chocolate containing a stimulant, huge quantities of soup cubes, money, loads of stuff. I didn't want to take anything. I told myself something very different is coming, the money will also be replaced. Some of the comrades were pocketing it, nevertheless. Meanwhile, we had become a larger grouping, several groups together. Then I found a nightgown. A human always retains some level of vanity. "It could be made into a blouse," I thought.

We came as far as Prenzlau. A shout rang out, "*Stoi!*" There was a large Soviet military HQ. The town had not been bombed, but had been totally destroyed except for a single street. It was the Nazis who had obliterated the town. They had a Wehrmacht garrison there. It was situated on one side of the railroad tracks, the town was on the other. The garrison had remained intact... There the Soviets had moved in. They stopped all contingents of people on the road and had set up a huge repatriation camp. Actually, it was amusing. Each of us was given a small area in the officers' and NCO's apartments, settlement houses with front gardens. The rooms were empty. Who had plundered them I don't know. In the gardens the Soviets had assembled empty bed frames to be used as toilets. There was no longer any water or sewage system. It was very French in style; you could see feet and heads. The Soviets, who themselves had nothing, because their supply lines were broken, distributed something every morning to each group, whatever they had at that particular moment. Usually it was horsemeat, but with no salt, that they dropped into your cap and told you to do with it as you please. To that extent, things were OK.

I said, "I want to come forward as an honest person." I wanted to go to the Soviet military HQ and say, "I'm a Communist." The potential consequences of such a move were something that Richard might well have been able to inform me about. I had no idea. And I wanted to say I had a false name. I went with Henri. In the military HQ was an officer who must have stemmed from somewhere in Siberia. He had somewhat slanting eyes and was totally bald, middle-aged—the commandant. They gave us a French–Russian interpreter. He was nicknamed *"Le chinois"* by the French. That man was a rascal. He didn't translate what you said. I'll come back to him later, he probably wasn't even a Soviet citizen. Later on, I saw the man once on the Kurfürstendamm in Berlin with the Allies. Naturally, it may also be that they simply hadn't translated what was said correctly.

In any case, we were immediately arrested and put in jail; Henri and I were separated. Henri was released twenty-four hours later, but I was confined for three-and-a-half days behind bars. It was very depressing. Being incarcerated was really a big issue for me. But before I was placed in prison, I was taken from the military HQ to an officers' prison of the Stalag, the Nazi POW camp. There were guards on duty, and they also had their quarters there. First, I was brought into a barracks for the enlisted ordinary soldiers. That was in the evening. The soldiers were all lying in their beds. And then began a terrible haggling… over who should get me. And I had never before begged and pleaded so much as there. I had never begged with the Nazis. But there, I…. I cried and pleaded and begged them to let me be. Afterwards they did leave me alone, but until then, they took their pleasure in shocking me and almost went all the way. It was just terrifying.

Then they took me to a small room, where an officer was lying in bed. They had a strange way of dealing with each other. He had to get up out of bed and I was told to get in. The commandant had ordered this. Thus I slept the first night in this officer's bed. The next day I was hauled off to prison. I was left in peace. They brought me an eiderdown quilt. And every few minutes the cell door was opened, the head of a soldier looked in around the corner, and then disappeared once again. They brought me something to eat too, so it was easy to bear. I also quickly noticed that those who came were not angry or mean, they wanted nothing but to take a look at who and what was there: a woman! A spy! "You spy, Gestapo!" Well, how often I heard them saying that.

After three days I was taken once more to the commandant's HQ to be interrogated. Henri had prepared a long, written declaration. I don't know where he had that translated by some interpreter. In any case, he had clarified the entire situation. I did not understand anything in this interrogation. The commandant was a very fun-loving, buoyant man who had considerable interest in the ladies. Consequently, he didn't have much time for me, because a lady was sitting there, waiting. In any event, he said to me, "*Domoi!*" [Go home!]. I didn't quite understand that I was being set free. I went back to the prison. I thought, maybe I hadn't understood correctly. But there were no longer any guards. Only then did my group come to pick me up.

Already at this point, we slept in a formation where four men slept on each side of me on the ground. When anyone came in, I was in the middle, out of sight. I was certainly thin enough to go unseen. They said, "Here only men!" So that worked out alright. Because such checks were frequent. I had another strange experience: I was outside, answering nature's call. Henri had come along to watch out for me and take care. And a little Soviet soldier approached us. They looked at times even younger than they were. And I thought the kid was maybe fifteen years old. He wanted to have me and started to haggle with Henri. Henri told him, "She's my wife." After a long discussion back and forth the boy patted Henri on the back and said, "OK, I'll leave her to you." Then another time, I was dragged down into a basement and had to endure that again. At that point I took a decision and told the others, "If that occurs one more time, I won't be able to continue living any more, I won't want to continue living. I'll find some way to end it!" It was so terrible, that basement that had apparently been used as a toilet by many. And I was thrown in there. For years afterwards, I remained really scared of uniforms.

Occasionally, we had wonderful parties. The commandant knew how to arrange them in style. Between the small houses along the street every evening another national group gathered and had to organize a celebration, a party. The Italians had already organized carts with horses and bells. They were somewhat similar to the Soviets with their habits, collecting and trading pencils.

Repatriation was conducted group by group. The French group had to wait a very long time. A week back then felt like a very long time for us! However, the trucks that were supposed to pick them up were immediately requisitioned by our commandant to drive to the nearby countryside and bring in potatoes. His actions were absolutely justified. After all, he was responsible for a large number of people.

One evening I was walking to the commandant's HQ and some man came and assaulted me, he wanted to take me with him. But since I was close to the HQ, I screamed hysterically, so the commandant's soldiers came and rescued me. I was brought to the commandant and described the soldier who had assaulted me. When he let go of me, the only thing I'd noticed is that his eyes had different colors. One was grey and one was brownish. This as well as the facial expression of him I remembered clearly. I didn't know more. I later heard that the commandant had the soldier whipped. So he did try to prevent such things. When I was upstairs in the commandant's HQ, I was crying, and I'd spoken a bit of German, because they understand that much better than French. The Soviet women who had witnessed this immediately took me along. There was an entire corridor in the headquarters reserved for the quarters of female foreign workers and the female Soviet doctor.

The Soviet doctor took me into her room, she had one for herself. I stayed with her in that room for three nights. Not more. But I liked her a lot. Anyhow, in those three nights I became acquainted with a very happy, youthful mode of life. She casually brought in men to be with her! That was psychologically interesting for me. She wasn't embarrassed in the slightest in front of me. She behaved as if I wasn't there, and I made myself invisible as well. I noticed that the lovemaking was very fast, very uncomplicated. And I made an interesting observation. I don't necessarily want to generalize. But it may be interesting for the place of women within the remnants of feudalism. I know that the Soviet woman had to work more than the men did.

Yet while this woman was powerful enough to get the men she found attractive—she was after all an officer—she served them in a highly subservient manner after becoming a woman through them. Early in the morning, she handed them the water to wash themselves—and it was there that I became familiar with the Russian way of washing yourself in the mornings, whereby you blow the water out over your hands and then rub yourself down. She served them in such a subservient way! I can only explain that as remnants of the earlier position of the woman. Then I also learned that the commandant had a girlfriend among the Russian women, and that that was his prerogative. But a wing had also been cleared for German women whom the foreigners had brought along or who otherwise had a special status. And the commandant had another girlfriend among them. I already noted that he was a very potent guy. First, he went to his German woman in the evening, and then to his Russian one. I met that German woman later on. She was young, pretty, a very nice mother with an infant. She did what she did to obtain milk for her baby and tried to make the best of the situation.

This commandant was afraid of himself when he got drunk. And he and the rest were often drunk. When they organized a binge—from where they got the alcohol, I have no idea—he told the Soviet women beforehand. Then they were to lock the rooms upstairs. He also told the German woman that she should watch out, that sometimes he'd make a mistake. So she received him—the whole thing always occurred among the other women—and brought him to her room so that he wouldn't make a mistake and go astray. He sent word to me that I could stay until my comrades were repatriated.

Already there I met Hungarian prisoners who were Jews. I always asked them to see if they could find someone from the Holzer family living at Szabor utca 3. If so, they should say I was still alive. I still knew nothing about Richard and was still very confused at that point.

And then, one day, our French group departed. I recall them sitting on the truck, waving to me, we promised we'd try to keep in touch. And I said to them that if I wasn't able to find anyone left, then I'd come to France, I wouldn't remain in Germany. That was my decision at that point. It wasn't like you said to yourself—only Germany! Believing things would be different… reconstruction and all that. No, it wasn't like that, not in my case. I thought, if nobody is alive anymore, then first of all I have to gain some distance. Then I'll go to my French comrades. People later held it against me that I had repeated this frequently at the time.

If I'd later been asked, "Why in the world did you do that with those soldiers?"—then I'd have felt it necessary to say, "Because I had no other choice." For my sake and that of my comrades. Perhaps otherwise they would have had to pay with their lives. You never knew exactly what would be. There were those kinds of threats. The second time in that basement the situation was such that had I started screaming, I would only have attracted others as well. And the third time, in front of the commandant's HQ, I did resist. In that case, the only thing that could happen was that help arrived. That was the objective angle. But in my own mind, I had serious thoughts about these assaults: Where does the mistake lie that such things can take place? Because these were young guys. They'd gone through the Soviet education system. And I considered their education the problem. But I didn't fully understand it until later, when I realized that it could also have been bound up with Stalinism. I said that I had known a bit about this, but only later did we learn details. In addition, there were the old concepts embedded in their minds. But basically, I think, the cult of personality[180] produced a sense of fear and submissiveness, but no genuine bond with the worldview. If a genuine Communist worldview had been inculcated and properly adhered to, the assaults would have never happened. Likewise, here in the GDR, I think hooliganism as reported in yesterday's paper are only possible because such phenomena were not completely eradicated by means of conviction and education.

When I was still living with the French workers in Prenzlau, I was a very close friend of Henri. We did everything together. That for me was especially important. If you'd experienced Fascism before and then what had transpired in Prenzlau, then you urgently needed some confirmation that you were still a human being and could still establish relationships with others. Henri helped me a lot in that respect. But the times were so abnormal, for example, that I never even thought of asking him what work he did, his profession. That was something so far removed from the

---

180 *Personenkult* (cult of personality) was a euphemism commonly employed by governments in the Soviet area of influence to retrospectively describe the years of terror under Stalin.

situation! I assume he had been involved in party work, perhaps a worker. But I don't know. That wasn't what we talked about. He talked a bit about Gaullism, I had no idea about that... On the side of Prenzlau where we lived, I used to go for walks with Henri, down as far as the lake, Uckersee. There's a very beautiful church there that had been destroyed. Yet it had such architectural beauty, or maybe it just moved me so strongly in that situation. This Gothic architecture really moved me.

Around that lake lay many corpses of the drowned. That was a kind of death I had never seen up to then. Many residents of Prenzlau had gone into the water and perished. There was no sanitation infrastructure at that point. Consequently, we had to get our water for cooking from this lake. You simply had to overcome your reluctance to do that. In addition, there was a kind of section with villas there, totally destroyed. We climbed around in these half-demolished houses, rummaged in their libraries, taking something to read. There were dishes buried in the gardens. You could check that by simply poking a rod into the ground.

When my French group, la belle équipe, departed, all my comrades emptied their pockets and pressed all the money they had collected into my hand—which I did not want to take—and they said, "Listen, maybe you'll need it after all!" It was 800 Marks.

Then the Soviets brought me over to the then already existing German municipal administration. I was escorted over with all honors and likewise nicely received there. The new mayor was a very young man named Schmidt or Schulze,[181] whom the Soviets had probably brought along from an anti-fascist school. The mayor told me they had no doctor and just one nurse, and he asked me if I could assist. I agreed to the extent that my knowledge and experience could be applied.

There was a thoroughfare where no Nazis lived. They had all absconded. Those residents now were actually—let me put it like this—good Germans. Initially it was a very difficult life. Basic foods were

---

181 Robert Schulz (1900–1969), a Communist politician and council member in Prenzlau. He was unlikely the person Charlotte met when she arrived in Prenzlau. Mayor at the time was not Schulz, but Hermann Kolb, only twenty-six years old in 1945 and thus fitting the description of a young man much better than the forty-four-year-old Schulz. For more on Schulz and Kolb, see the biographical entries in the appendix.

distributed, but only to those who were fit to work. And there were not many. I had no place to stay. People asked the other nurse whether she could take me in. Valeria Kothe was a very dear and kind young girl of nineteen or twenty, she lived with her grandparents, mother, and maybe four small brothers and sisters. The family lived in a large parlor, and opposite it, separated by a hall, was a very tiny room. It contained a bed, across from it a couch, in between a narrow space you could walk through, then a window, a door, behind that a small table with a chair. When I came, Valeria said I could sleep there, but that she had to take care of her brothers and sisters. She said, "If that doesn't disturb you and is OK—I have a steady boyfriend—then you can stay." I said fine, I would sleep there.

Every evening a Soviet soldier came and slept in the room. In the course of the day he would come by with a small handcart and bring sugar or horsemeat, sometimes both. I have to say I thought that a highly moral relationship. First, because this girl did not have any of the characteristics other German women had, "Oh, those Russians!" Rather the Russians for her were human beings like all others. And what she earned by doing this was for her brothers and sisters. She thought that was fine and so did I. I think the soldiers could have had that kind of relationship everywhere had they just waited a bit. Because, after all, the Americans had had that for a mere bar of chocolate. But actually, it was prohibited by the Soviets. Maybe that was an error on their part. Yet they probably forbade it because of all the other stuff that had occurred. One really detrimental thing was that the Soviet soldiers had engaged in this practice all the way from East Prussia down to us— and now were largely infected.

This was another example of how a problem was wrongly approached on their side. I had learned that this illness is not a moral deficiency but simply a disease that has to be treated like all others. But the Soviet soldiers were accused of engaging in some kind of moral transgression. In the wake of the wars of intervention the authorities had presumably wanted to curb and contain it. But they had maintained that stance for much too long. One thing I learned from experience was: Moral concepts mustn't be guided by the exigencies of the day; you have to find other ways. Because moral distortions have ramifications.

The infections the soldiers now had were being spread ever further because they didn't report what they had. In addition, we didn't have enough medicines.

Regarding my comrade Valeria: Naturally, I also lived on what she was "acquiring." The everyday German word anschaffen (acquire) is also used to describe prostitution. But she wasn't engaged in that at all. She was just a simple, modest girl, probably very clean and honest.

During the day I worked in the municipal administration and established a kind of first aid office. I was there on hand when someone needed something and did what I could without a doctor. Then I had an awful experience. I was called to a family living somewhat outside of town. In a small house a couple lived with a daughter, about seventeen years old. They brought me up into a small attic room. The daughter lay there in a coma. The parents told me she'd had diabetes from her early teens and had constantly been getting insulin shots. But they had no more insulin. So what should be done now? The girl would have died, like in the past before insulin injections were discovered. Nothing could be done. I was in a terrible situation.

I immediately sent the parents off with a small note to the Soviet military base hospital that had been set up in the meantime. I wrote that they should try to procure insulin as fast as possible. With good reason, I prudently sent the parents. Communication with the Russians was linguistically just as difficult for me as for them, but when a mother arrives, that would more likely move the Soviet doctors to act... And they really did return with insulin! I had learned at the hospital that administering intravenous shots was forbidden for nurses. Although I knew how, I'd never actually done it. And second: How much insulin should I use? I was sitting in front of the girl in a coma, she was already choking, her tongue curved backward, and I told myself, now it makes no difference, you can't do worse damage. I found the vein and injected the insulin very slowly, until I noticed that she was starting to move. I was able to save her and was really happy about it. She stayed alive.

Then a doctor, who had fled somewhere, returned. He took over the medical service, and we established something like an outpatient clinic. We had a lot of scabies to treat, and those open wounds on the legs, which I also had later on; everything a product of maladies due to deficiency and lack of care, injuries, and naturally, infected women. In the neighboring village was a Soviet major who arrived every few days with a horse cart packed full of women and said, "They've all got the ladies' sickness!" In the meanwhile, we'd received a supply of penicillin. That came via some channel or other of the International Red Cross, from the Americans, and now we too could help. But then this doctor began to do a business, making deals. Later I heard he'd been executed in a campaign by the Soviets against profiteers. So he belonged to those circles, and I'm not even fully sure he was actually a physician.

I probably don't have to tell you that the immediate postwar period was not very nice. The Prenzlau residents naturally felt they were being mistreated by the Soviets. They saw themselves as opponents to the Nazis who had stayed on voluntarily. And now their upholstered furniture was being taken away from them. For me that wasn't an issue, I just laughed at their talk, it was clear to me that all that was nonsense. Before it was transported to the Soviet Union it had either been stolen elsewhere or it was sent as junk. But I tried to tell the people that ultimately the Germans had destroyed or stolen more in the Soviet Union than just a few pieces of furniture. The people were now coming in regularly to the office of the mayor installed by the Soviets to complain and whine. He was often quite depressed, and around noon one day I happened to be present when he said something very quietly and sincerely, "Someday you're going to be happy that this place was not occupied by the other side—but by the Soviets." He didn't say anything further, but I understood what he was getting at. And that comment also actually helped me, because naturally sometimes I found it difficult, too.

But now I wanted to get back to Berlin. I wished to learn if my child was still alive. If I've rarely spoken about Eva in this narrative, it corresponds with the situation I was in at that time. I was consciously trying to suppress thoughts about the child. I told myself I couldn't do anything to help. And when I can't do anything but am being thrown back and forth like some kind of package—I have to let myself be thrown around and have to disconnect, to tune out. Only when I myself can do something, that's when I can think again! And in general, by means of this philosophy, I was able to bear up and pull through.

When I sometimes spoke with Richard about this later, he said I'd just been tormenting myself. There was, however, no other way. I could either push to make it through all of this, if they did not murder me, or I could give up. But for the former, I had to push even the hint of a negative thought away! And I trained myself to be like that. I didn't know about Eva; I didn't know about Richard. And then there were personal anxieties I had to push away. The image of my beheaded comrades, that repeatedly entered my mind, I had to suppress. And I did just that!

I had made a request to the Soviets right from the beginning to go to Berlin. But Berlin was closed for entry. Typhus was raging, there were loads of people, and not enough places to live. I'd arrived on May 4 or 5 in Prenzlau. I was imprisoned first for three or four days, then I was released, probably on May 8. When I was released, there was so much shooting we thought the war had returned. But it was the war's end. The Soviets celebrated by shooting off whatever they could. I returned to Berlin on July 2. I was in Prenzlau for seven or eight weeks. Of those, three were together with the French workers, and then afterwards with the Germans.

Return to Berlin

Then a so-called *propusk* came, an entry permit, "for certain privileged persons." I was included in that category. A flatbed large cart, pulled by two horses, rode on into the German municipality grounds. In the coach box were two Soviet soldiers. A bunch of different chairs were arranged in the cart, and the privileged people were then placed on the cart. Among them were several older people about whom I only know that they complained terribly on the road, plus a young couple. There was a man, a civilian, who looked very dubious to me, who came from the Soviet Union, he said from the anti-fascist schools.[182] But I didn't

---

182 Antifaschistische Frontschulen (Anti-fascist Front Schools) were reeducation facilities for captured German soldiers that were supposed to indoctrinate them and turn them into allies of the Communist cause.

believe a word of it. With him was a girl who came from East Prussia, decent and nice, whom he had acquired for himself.

The trip from Prenzlau to Berlin took about five days. The Soviet soldiers took care of us wonderfully during the journey and managed to get us food. We obtained potatoes and sometimes onions, at times also nothing at all. Whatever they managed to get their hands on. They repeatedly stopped somewhere and said, "*spatj!*" when they felt the need to sleep. Wherever there was a nice, empty house, they decided to stop and stay, I think. It was enjoyable, though, I was able to look around these places in quiet contemplation. We rode into Berlin from the north and came through Neue Königstrasse. From the other direction, speeding, a Soviet car drove by, they really managed to drive fast! And it crashed into us. The impact caused just damage, the coach box broke off, the front wheels of the cart separated, the flatbed tilted down, and we tumbled out onto the street. The journey was at its end.

When I had picked myself up from the street, I saw a large paper placard. It stated, "All comrades from the concentration camps: Report for a meeting at Köllnischer Park!" Well, I thought, that's nearby. I went toward the place, just as I was, and this young couple came along too. I think it was in the building that today houses the social insurance authorities. I arrived, and sitting there was a communist woman who had been one of Richard's comrades, and who later was in a relationship with him. She knew about Richard's membership in the Herbert Baum Group, and thus mine as well. In addition, there were many connections with our group. My story was immediately validated. I had no difficulty in being recognized by the VdN—the Association of Persecutees of the Nazi Regime.[183] The two others were also accepted, because they had a document from the Soviets in their pocket.

---

183 *Verfolgter des Naziregimes* (VdN—Persecutee of the Nazi Regime) was not an organization, but the accepted designation in East Germany for Anti-Nazi resistance operatives and people persecuted by Nazis. The association itself was the Vereinigung der Verfolgten des Naziregimes (VVN—Association of Persecutees of the Nazi Regime). The stark difference in treatment of Jewish communists and Jewish victims that Charlotte points out several sentences later was also structural, those among the persecuted who were aligned with the Communist Party received a higher pension payment in the GDR than those who were "just" victims.

Special ID for Charlotte Holzer, issued by the authorities in Prenzlau.
Jewish Museum Berlin, item no. 2009/86/2.

This communist woman told me that the comrades from the concentration camps were staying at a home on Wrangelstrasse, in southeastern Berlin, very near the neighborhood where I'd grown up. But she wanted to place me somewhere different and searched in a stash of addresses, pulling one out for me in Moabit. She said the other couple and I could live there together because we'd arrived together. But at the same time, others came, also Jews. They hadn't been anti-fascists, nor active fighters, as we today distinguish between fighters and victims. And this woman treated those Jews in such a rotten, nasty way—so badly that to this day, I've retained a poor relation with her. Right from that day I first met her on the street in Berlin. Because I can't forget and excuse what she did. I found it horribly wrong to treat people so badly who had suffered so badly at the hands of the fascists. Unfortunately, among us there are still those who distinguish between people. When I see that, I want nothing to do with those people, in my eyes they're finished. To be sure, there is a Party principle to be vigilant regarding people, but I considered it wrong from the outset to snub people a priori that way. Mistrust has nothing to do with vigilance. And a fortiori most certainly not with our worldview. I mean, to discard people who don't share and espouse that view.

In the meantime, things have changed, and we accepted many people who back then weren't yet Communists.

We three then walked from Köllnischer Park to Moabit. We had to take a boat across the Spree because there was no bridge left. There was a kind of ferry. I walked along Alt-Moabit. No, let me think, along Turmstrasse, and there on a side street was our destination, the address we'd been handed. The apartment belonged to a woman whose son and daughter-in-law had been active Nazis and had been arrested; now we were supposed to move into their rooms. That naturally was a very difficult situation for us. There was a wardrobe in the room full of clothes. The girl in the couple wanted to take some for herself, but I thought that was wrong. And I said, "As long as I'm here, that won't happen. I will oppose that." I also spoke with the mother living there. I told her some things that the Nazis had done which she perhaps had never heard about. And I said to her, "If your children did anything like that, then you have to accept that this is going to be investigated. And if they have suffered an injustice, it has to be added to the huge injustice, that was committed by fascism and the entire war." I don't know for sure, but I suspect that I made her feel a bit more at peace with these words.

The very next day I wanted to head off in search of my child. Where to begin? There was only one homeland for me, the Jewish Hospital. In addition, it wasn't so far from Moabit. I went back across the Spree[184] and was now in the other part of town, and I walked to the hospital. After I was welcomed in, I was told right away out near the gatekeeper's office that Gustav, my first husband, was in the hospital in one of the wards.

"Where is he?" I asked. "In the TB ward," I was told, "Just over here." I found him in a horrible condition. He was thinking clearly at this point, but I saw that he probably would pass away soon. I immediately contacted the doctor. He told me Gustav had TB in both lungs. In addition, he had a serious leg injury on the thigh, teeming with maggots. He said they couldn't operate because he wouldn't survive it. He'd probably only live a few more days. I then stayed with him.

---

184 She likely did not cross the Spree, but the Hohenzollernkanal, which connected the rivers Spree and Havel and separated the mentioned part of Moabit from the Wedding quarter.

He no longer remembered that we'd separated. But otherwise he was thinking clearly. He told me that after his two years in jail in Brandenburg-Görden he'd been transferred to Neuengamme concentration camp, and that he'd been confined there in the sick bay with TB. He also told me that the prisoners were put on ships but that the invalids were not. Instead they were forcibly removed from the camp and sent on a march. He and his group had been driven away and marched as far as somewhere near to Ludwigslust. There they were chased into a forest. Then most were murdered. The forest was surrounded. But he tried to push out and escape together with a comrade and was successful. He merely suffered a few blows from a rifle butt on his thigh. The terminally ill man had dragged himself with his injuries all the way to Spandau. On foot! There he collapsed in the street. A woman had picked him up, taken him home with her, and taken care of him. When the battles in Berlin were over, she brought him as he requested to the Jewish Hospital. He told me that my Eva was still alive, living with his mother. He warned me that it was going to be very difficult for me with her.

I don't recall how much I've already told you about his mother. Gustav's father was a potter. There were three brothers. The father returned from World War I with paralysis of the spinal cord. He lived thus paralyzed for another eleven years. Gustav's mother, a very energetic and hard working woman, was then left alone with the three boys. She descended into the lowest rungs of the proletariat, the *Lumpenproletariat*. She doubtless also did many bad things. She was young, she brought men back home—next to her husband, in the same bed... And the boys witnessed that. They had only one room. They held that very much against their mother. All three were quite gifted. But Gustav at least was headed likewise for the gutter. He'd started to drink heavily when I met him.

When he was arrested the first time, his mother, who has some residual antisemitism in her character, criticized me viciously. I was terribly afraid of her. She had the mouth of a market crier. And my child was now staying with her.

I promised Gustav I would do nothing against his mother. And I kept that promise. But the whole situation made it terribly difficult for me. The next day his mother came with little Eva. I was there, as I was taking care of Gustav. And my child did not shake my hand. Later I learned from Mariechen—she was a girl who earlier had assisted us in illegality—that she had tormented the child horribly. The only physical contact Eva had with her was being hit and slapped. She'd picked on the child for so long that Eva had started to curse me. Through that, the child found a kind of peace and quiet. Therefore now, Eva, very frightened, clung to her grandmother and didn't know how she should behave, what she should think. I told Eva not to worry, I'd never force her to be with me. I said she should just visit me as often as she liked. She would have a home in my place only if she wanted that herself.

And in fact, the very next day, after I'd been with Gustav, I moved out of the apartment in Moabit to my own apartment, where I'd lived earlier, at Zechliner Strasse 6. That proved possible because Gustav owned this apartment and it had not been considered a Jews' apartment. So when he was arrested the apartment was not confiscated. Rather, his mother had rented it out to two women, furnished and all, for the entire time. When Gustav returned, he was placed in the hospital, but she immediately had the apartment vacated. And she had not done anything against her son. Although they both got into terrible arguments. He didn't know he was dying; he didn't ask me at all. Rather he said, "When I regain my health I'll come back home." And he told me to go to that apartment to stay. Because I knew his situation, naturally I said OK. And I think that was the right thing to do. Why should I do anything differently?

Gustav died on July 21. I didn't press Eva. I lived there in the apartment and during the day I took care of him. Rita Zocher was in the same ward, likewise with a form of TB, and it was expected that she wouldn't live. As soon as she was capable of being moved, a year later, she was transferred to Sülzhain, to a sanatorium, and remained there for two years.

After Gustav died, Eva visited me every day. Every single day. I had not done anything, as I had been advised, to gain back custody of the child. That would have been foolish. In this period Eva very secretly, on the quiet, brought back all my things from her grandmother. One day she arrived, bringing me an iron, a heating pad, and several books. And then one day she told me she wished to come back to live with me.

Something else: People still didn't know at that point what they should do with the many corpses. When Gustav died, they kept his body on ice and put it in the basement. Together with his brother Max, they brought him in a handcart to the crematorium on Gerichtstrasse. We had provided a cardboard coffin. It was a great accomplishment that we'd managed to find such a coffin. And just like that, he was cremated. Then his funeral at the cemetery on Seestrasse was to take place. And the old hag, his mother, decided to set the day of the burial for August 21, exactly on little Eva's birthday. So now the child had to go to the burial of her father on her birthday. I wouldn't have taken her along myself. But then she placed her little hand in mine. In September she wished to return to stay with me.

But the old hag didn't want to let her go. I had to negotiate with Gustav's mother. All who returned from the camps back then received 400 Marks to start a new life. I gave her my 400 Marks and my ration coupons. In return I got the child. Easy to narrate but it was hard to live through. I got my child back; she was totally confused.

Her grandmother had helped her survive, kept her alive. And that was certainly not easy for her. Neither economically nor in terms of the law. Sometimes Eva was illegal, at times semilegal, depending on the attitude of the Nazis toward her case. Then there was the whole story with the Gestapo, that I myself had staged. Certainly, that had become an overwhelming situation for her. Eva for a time had worked a bit, pasting ration coupons in a food shop, collecting bottles, and selling them. All that wouldn't have been so bad.

But when the Soviets came, the old hag told her repeatedly that her mother wasn't worth a damn. She hung a sign around her neck—someone in the building there who knew Russian had written it. It said, "I'm a Jew, my mom's a Jew and was gassed in a concentration camp." That's how she sent her to the Soviets to beg for food. Now you can imagine what kind of a state I found her in when she came back. To the extent I was able to, I invested in the child's development. She attended a school, on Gotenburger Strasse. A secondary school. She had not attended any school before that. In the course of a month she skipped one grade, and then another, because initially she had been placed according to her actual school-based knowledge. But Eva had already matured. And during the time I wasn't there, she had been reading my books at random. So she had already learned something. Nonetheless, Eva had never forgotten that once as a small child wearing the yellow star she had been attacked and beaten bloody. And after a short time, she said she didn't want to go to school with German children.

Charlotte Holzer, after the war, in 1952.

AFTERWORD

by Helmut Peitsch

Charlotte Holzer told the story of her survival of persecution not just to the journalist Dieter Heimlich in 1966–1967, but also previously and later; however, her report was never so detailed as in the transcribed conversation that forms the basis for the present text. In a memo in February 1976, she called it "my story." In this text, these memoirs will be discussed in the context of Charlotte Holzer's earlier and later statements in order to encourage a historical reading that considers the conditions of expression back then which weren't the same as today.

As she herself noted, Charlotte Holzer's story combines "personal" memories of family, school, and vocational training with "political" memories of the German Communist Party and the resistance group around Herbert Baum. The greater part of the story and its longest temporal segment centers on the Jewish Hospital, operated by the Jewish community, where Charlotte worked as a nurse from 1927 until 1944, with two interruptions. These interruptions, characteristic of the fusing of private and political elements in her story, spanned 1933 to 1935, when her first husband, Gustav Paech, was under arrest, and

277

she had to care for her newborn daughter Eva; and October 1942 to October 1943, when she was confined in various prisons following the arrest of members of the Baum Group in the wake of the arson attack on the exhibition "The Soviet Paradise." In the Jewish Hospital Charlotte made the acquaintance of Communists, a group which she subsequently joined. She also encountered Herbert Baum again there in 1939, and through his resistance group met Richard Holzer, whom she married in 1947. His story is succinctly told on the gravestone she erected for him in the Jewish cemetery in Berlin-Weißensee in 1975, "Born Jewish—became a Communist—that's what he lived for."

In the interview, conducted by the GDR journalist—a "guided" interview, long before the concept had been coined—Charlotte responds to questions (which were not recorded) and gives a narrative account of her life history. Both her own published and unpublished personal texts and her oral memoirs recorded by others deal with more narrowly limited periods of time or circumstances. In the following, I would like to present an overview of these texts.

On November 20, 1963, Historian Kurt Jakob Ball-Kaduri provided Yad Vashem with a four-page report on a short interview he had conducted with Charlotte Holzer about the Baum Group and the attack on the Soviet Paradise exhibition.[1] It included references to Günther Weisenborn's *Der lautlose Aufstand*, in which—based on an unspecified report—the Baum Group was referred to as "purely Jewish."[2] It also references a text attributed to Charlotte and her husband Richard Holzer, which Charlotte had passed on to Bertha Cohn of the Wiener Library in 1956 or 1957.[3] The first section bears the heading "The Development of the Fighters," and only briefly sums up the background of the members and the conditions under which the group was formed.

---

1   "Bericht über eine Besprechung mit Frau Charlotte Holzer zum Thema: Attentat auf die Ausstellung Sowjetparadies in Berlin im Jahre 1942," November 20, 1963, Yad Vashem Archives (YVA), Ball-Kaduri Collection, O.1/298.

2   Günther Weisenborn, *Der lautlose Aufstand: Bericht über die Widerstandsbewegung des deutschen Volkes, 1933–1945* (Hamburg: Rowohlt, 1962), p. 150.

3   "Die jüdischen Widerstandskämpfer in Berlin: Gruppe Baum," YVA, Ball-Kaduri Collection, O.1/297.

Charlotte Holzer's autobiographical texts written for readers in the GDR show a similar thematic limitation. In 1958, Walter A. Schmidt published *Damit Deutschland lebe*, according to the subtitle "a source book on the German anti-fascist resistance struggle," in the GDR. It contained the abovementioned report, co-written by Charlotte and Richard Holzer "Die jüdischen Widerstandskämpfer in Berlin: Gruppe Herbert Baum"[4] (with only minor changes). Schmidt's book was criticized as "popular-scientific" because of the "extensive subjective coloring" present in the sources.[5]

Charlotte and Richard Holzer referred to this text and provided only "supplementary details" pertaining to their own respective roles in resistance in "Protokoll über Erinnerungen der Genossen Charlotte und Richard Holzer über ihre Tätigkeit in der Herbert-Baum-Gruppe in Berlin 1939–1942." That text was written for the historian Margot Pikarski, who—in 1968—published a portrait of the Baum Group under the title *Sie bleiben unvergessen*.[6]

The concluding sentences in the report of 1956/1958 on the Herbert Baum Group state, "All fighters in this resistance group, faithful to their convictions, stood with pride and dignity accused in the dock before the fascist court. Fellow prisoners report that in response to their final request before their execution, the doors of their cells were opened, so that they could see each other once more and could sing together their songs. They died as heroes."[7]

Irene Runge quoted Charlotte Holzer at length in an article on a visit with her in 1979, published in *Sonntag*, the weekly of the

---

4   Walter A. Schmidt, *Damit Deutschland lebe. Ein Quellenwerk über den deutschen antifaschistischen Widerstandskampf, 1933–1945* (Berlin: Kongress-Verlag, 1958), pp. 375–378.

5   On that criticism, see Simone Barck, *Antifa-Geschichte(n). Eine literarische Spurensuche in der DDR der 1950er und 1960er Jahre* (Cologne, Weimar, and Vienna: Böhlau, 2003), pp. 151, 153.

6   Margot Pikarski, *Sie bleiben unvergessen, Schriftenreihe zur Geschichte der FDJ*, 10 (Berlin: Verlag Junge Welt, 1968).

7   See "Bericht über eine Besprechung mit Frau Charlotte Holzer," YVA O.1/298, p. 4; Schmidt, *Damit Deutschland lebe*, pp. 377–378.

GDR Cultural Alliance. Its title was a quote from the conversation that indicated a different view: "I don't like the word hero."[8]

The story of Charlotte Holzer's life wasn't told only by her, as Michael Kreutzer writes in his historical study of the resistance groups around Herbert Baum. It was not only her who "narrated the story of her survival time and again, and tried to draw conclusions for herself and others."[9] Rather, even before historians became interested in the resistance group of Herbert Baum and the arson attack on the Nazi exhibition, SED functionaries had also written *their* story of Charlotte Holzer. A 1952 report on Charlotte and Richard Holzer stated that, "Charlotte Holzer previously did not tell the party the truth about her past. Only after an extended admonition did she admit to having incriminated comrades to the Gestapo. To date she has not revealed the full truth about the extent of her activity for the Gestapo [sic]."[10] As part of this alleged "truth," established by treating Gestapo files as objective and factual, it was claimed that "In her interrogation by the Gestapo, she provided extensive details about Jewish anti-fascists who were arrested and almost all perished."[11] The investigators then conclude that "Charlotte Holzer was assigned the task to join the SED by the agencies of the enemy."[12]

This conclusion is the only thing absent in a historic nonfiction book that praises the Central Party Control Commission (CPCC) of

---

8   Irene Runge, "'Das Wort Held mag ich nicht'. Nach einem Gespräch mit der Antifaschistin Charlotte Holzer aufgezeichnet," *Sonntag*, 36 (1979), p. 7.

9   Michael Kreutzer, "Die Suche nach einem Ausweg, der es ermöglicht, in Deutschland als Mensch zu leben. Zur Geschichte der Widerstandsgruppen um Herbert Baum," in Wilfried Löhken and Werner Vathke, eds., *Juden im Widerstand. Drei Gruppen zwischen Überlebenskampf und politischer Aktion 1939–1945* (Berlin: Edition Hentrich, 1993), p. 147.

10   "Ergebnis der Überprüfung der Eheleute Charlotte und Richard Holzer," Bundesarchiv, Stiftung Archiv der Parteien und Massenorganisationen der DDR (BA-SAPMO), RY 1/I 2/3/162, fol. 96, p. 3.

11   "Ergebnis der Überprüfung der Eheleute Charlotte und Richard Holzer," BA-SAPMO, RY 1/I 2/3/162, fol. 96, p. 2.

12   "Ergebnis der Überprüfung der Eheleute Charlotte und Richard Holzer," BA-SAPMO, RY 1/I 2/3/162, fol. 96, pp. 2–3.

the SED for its "ability to detect inconsistencies" in Charlotte Holzer's handwritten party files, which include a "resume" dated July 4, 1945, a "report," dated April 29, 1952, a "declaration," dated April 30, 1952, and an "amendment" of May 2, 1952.[13] In evaluating the self-incriminations without taking into account the method of blackmail explicitly aimed at unmasking the "agent," author Regina Scheer adopted the suspicions regarding Lotte Holzer as her own, embedding these in her discourse. The upshot is that the reader seemingly perceives Charlotte Holzer through the ears and perspective of a member of the Herbert Baum Group when the text notes: "He grew numb when he heard the voice."[14]

What this fictionalization hopes to achieve becomes clear when the author imagines herself transposed in the body of her mother along with the deceased Edith Fraenkel, as a witness of Herbert Baum's burial in the Jewish cemetery in Berlin-Weißensee on the memorial day for victims of fascism in 1949. There, the fictional Edith Fraenkel stands "amongst the fellow students of my young mother, not wearing the shirt of the Free German Youth, but likewise not present up in the official gallery next to Richard and Lotte."[15] In the belated introduction of "Charlotte Holzer," the author states that. "Charlotte Holzer, as was her name after the war, was a well-known anti-fascist often interviewed by party historians."[16] In the first mention of Lotte Holzer in a conversation with Ilse Stillmann, reference is to "the former Lotte Paech, [I have] only known her from the GDR."[17]

Scheer's manipulation, the way in which she turns the "truth" as it is reported by the CPCC into a moral unmasking of the official anti-fascism of the GDR, and then portrays Charlotte Holzer as the representative of that kind of anti-fascism—stands in stark contrast with another fictionalization of Holzer's story that appeared in the year of the honoring of Herbert Baum: Elfriede Brüning's novel

13 Regina Scheer, *Im Schatten der Sterne. Eine jüdische Widerstandsgruppe* (Berlin: Aufbau, 2004), p. 421.
14 Ibid., p. 385.
15 Ibid., p. 142.
16 Ibid., p. 120.
17 Ibid., p. 33.

...*damit du weiterlebst*,[18] which the director of the publishing house of the Association of Persecutees of the Nazi Regime (VVN) declared in 1952 to be "valuable resistance literature." It was a novel "containing poetic renderings of the theme of resistance extending far beyond pure documentation,"[19] and it remained in print until the demise of the GDR, boasting sales of some 150,000 copies.[20]

Brüning interviewed Frieda Coppi in 1946, who provided her with the letters of Hans and Hilde Coppi, two members of the Schulze-Boysen/Harnack Organization, known as the Rote Kapelle,[21] as well as Charlotte Holzer, who told her "the adventurous story of her escape."[22] In the novel she retained the first names of the five central characters: Hans, Hilde, her son Hans born in detention, Lotte (Charlotte), and her daughter Eva. In 1970, Brüning commented in a new afterword, "Not only Hans and Hilde [...] Coppi are based on real life, but also the figure of Lotte Burkhardt and her daughter Eva [...], who belonged to the Jewish resistance group of Herbert Baum [...]. Likewise in her case, it was the desperate struggle which the mother waged for her child that touched me the most profoundly. In my book I interconnected the two resistance groups—that of Herbert Baum and the Schulze-Boysen-Harnack Organization—in terms of the action, as the conception of the novel demanded."[23]

18 Elfriede Brüning, ...*damit du weiterlebst*. (Berlin: Neues Leben, 1949; Berlin, Potsdam: VVN, 1949).

19 Simone Barck et al., eds., *"Jedes Buch ein Abenteuer"*. *Zensur-System und literarische Öffentlichkeiten in der DDR bis Ende der sechziger Jahre* (Berlin: Akademie, 1997), p. 288.

20 See Monika Melchert, "Die Zeitgeschichtsprosa nach 1945 im Kontext der Schuldfrage," in Ursula Heukenkamp, ed., *Deutsche Erinnerung. Berliner Beiträge zur Prosa der Nachkriegsjahre (1945–1960)* (Berlin: Schmidt, 2000), p. 140; on its contemporary reception, see Elfriede Brüning, *"Ich mußte einfach schreiben, unbedingt..."* *Briefwechsel mit Zeitgenossen* (Essen: Klartext, 2008), pp. 14, 32, 40, 49.

21 See the revised edition of Elfriede Brüning, ...*damit du weiterlebst* (Halle/S. and Leipzig: MDV, 1978), pp. 241–243.

22 Ibid., p. 244.

23 Ibid.

On the level of the development of the action, a clear hierarchization of the two mothers emerges—the survivor among the mothers is placed in a lower status as the female martyr. In the final scene, the child Eva hesitantly transfers her reverence for the exemplary mother—the dead resistance fighter Hilde, who died while rescuing her child—onto her own mother, the surviving resistance fighter. The 1970 afterword closes by pointing out what "has become" of the child of Hans and Hilde, "He studied foreign trade. Recently he completed his service in the People's Army. His mother would be proud of him today."[24] However, this contemporary updating of the anti-fascist resistance as a legacy of the dead fulfilled in the GDR becomes especially questionable when Brüning continues, "And Eva Burkhardt, the child of the Jewish woman, whose harmonious development was disturbed as a result of the criminal racial fanaticism and who was driven to the very edge of depravation, Eva found the way back to her mom. Today she herself has two children whom she loves tenderly, and who for their part are strongly attached in tender love to their grandmother."[25] While in the case of Hans Steffen the documented name Coppi is mentioned, the corresponding surname for Eva Burkhardt—Holzer—is missing. Moreover, while there is mention of the relation between daughter and mother, and grandchildren and grandmother, the fact that while Charlotte Holzer was living in the GDR in 1970, her daughter had emigrated to Mandatory Palestine in 1947—one year before the State of Israel was declared—is concealed.

On the one hand, the novel proves that generalizing theses about the tabooing or marginalization of the persecution of the Jews in the literature of the Soviet Occupation Zone/GDR are untenable and indefensible.[26] On the other hand, however, it shows that the hierarchization of resistance over persecution—also institutionalized in

---

24 Ibid., p. 247.
25 Ibid., p. 248.
26 For a general discussion of this topic, see Bill Niven, *Das Buchenwaldkind. Wahrheit, Fiktion und Propaganda* (Bonn: Bundeszentrale für politische Bildung, 2009), pp. 205, 211; for a discussion relating to Brüning's novel, see Joanne Sayner, *Women without a Past? German Autobiographical Writings and Fascism* (Amsterdam and New York: Rodopi, 2007), pp. 277–279.

the official recognition as victims of fascism—could and necessarily did lead to the concealing of certain facts.

Charlotte Holzer's family-based relation to Israel led to her playing a role in connection with a resistance novel that was not only successful domestically, in the GDR, but internationally, namely Bruno Apitz's *Nackt unter Wölfen*, which in the first five years was translated into eighteen languages.[27] Now the novel's worldwide print-run in thirty languages is more than three million copies. At the showing of the DEFA film version of the novel in the framework of the Moscow Film Festival, a married couple living in Moscow recognized the story of the Jewish child rescued in the Dachau concentration camp the story as that of their nephew, Stefan-Jerzy Zweig, and of his father Zacharias, who lived in Israel at the time. Charlotte Holzer was contacted by the *BZ am Abend* (BZA), which had learned of this from the Film Festival journal, "A reader, Charlotte Holzer, who was planning a trip to this country, was engaged with the task, in the name of the editors, to continue the search for the Buchenwald child in Israel," the *Neue Berliner Illustrierte* (NBI) reported.[28] In the special issue of the BZA, there was no mention whatsoever of Charlotte Holzer's own story, "Stefan-Jerzy Zweig: Der große Bericht über das Buchenwaldkind." However, it did contain her report on the "dramatic encounter with the father, Dr. Zweig."[29] There she shared with readers of the BZA the "slight doubts" she had harbored before their first meeting, "There are in Israel many people who experienced fascism in Auschwitz or Buchenwald and whose families were exterminated by the Germans. They don't wish to hear and read the German language any more. They do not wish to be reminded of the horrific years of their former lives. Are the Zweigs also among these people?"[30]

---

27 The original German edition was Bruno Apitz, *Nackt unter Wölfen* (Halle and Leipzig: Mitteldeutscher Verlag, 1958), the first English edition under the title *Naked Among Wolves* was published by Seven Seas in East Berlin in 1960.

28 See *Neue Berliner Illustrierte* (NBI) 11/1964, p. 18.

29 See "Stefan-Jerzy Zweig: Der große Bericht über das Buchenwaldkind," *BZA* special issue (1964), p. 5.

30 Ibid.

Charlotte Holzer described the first encounter with Zacharias Zweig as a negation of such doubts: "It is still unclear to him what side of Germany I am coming from. He speaks full of emotion, excitedly: "There is one thing I want to tell you right away, whether you like it or not. The Buchenwald prisoners saved the life of my child, the international camp committee, and those were mainly German Communists."[31]

Fourteen pages in the special issue of the BZA were taken up by extracts from a text that Zacharias Zweig had written in January 1961 for Yad Vashem. They were first published in twenty-four installments between February 5 and 29, 1964, in the BZA.[32] In December 1963, immediately after her return from Israel, Charlotte Holzer had written to Yad Vashem together with Bruno Apitz in the name of the Committee of Anti-Fascist Resistance Fighters in the GDR and the Lagergemeinschaft Buchenwald (the association of former inmates of the Buchenwald concentration camp), with a request, "The lawyer Dr. Zweig has composed a documentary report on the fate of his son and about his own fate; it is in your possession. We would like to request that this report kindly be placed at our disposal for the purpose of our own documentation." The BZA published the report with a note by the editors noted stating that it had originally been submitted "to the documentation center of the State of Israel, which keeps a registry of the fascist crimes against the Jews." It described the report as "Ninety typewritten pages, which have the appearance of an ordinary office file, written in an almost unemotional tone. And yet—what a harrowing document. It is the official counterpart to Bruno Apitz's masterful fictional creation about the rescue of the Buchenwald child."[33]

Charlotte Holzer herself delivered her personal testimony in Yad Vashem on February 18, 1964[34]—going far beyond the "discussion"

31 Ibid.
32 The way the text was abridged and the intention behind it is discussed in Niven, *Das Buchenwaldkind*, pp. 187–194.
33 "Ein Kind unter Wölfen. Aus dem amtlichen Bericht des Dr. Zacharias Zweig," *BZA* special issue (1964), p. 18.
34 See the testimony, given by Charlotte Holzer in Yad Vashem, February 18, 1964, YVA, O.3/3096.

she had conducted with Kurt Jakob Ball-Kaduri at the end of her visit to Israel in November 1963 about the arson attack on the "Soviet Paradise." And she told her story in the taped discussion with Dieter Heimlich from May 1966 to July 1967.

A second track leads from Zacharias Zweig's statements at Yad Vashem to Charlotte Holzer's testimony. Her interlocutor, Dieter Heimlich, was a journalist on staff at the *Neue Berliner Illustrierte* (NBI). Since 1963, this magazine has been actively engaged with promoting new journalistic talent, inter alia by means of a course led by Jean Villain on reporting, in which, for example, the author Klaus Schlesinger had become aware of "chronicles, diaries, and reports, on the Warsaw Ghetto Uprising" and had tried to write about this: "where [...] then does our current situation, politically and socially, derive from, if not from the past? Isn't everything that came 'thereafter' a reaction to the past?"[35]

"Schlesinger's most important reportage by far in the course" was later described by the course director as his "devastating report on the Jewish Cemetery in Weißensee." "And this by no means only because, as far as I know, we were the first to dare to deal with this difficult topic."[36] Villain's concept of the course sprang from the notion that readers had a need for "undoctored, unadorned biographies."[37]

When the BZA published parts of Zacharias Zweig's testimony, the NBI came out with a summary under a heading "Contents of the Testimony," which Yad Vashem staff member Mata Hollender had written.[38] In that same and in subsequent issues of the NBI, photos were published that the photographer Barbara Meffert, then the wife of Dieter Heimlich, had made during Jerzy Zweig's visit to Buchenwald

---

35   Jean Villain, *Bitte nicht stören! Wie der DDR "Profil" abhanden kam und weitere Zeitungsmacher-Geschichten aus Deutsch-Fernost* (Rostock: MV Taschenbuch, 2004), p. 23. On Schlesinger's "Michael" see Jan Kostka, *Das journalistische und literarische Werk von Klaus Schlesinger 1960 bis 1980. Kontext, Entstehung und Rezeption* (Berlin: be.bra wissenschaft verlag, 2015), pp. 173–221.

36   Ibid., p. 30.

37   Jean Villain, *Plädoyer für Aschenbrödel. Über Reportagen und Reporter* (Halle: Mitteldeutscher Verlag, 1978), p. 209.

38   See *NBI* 10/1964, pp. 24–25.

and Weimar, and also one photo with Charlotte Holzer,[39] about which the Free German Youth paper *Junge Welt* wrote: "Comrade Holzer, who is sitting next to Jerzy, attentively follows our conversation. He calls her 'mother,' because she was the person who brought him together with his protectors."[40]

In 1982, the department in charge of memoirs at the Central Party Archive at the Institute for Marxism-Leninism of the Central Committee of the SED evaluated the typescript of the Heimlich interview. The Röderberg-Verlag, the publishing house of the VVN, with its main office in Frankfurt/Main in West Germany, had forwarded it via the Dietz-Verlag to the SED. "It is obvious that publication is out of the question," concluded Ilse Sch. already beforehand in her letter, requesting Margot Pikarski to provide an expert opinion on the text.[41]

The justification that the historian Kurt Gossweiler gives in his comments on the memoirs of Charlotte Holzer[42] prompted Margot Pikarski to ask "whether we aren't perhaps obligated, also posthumously so to speak, to inform the CPCC. Because the details that Kurt here has brought to light, when read in such conciseness, are even more outrageous than when you explain all that in general terms."[43] The details that Gossweiler enumerated amounted to the following: "A publication would, by the way not only be irresponsible because the party, its struggle, and desire—including the Herbert Baum Group—is vilified; Ch. H. also presents a picture of herself that would deeply disappoint all comrades and friends who recall her in positive memory, and would cause them in retrospect to turn their backs on her."[44]

---

39 *NBI* 11/1964, p. 18.
40 *Junge Welt*, February 11, 1964.
41 Letter from Ilse Sch. to Margot Pikarski, May 11, 1982, BA-SAPMO, SgY 30/2014/1, fol. 367.
42 Kurt Gossweiler, "Bemerkungen zu den Erinnerungen von Charlotte Holzer," BA-SAPMO, SgY 30/2014/1, fol. 351.
43 Letter from Margot Pikarsky to Ilse Sch., September 29, 1982, BA-SAPMO, SgY 30/2014/1, fol. 343.
44 Kurt Gossweiler, "Bemerkungen zu den Erinnerungen von Charlotte Holzer," BA-SAPMO, SgY 30/2014/1, fol. 351.

The necessity to take into consideration Charlotte Holzer's reputation was also echoed in the final "advisory opinion on the manuscript in the Röderberg-Verlag" by the department for memoirs, "The publication would greatly damage the reputation of the comrade and above all of the party."[45] The refusal to publish was designed to preserve an official image of the resistance fighter as had been set out two years before in the death notice issued by the Committee of Anti-Fascist Resistance Fighters in Berlin-Pankow, "Condemned to death by the fascists, escaped from the executioners, she fought up to her final breath for our cause." The department for memoirs came to the final judgment on Lotte Holzer's memoirs, "The manuscript is replete with inaccuracies, politically incorrect assessments, private, intimate details about the author and other comrades. [...] On the whole, this is an excessively emotional, politically immature, naive portrayal."[46] Gossweiler's expert opinion also pointed to the fusing of the private and the political, even if in closing he acknowledged that "this manuscript contains passages that are not only instructive but devastating."[47] He also made reference there to the "description of her own fate and that of many others, above all Jews, under fascism" and remarked, "What comes alive here in a multitude of episodes is the sheer incomprehensible barbarism of fascism, the unimaginable horrific everyday life above all of the Jewish population under fascism."[48] Yet this qualification did not change anything in the final judgment, "But you can't cut anything out in the memoirs. The good and bad are inextricably interwoven."[49]

The fact that the text of 1966/1967 was also not deemed publishable in the eyes of the SED in 1982 derives from the particular way in which Charlotte Holzer told the tale of her survival: corresponding to her candor in relating personal matters was the shifting vantage point from which political differences of opinion

---

45 "Stellungnahme zum Manuskript im Röderberg-Verlag," BA-SAPMO, SgY 30/2014/1, fol. 365

46 Ibid.

47 Gossweiler, "Bemerkungen zu den Erinnerungen von Charlotte Holzer," BA-SAPMO, SgY 30/2014/1, fol. 363.

48 Ibid., fol. 348.

49 Ibid., fol. 363.

are described. Thus, she commented, on the one hand, that she was "arrested with a copy of Freud's [*An Outline of*] *Psychoanalysis*" and how its repeated reading had "proved a great help" while in detention. On the other hand, she placed stress on the differing positions within the resistance group when it came to the attack on the anti-Soviet exhibition. The spectrum of persons whom she encountered suffering persecution is correspondingly broad, encompassing Jews and non-Jews, and members of different, and by no means only Communist resistance groups, such as Max Fürst and other former members of the Schwarzer Haufen, members of the Schulze-Boysen/Harnack Group and Harald Poelchau.[50]

Richard Holzer, ca. 1970, and Charlotte Holzer before her passing, March 1980.

50 Harald Poelchau was a prison chaplain who was connected to the underground resistance against Nazism, namely to the Kreisauer Kreis and the July 1944 attempt to overthrow Hitler. In early 1945, he also saved the lives of two Jews who had escaped from Gestapo custody and hid them in his apartment until the end of the war. He was declared a Righteous Among the Nations by Yad Vashem on November 30, 1971.

The honorary grave of Herbert Baum, a memorial stone for the murdered
members of the Baum Group, and the grave of Charlotte and Richard
Holzer, at Weissensee Jewish Cemetery in Berlin.

BIOGRAPHICAL ENTRIES

by Wolf Kaiser

This list contains supplementary data on important persons mentioned in Charlotte Holzer's memoirs. Not included are individuals especially well-known internationally, persons whose biographies contain no information that might contribute to a better understanding of the text and Charlotte's life world, as well as persons for whom it was impossible to find sufficient biographical data. Names in parentheses, which were presumably code names or nicknames, are citations from the text.

Abegg, Dr. Elisabeth (1882–1974), German educator and savior of Jews during the Nazi period. Born into a military family, she was one of the first women to obtain a university degree. Abegg earned a PhD in history and taught from 1923 at the *Luisen-Oberlyceum* (Luisen Girls' High School). She made no secret of her opposition to Nazi ideology, and was punitively transferred to another school in 1935, after persisting in teaching humanitarian and democratic values. In 1941, she was forced into premature retirement. When the deportations of Jews to the ghettos and camps in the East started, Abegg assisted Jews who wanted to go underground. She offered shelter and organized hiding places with other people. On May 23, 1967, Yad Vashem bestowed the title "Righteous Among the Nations" on Elisabeth Abegg. She passed away in Berlin in 1974, age 92.

Abraham, Margarete, née Döblin (1886–1943), Charlotte Holzer's mother; trained as a milliner, later as a nurse's helper. She was deported March 12, 1943, to Auschwitz and probably murdered there.

Abraham, Max (1872–?), Charlotte Holzer's father, a merchant. According to Charlotte, he immigrated to Argentina and died there of starvation.

Abraham, Rose Augusta (Gustchen), later Augusta Noher (b. 1908), Charlotte Holzer's sister.

Abrahamson, Günther (b. 1920, presumably died in the 1990s), employed by the Jewish community of Berlin as a sports teacher and educator. From 1941, he worked as a steward of the Jewish community in connection with deportations, assigned from 1942 to the *Sammellager* (transit camp) at Grosse Hamburger Strasse. He was active with the Gestapo in tracking down Jews who had gone into hiding, but warned victims of persecution in some cases, and for that reason shortly before the war's end was imprisoned in the "bunker" of the camp. After legal proceedings extending over five years, he was given a five-month prison sentence for crimes against humanity and was accorded an amnesty and released a short time later. He earned his doctorate in architecture in 1957.

Adler, Rosa, née Fürst (1907–?), younger sister of Edith and Max Fürst; educator, worked in the *Kinderheim* (children's care home) of her sister Edith. In 1939, she immigrated together with her husband Siegfried to Bolivia, and in 1950 returned to the GDR.

Adler, Siegfried (husband of Rosa Adler), from 1928 editor of the communist *Ruhr Echo* newspaper in Essen, 1933–1934 imprisoned in the Börgermoor concentration camp near Papenburg. He later worked in the children's home of Edith Fürst as a janitor and cook; immigration in 1939 to Bolivia, return 1950 to the GDR.

Ansbach, Herbert (1913–1988), journalist, member of the Communist Youth Association and the German Communist Party (KPD), from 1934 cooperation with Herbert Baum and Werner Steinbrink; arrested in 1935 and sentenced to two and a half years in prison. He immigrated in 1938 via Czechoslovakia to Great Britain; from 1939, was interned in Australia. In the period 1975–1988, he headed the "Working Group Herbert Baum" at the District Committee Berlin of the Committee of Anti-Fascist Resistance Fighters in the GDR.

Arnould, Rita (1914–1943), courier and radio operator of the Rote Kapelle (Red Orchestra) resistance group in Belgium; arrested in December 1941 in Brussels and long detained in the Moabit court prison; sentenced to death by the People's Court and executed on August 20, 1943.

Bahnmüller, Dora (Dorle), née Marcuse (1901–1945? [or earlier]), kindergarten teacher, director of the children's home Ahawah in Berlin; a member of the Herbert Baum Group. She was arrested on November 30, 1942, subsequently deported, presumably to Auschwitz, and murdered there.

Baum, Bruno (1910–1971), electrician, engineer, functionary in the Communist Youth League and the Alliance of Red Front Fighters; arrested in 1935, together with Erich Honecker, and sentenced to ten years imprisonment for high treason in 1937. He was transferred in 1943 from Brandenburg-Görden prison to Auschwitz, and later liberated in the Mauthausen concentration camp. In 1949, he wrote a book about his ordeal, titled *Widerstand in Auschwitz. Bericht der Internationalen Lagerleitung* (Resistance in Auschwitz. Report of the International Camp Direction) (Berlin and Potsdam: VVN, 1949).

Baum, Herbert (1912–1942), electrician, active as a youth in the Rote Falken (Red Falcons) and the German–Jewish Community (DJG); from 1931 member in Berlin of the Communist Youth League and the German Communist Party. He was at the center of a circle of friends whose members distributed anti-fascist leaflets, sent letters to soldiers, listened to foreign radio stations, and conducted political education courses. From 1940, he was in conscript forced labor at Siemens; arrested after the the May 18, 1942, arson attack on the national socialist propaganda exhibition "The Soviet Paradise." Herbert Baum died in custody on June 11, 1942, probably by suicide or from the consequences of brutal torture.

Baum, Marianne, née Cohn (1912–1942), children's nurse, worker, member of the Communist Youth League and the German Communist Party. She met Herbert Baum in 1928, and they married in the mid-1930s; executed on August 18, 1942.

Bebel, August (1840–1913), influential politician, in 1869 he founded (together with Wilhelm Liebknecht) the Social Democratic Workers' Party (SDAP), which later became the SPD. His book *Die Frau und der Sozialismus* (Zurich: Verlag der Volksbuchhandlung, 1879), in which he called for professional and political equality for women, found exceptionally widespread distribution and interest.

Behrens, Margarete (1888–1961), social democratic educational reformist; appointed as director of the *Luisen Oberlyzeum* in the early 1920s against conservative resistance; she sought to create a more liberal climate there. Under her direction, educators such as Elisabeth Schmitz and Elisabeth Abegg taught at the school, teachers who later also became rescuers of persons in danger.

Benjamin, Dr. Georg (1895–1942), brother of the philosopher Walter Benjamin, physician, member of the German Communist Party, municipal school physician in the Berlin-Wedding district. In 1933, he was detained in Sonnenburg concentration camp; in 1936, convicted of high treason and sentenced to six years imprisonment. He was transferred from Brandenburg prison to the Mauthausen concentration camp, where he died on August 26, 1942. See Bernd-Peter Lange, *Georg Benjamin. Ein bürgerlicher Revolutionär im roten Wedding* (Berlin: Walter Frey, 2019); Uwe-Karsten Heye, *Die Benjamins. Eine deutsche Familie* (Berlin: Aufbau-Verlag, 2014).

Benjamin, Hilde, née Lange (1902–1989), wife of Georg Benjamin, lawyer, politician, from 1927 member of the German Communist Party. In 1933, she was banned from professional practice, from 1939 conscripted as a worker in the clothing industry. From 1947 to 1949 head of the personnel department in judicial administration of the GDR, responsible for the cleansing of the judicial system in favor of "people's judges." In the period 1949–1953, she served as vice president of the GDR's supreme court, in this role bearing chief responsibility for a series of show trials against purported "enemies of the state" and saboteurs; she handed down death sentences and long sentences of imprisonment. From 1953 to 1967 GDR minister of justice; 1954–1989 member of the Central Committee of the SED party. In the 1950s and 1960s, she had principal responsibility for changes in legislation on the equality of women and for the reform of the criminal justice system in regard to homosexuality and abortion. In 1967, Hilde Benjamin resigned from her post as minister for "reasons of health." In 1977, she published *Georg Benjamin. Eine Biographie* (Leipzig: S. Hirzel, 1977). See also Uwe-Karsten Heye, *Die Benjamins. Eine deutsche Familie* (Berlin: Aufbau-Verlag, 2014).

Benjamin, Michael (Micha, Mischa) (1932–2000), son of Georg und Hilde Benjamin, professor of jurisprudence, and politician. From 1990, he was centrally active in the newly created Partei des demokratischen Sozialismus (PDS).

Berkowitz, Liane (1923–1943), student in Berlin, member of the Schulze-Boysen resistance group. She protested on May 17, 1942, with a sticker campaign, against the propaganda exhibition "The Soviet Paradise." Liane Berkowitz was arrested, together with other members of the group, in September 1942. The pregnant Berkowitz was sentenced to death in January 1943 and had to give birth to her daughter Irene in prison in April. Her fate was sealed when Hitler personally refused to allow a pardon of the young mother despite a recommendation of the court to do so. Liane Berkowitz was executed on August 5, 1943.

Bernhard, Dr. Hans (Henschel) (1899–1969), dismissed from his post at the Municipal Hospital "am Urban" in 1933; assistant doctor 1934–1939 at the Jewish Hospital Berlin; subsequently immigrated to the United States.

Birnbaum, Heinz (Buber, Bobby) (1920–1943), lathe operator, partner of Irene Walther, belonged to the Herbert Baum Group; arrested in June 1942, sentenced to death in December 1942, and executed on March 4, 1943.

Bode, Cäcilie (Cilly) (1907–1971), payroll clerk, life companion of Joseph (Beppo) Römer. Arrested and charged with activity in the resistance in February 1942, imprisoned in the jails at Alexanderplatz and on Lehrter Strasse, and from December 1, 1942, to April 13, 1943, in the "Women's Reeducation Camp" Fehrbellin. Subsequently transferred to the Ravensbrück concentration camp. Sentenced to five years imprisonment on June 19, 1944. After establishment of the GDR, active until 1959 in the State Secretariat for Vocational and Tertiary Education.

Bolz, Kurt (1908–1985), an artist who, in 1935, was banned from practicing his profession because he was classified as Jewish. From 1936, successive, temporary stays in several countries, in some illegally. Bolz married and divorced several times. In March 1943, after serving time in jail for extortion, was expelled from Denmark to Germany. In April 1943, placed on a deportation train to Auschwitz, but managed to flee. Subsequently recaptured and imprisoned in the Grosse Hamburger Strasse transit camp. After further unsuccessful attempts to escape, he cooperated with the Gestapo as a *Greifer* (catcher) in tracking down Jews in hiding. He disappeared from the transit camp shortly before the war's end, reaching Copenhagen with the aid of the Swedish Church.

Detained in Denmark, he escaped from a Danish camp to Sweden in 1946. Filed a claim for reparation in Berlin in 1957.

Brockdorff, Erika Gräfin von, née Schönfeld (1911–1943), an office worker. She made her apartment available to Hans Coppi, who belonged to the circle around Libertas and Harro Schulze-Boysen, for sending and receiving radio messages. Arrested in September 1942 and sentenced to ten years imprisonment in December; after an intervention by Hitler resentenced to death and executed on May 13, 1943.

Budzislawski, Herbert (Butz) (1920–1943), locksmith, a member of the Herbert Baum Group; arrested on November 13, 1942, sentenced to death on June 29, 1943, and executed September 7, 1943.

Charlotte, see Hannover, Sophie Charlotte von.

Cohen, Dr. Helmuth, internist; he was an assistant doctor in the Department of Internal Medicine at the Jewish Hospital and took over as head of the department when its director was deported at the end of July 1942. After the war until 1949, he served as director of the Jewish Hospital, and in 1949 immigrated to the United States.

Cohn, Lothar (1908–1944, brother of Marianne Baum), worker, garment maker, member of the Communist Youth League. He belonged to the Herbert Baum Group and the Hans Fruck Group; arrested in January 1944 and shot to death shortly after, on January 21, in the Sachsenhausen concentration camp.

Cühn, Harry (1913–1994), partner of Edith Fraenkel, father of her son Uri, who was born in 1941 and died after just six months, friend of Berta Waterstradt. He was politically active in an organization already before 1933; took part in meetings of the Herbert Baum Group, survived by hiding his real identity, living in illegality.

Deutschkron, Hans (1902–?), Charlotte's first love. Arrested in 1938 and imprisoned in Sachsenhausen, released in December of that year. Subsequently immigrated to the United Kingdom where he was registered in the Kitchener Refugee Camp. Became an economist.

Dobberke, Walter (1906–1946), *Kriminalobersekretär* (a junior officer rank) in the criminal police, from 1941 an employee of the *Judenreferat* (Jewish Affairs Department) of the regional Gestapo headquarters in Berlin, and from spring 1943 in charge of the transit camp at Grosse Hamburger Strasse. After the war he was tracked down by a survivor and handed over to the Soviet occupation authorities; he died in the Soviet detention camp Posen.

Döblin, Alfred (1878–1957), writer; well known inter alia for his works *Wallenstein* and *Berlin Alexanderplatz*. Alfred Döblin's father was a master tailor and a cousin of Charlotte Holzer's maternal grandfather.

Drach, Anna (1887–?), mother of Hans Eduard, Thomas, and Rosa; arrested in 1933 for possession of leaflets critical of the regime, she spent four months in prison. Anna became a nurse, thereafter, working in the Jewish Hospital and the Jewish Nursing Home. She went into hiding in connection with the *Fabrikaktion* (Factory Operation) mass roundup of Jews in March 1943. Apprehended in November 1943, she was incarcerated in the transit camp at Grosse Hamburger Strasse but managed to escape while part of a work detail sent to clean out the ruins of a bombed building. Anna survived the rest of the war in hiding and was reunited with her daughter Rosa in England in the late 1940s.

Drach, Hans Eduard (1914–1941), son of Anna Bertha (Anja) Drach; actor, immigrated to the Soviet Union after the Nazis took power, where in 1935, he wrote the lyrics to the song *Mein Vater wird gesucht* (My Father Is Wanted) about the persecution and murder of his father at the hands of the SA. He was arrested in 1936 in the Soviet Union and handed over to the German authorities in 1939, after the signing of the Hitler-Stalin Pact. Transported from one concentration camp to another, he was sent in October 1941 from the Sachsenhausen concentration camp to the Niederhagen concentration camp, where he perished on December 10, 1941, under unknown circumstances.

Drach, Thomas (Gideon) (1916–1990), brother of Hans, immigrated in 1933 to Lithuania, and in 1936 to the Netherlands. After the German occupation of the Netherlands, he joined the resistance group Westerweel. In 1944, he was arrested by the Gestapo and interned in the Westerbork transit camp. He escaped but was apprehended again in early 1945 and brought back to Westerbork, where he remained until liberation. In 1947, Drach immigrated with his wife to Mandatory Palestine. He died in Israel in 1990.

Drach, Rosa (1912–2017), sister of Thomas and Hans Eduard. Rosa was arrested already in 1933 because of a leaflet campaign, charged with "conspiracy to commit treason," and incarcerated for twenty-two months in the Moabit and Barnimstrasse prisons. She subsequently left Germany and immigrated to England, where she worked as a nurse. Rosa Drach died in 2017, aged 105.

Dubinsky, Jutta, née Jegeth (1917–1985), stenographer, economist, member of the Communist Youth League; married to Victor Dubinsky. She belonged to the circle around Libertas and Harro Schulze-Boysen. She was among the founders of the Hochschule für Ökonomie (University of Economics) of the GDR in Berlin.

Feldmann, Vera (Püppe) (1925–1943), small child that Charlotte took care of in the infants' nursery. According to the *Book of Remembrance* of the German Federal Archives, Vera was taken on February 17, 1943, to Grosse Hamburger Strasse transit camp and deported on February 26 to Auschwitz. There is no record of her entering the camp as a prisoner, so she was likely murdered shortly after arrival.

Figner, Vera (1852–1943), Russian revolutionary socialist, led the organization Narodnya Volya (Will of the People), which aimed to overthrow the tsarist monarchy by terrorist action. She spent many years in tsarist Russian prisons. Her memoirs, published in English translation as *Memoirs of a Revolutionist* (DeKalb/IL: NIU Press, 1991 [most recent edition]) became famous worldwide. See also Lynne Ann Hartnett, *The Defiant Life of Vera Figner: Surviving the Russian Revolution* (Bloomington: Indiana University Press, 2014).

Fox, Erich (1900–1969), toolmaker, member of the KPD, a leading worker in the Berliner Verkehrsbetriebe (Berlin Public Transport Company), significantly involved in organizing the 1932 Berlin Transport Strike. In November 1934, sentenced to two years and three months in prison for participating in communist resistance.

Fraenkel, Edith (1922–1944), worker, belonged to the Herbert Baum Group. She was transported on October 15, 1943, to Theresienstadt; deported on October 16, 1944, to Auschwitz and murdered there.

Franke, Joachim (1905–1942), engineer, worked at Kabelwerke Oberspree (Cable Works Upper Spree), a member of the German Communist Party since 1932. Together with Werner Steinbrink, Franke headed a resistance group, and along with Steinbrink and Herbert Baum they placed the incendiary devices in the arson attack on the "Soviet Paradise" exhibition. Allegedly revealed numerous names during his interrogation by the Gestapo in order to rescue his wife and child. His wife Erika Franke was likewise arrested but was pronounced not guilty on April 19, 1943. Joachim Franke was already executed on August 18, 1942.

Freud, Sigmund (1856–1939), founder of psychoanalysis; his central work *Über Psychoanalyse. Fünf Vorlesungen* was published in 1910, *Abriss der Psychoanalyse* in 1938; Freud immigrated with his wife and daughter in June 1938 to England; his four sisters who remained in Vienna were murdered by the Nazis.

Fruck, Hans (1911–1990), member of the KPD, had contacts with the Herbert Baum Group. He was sentenced to five years imprisonment in 1943 for resistance activities. From 1945 a member of the criminal police in the Soviet sector of Berlin, from 1953 to 1977 major general in the Ministry of State Security, GDR.

Fürst, Edith (1904–1997), the older sister of Max Fürst; director of an infant's nursery and children's care home in Pankow, which she managed together with her sister Rosa. She had to close it down in September 1938. Subsequently she was active in the children's home Ahawah. She subsequently went into hiding, was tracked down in 1944, and imprisoned in the Ravensbrück concentration camp until liberation.

Fürst, Max (1905–1978), cabinetmaker and writer, member of the German–Jewish youth group Kameraden (Comrades) in Königsberg. Together with Hans Litten one of the founders of the left-socialist youth group Schwarzer Haufen (Black Bunch). He relocated in 1925 to Berlin; 1933/34 detained in Oranienburg concentration camp. In 1935, he immigrated to Mandatory Palestine, then returned to Germany in 1950. In 1973, he published *Gefilte Fisch. Eine Jugend in Königsberg*, in 1976 *Talisman Scheherezade. Die schwierigen zwanziger Jahre*. His last book *Gefilte Fisch und wie es weiterging* was published posthumously in 2004.

Götze, Ursula (Ursel) (1916–1943), participated already as a schoolgirl in resistance operations of the Communist Youth League, held contact with the circle around Libertas and Harro Schulze-Boysen. Together with her friend, the Romance philologist Werner Krauss, took part in a sticker campaign against the propaganda exhibition "The Soviet Paradise." Arrested in October 1942, sentenced to death in January 1943, and executed on August 5, 1943.

Gogoll, Fritz (1909–?), police officer, low-ranking member of Department IVD1 (Jewish Affairs) of the Berlin Gestapo. Rarely mentioned in postwar witness testimonies, he ostensibly was relatively rarely present in the assembly camps. The available testimonies are contradictory in their characterization of Gogoll. In some, he appears as a compassionate person who would occasionally provide information or help to Jews, in others as someone who participated in brutal abuse.

Goldschlag, Gerhard (1889–1944), father of Stella Kübler-Isaaksohn, journalist, musical conductor, pianist, and composer. Deported in February 1944 to Theresienstadt and, in October 1944, deported onwards to Auschwitz, where he was murdered.

Goldstein, Bruno ("tall Goldstein") (1894–?), merchant, municipal official, in 1935 forcibly retired due to the "Law for the Restoration of the Professional Civil Service"; employee of the Jewish community; from the end of 1942 head of one of the two groups of Jewish orderlies in the Grosse Hamburger Strasse transit camp. He ruthlessly implemented the orders of the Gestapo and from 1944 also supported their search and manhunt operations. On July 20, 1944, he was transported to Bergen-Belsen concentration camp together with his family for a planned swap with ethnic Germans from Mandatory Palestine. From there he was sent to Theresienstadt but was liberated underway. Sentenced to seven years imprisonment in 1949, he was released from prison in 1951 due to a severe illness.

Goldstein ("short Goldstein"), worked as an orderly in Grosse Hamburger Strasse transit camp.

Goldstein, Rudolf (Rudi) (1908–after 1990), pediatrician and pathologist, dismissed in from the Moabit Hospital, he worked in pathology in the Jewish Hospital; friend of Charlotte Holzer. He immigrated in 1944 to Mandatory Palestine.

Haak, Ilse, née Lewin, later Stillmann (1911–1988), editor; member of the youth group Schwarzer Haufen (black bunch), then joined the Communist Youth League and the KPD. In 1933 she entered a short-lived sham marriage with a non-Jew named Haak in order to be able to drop her Jewish last name. She had contact with Richard Holzer. From September 1940 conscripted into forced labor at Siemens in the same "section for Jews" there as Herbert and Marianne Baum.

She went into hiding shortly before the *Fabrikaktion* mass roundup of Jews in March 1943 and survived in hiding. In the years 1945–1949, she was active as a worker in the Hauptausschuss für die Opfer des Faschismus (Main Committee for the Victims of Fascism); married to Günter Stillmann.

Hannover, Sophie Charlotte von (1668–1705), Duchess of Brunswick-Lüneburg, nicknamed "Figuelotte" by her family, married Frederick of Hohenzollern and became the Queen of Prussia when her husband ascended to the throne in 1701. The mother of the "soldier king" Friedrich Wilhelm I., she was known for her unusually high level of education and her friendships with some of the leading scientists of the time, particularly with Leibniz, together with whom she successfully advocated for the establishment of the internationally renowned Prussian Academy of Sciences.

Harder, Minna, née Cohn (1886–?), communist from a Jewish background; arrested on October 27, 1942, sentenced in March 1943 to five years imprisonment.

Harnack, Elisabet von (1892–1976), cousin of Arvid Harnack and daughter of the theologian Adolf von Harnack. She earned her doctorate with a thesis on care for school-age children in day nurseries. She was a member of the Bekennende Kirche (Confessing Church) and had a leading position in inner mission work. Harnack assisted persecuted Jews. After the war she became one of the most important persons in social work in Berlin and West Germany. Her older brother Ernst von Harnack was tried and sentenced to death for his participation in the July 20 resistance plot and executed on March 5, 1945. See Manfred Berger, "Harnack, Elisabet von," in Hugo Maier, ed., *Who is who der sozialen Arbeit* (Freiburg im Breisgau: Lambertus, 1998), pp. 229–230.

Harnack, Mildred, née Fish (1902–1943), an American scholar. She lived from 1929 with her husband Arvid Harnack in Berlin; in 1941, she earned her doctorate at Giessen University with a thesis on

American literature. Engaged in resistance activities with groups in the Rote Kapelle spectrum, she was arrested and initially sentenced to six years imprisonment, subsequently changed to a death sentence. She was executed, together with her husband, on February 16, 1943. Her book *Variationen über das Thema Amerika. Studien zur Literatur der USA* was published posthumously (Berlin: Aufbau-Verlag, 1988).

Helischkowski, Dr. Siegmund (1888–1963), gynecologist, in 1942 assistant doctor in the Jewish Hospital Berlin; protected by a "mixed marriage." From 1945–1956, he served as head of the Jewish Hospital's gynecological ward.

Heymann, Bernhard (Hardel) (1909–1942), member of the resistance group around Hans Fruck; he was probably executed in 1942. There are contradictory data on the place and date of his death.

Heymann, Felix (1917–1943), partner of Hella Hirsch; lathe operator, member of the Herbert Baum Group. It is purported that he provided information under torture about supporters; executed on September 7, 1943.

Hindenburg, Paul von (1847–1934), military commander and politician. Became a national hero as a result of the victory in the Battle of Tannenberg (1914) and further partial successes in World War I. He subsequently rose to the rank of general field marshal; in this position he initially led the army to several victories and then to complete defeat. Despite his failure he remained the center of a celebrity cult as a military commander. He served from 1925 to 1934 as Reich president. His support of Hitler as chancellor, of the Reichstag Fire Decree (issued February 28, 1933) and of the Enabling Act (signed by von Hindenburg, March 23, 1933) paved the way for the Nazi dictatorship.

Hirsch, Alice (1923–1943), sister of Hella Hirsch; worker, belonged to the Herbert Baum Group; arrested in July 1942, sentenced to three years in prison in December. Alice Hirsch was deported on October 14, 1943, to Auschwitz and murdered there.

Hirsch, Dr. Franz (1893–1942), gynecologist, deported on January 19, 1942, to Riga and murdered there.

Hirsch, Helene (Hella) (1921–1943), sister of Alice Hirsch. She completed a commercial apprenticeship and worked as a receptionist; was a member of the Herbert Baum Group. Arrested in July 1942, sentenced to death in December, and executed on March 4, 1943.

Hoelz, Max (1889–1933), politician, Communist leader in the "March Action" of 1921, a failed Communist uprising by the KPD and other allied groups. Sentenced to life imprisonment that same year based on a false accusation. He published his *Zuchthausbriefe* (Prison Letters) in 1927, was accorded amnesty in 1928, released and subsequently immigrated to the Soviet Union.

Holzer, Gerhard (1912–1937), Richard Holzer's brother; arrested in 1935, was later sentenced to death by the People's Court for his resistance activities for the KPD; executed July 31, 1937.

Holzer, Richard (1911–1975) Charlotte Holzer's second husband, married 1946; textile merchant, Jew with Hungarian citizenship. He was a member in the 1920s of the Jewish youth group Schwarzer Haufen (Black Bunch) around Hans Litten and Max Fürst; joined the KPD in 1930. He became a member of the Herbert Baum Group after his brother Gerhard had been executed. Richard fled in July 1942 to Budapest and was placed by the Hungarian army in conscript forced labor on occupied Soviet territory. In March 1944, he deserted to the Red Army, returning to Hungary in 1945 and to Germany in 1946. He was active in foreign trade in the GDR.

Isaaksohn, Rolf (1921–1957 [declared dead]), commercial apprentice, he went into hiding at the end of 1942 and lived by selling false identification papers. In June 1943 met Stella Kübler, was arrested together with her at the beginning of July 1943. At the end of that year he was transferred to the Grosse Hamburger Strasse transit camp and from then on worked as a *Greifer* (catcher) for the Gestapo.

Together with Stella Kübler and monitored by Bruno Goldstein, and later by Kurt Bolz, he extorted large sums of money from Jews in hiding. He married Stella Kübler in October 1944 and vanished from Berlin on April 17, 1945. Searches for him in the postwar years proved unsuccessful.

Jadamowicz, Hildegard (Hilde) (1916–1942), active in 1935 in the illegal Workers International Relief, she participated in leaflet campaigns organized by the group around Joachim Franke. Arrested in 1936, she was released after nine months in custody due to a lack of evidence; engaged to Werner Steinbrink; she belonged to the Herbert Baum Group and participated in the attack on the "Soviet Paradise" exhibition on May 18, 1942. She was caught shortly after, sentenced to death in July 1942, and executed on August 18, 1942.

Jegelka, Ernst, communist, a member of the resistance group Neu Beginnen (New Beginning), a friend of prominent Social Democrat Herbert Wehner. Jegelka managed to remain undetected by the Gestapo after many members of Neu Beginnen had been arrested. After the war, he was active as a trade union functionary, and later relocated to West Berlin.

Joachim, Heinz (1919–1942), music student, placed in conscript forced labor at Siemens in the same "section for Jews" as Herbert and Marianne Baum; a member of the Herbert Baum Group; married to Marianne Prager. Heinz Joachim was arrested together with Herbert Baum on May 22, 1942, and executed on August 18, 1942, at Plötzensee Prison.

Joachim, Marianne, née Prager (1921–1943), wife of Heinz Joachim, kindergarten teacher. She was placed in conscript forced labor in the "section for Jews" at Siemens, and was, like her husband, a member of the Herbert Baum Group. Marianne Joachim was arrested in June 1942, and executed on March 4, 1943, at Plötzensee Prison.

Kahn, Siegbert (Siecke) (1909–1976), goldsmith, member of the Communist Youth League, imprisoned 1934–1936 in the Brandenburg-

Görden Prison; member of the group around Günther Stillmann. He went into exile in Czechoslovakia, and from 1939 to 1946 in Great Britain. In 1949 he cofounded the German Economics Institute of the GDR, in which he worked as a professor. He wrote *Antisemitismus und Rassenhetze. Eine Übersicht über ihre Entwicklung in Deutschland* (Berlin: Dietz Verlag der SED, 1948).

Kochmann, Martin (1912–1943), office employee, member of the Herbert Baum Group; arrested in October 1942, it is purported that under torture he provided information about supporters; executed on September 7, 1943.

Kochmann, Sala, née Rosenbaum (1912–1942), wife of Martin Kochmann; kindergarten teacher, member of the Herbert Baum Group; arrested shortly after the attack on the "Soviet Paradise" exhibition, tried to take her own life by jumping down a light shaft in the Berlin police headquarters, she survived severely injured, was sentenced to death in June, and executed on August 18, 1942.

Körner, Theodor (1791–1813), young poet who fought as a soldier in the Lützow Free Corps during the Napoleonic Wars. The militaristic and patriotic tone of his poems and his untimely death in battle rendered him popular with a German readership during the nineteenth and the first half of the twentieth century.

Kolb, Hermann (1918–?), first mayor of Prenzlau appointed by the occupying Red Army, member of the National Committee of *Freies Deutschland*. He was presumably the person whom Charlotte Holzer met after her arrival in Prenzlau and in recollection mistakenly identified him as Robert Schulz. Kolb, twenty-six years old at the time, clearly fits in better with Holzer's description "very young" than Schulz, who was then forty-four. More on Schulz in the entry on him below.

Krahl, Dr. Franz (1914–1990), office worker, member of the Communist Youth League; imprisoned 1934–1936 in the Brandenburg-Görden Prison, in 1936–1939 in exile in Czechoslovakia, from 1939 to 1946 in Great Britain. After returning to Germany, he served as an editor of the official SED party daily newspaper *Neues Deutschland*.

Kübler, Stella, in her second marriage **Stella Kübler-Isaaksohn, née Goldschlag** (1922–1994), daughter of the singer Antonie Goldschlag and the composer Gerhard Goldschlag; trained as a fashion designer; from 1941 forced to work. Her first marriage in October 1942 was with Manfred Kübler, whom she divorced after his deportation. During the *Fabrikaktion* roundup of Jewish forced laborers at the end of February 1943, she went into hiding together with her parents. In early July 1943, she was reported to the police by an informer and arrested. She escaped from a jail on Bessemerstrasse and was rearrested. From August 1943, she cooperated with the Gestapo in searching for Jews in hiding, and soon was among the most active Jewish "catchers" for the Gestapo, exposing and betraying Jews in hiding. She relocated to Luckenwalde shortly before the war's end; in March 1946, she was arrested after she had applied for recognition as a victim of fascism, using a false name. She was sentenced to ten years forced labor for crimes against humanity. After her release she was charged once again and sentenced, in 1957, to ten years imprisonment, but it was ruled the sentence had already been served. She committed suicide in 1994 at the age of seventy-two. For greater detail on Stella, and also on the Zajdmann family (cf. below), see Peter Wyden, *Stella: One Woman's True Tale of Evil, Betrayal, and Survival in Hitler's Germany* (New York: Simon & Schuster, 1992).

Latte, Konrad (1922–2005), musician; tried to elude deportation and was arrested in September 1943 during a police raid. He was scheduled to be deported to Auschwitz in October together with his parents, but then was deferred because he was to present witness testimony. Konrad escaped on November 27, 1943, from Grosse Hamburger Strasse transit camp, surviving in Berlin in hiding. In 1953, he founded the Berlin Baroque Orchestra, which he directed. See Peter Schneider, *"Und wenn wir nur eine Stunde gewinnen..." Wie ein jüdischer Musiker die Nazi-Jahre überlebte* (Berlin: Rowohlt, 2001).

Lewkowitz, Dr. Julius (1876–1943), uncle of Charlotte Holzer; from 1913 rabbi of the Berlin Jewish Reform community. He taught philosophy of religion at the *Hochschule für die Wissenschaft des Judentums*; deported on March 12, 1943, to Auschwitz and murdered.

Lewkowitz, Selma, née Abraham (1880–1943), Charlotte Holzer's aunt; deported on March 12, 1943, to Auschwitz and murdered.

Liebknecht, Karl (1871–1919), social democratic politician and a cofounder of the German Communist Party. On August 4, 1914, he remained absent from the vote for war credits in order not to oppose his own party in the Reichstag, which voted unanimously to approve the credits. On December 2, he was the sole Reichstag deputy to vote against extending the credits. On May 1, 1916, Liebknecht made a speech against the war, for which he was sentenced to four years imprisonment. He was murdered by marine officers in Tiergarten, Berlin on January 15, 1919.

Liliencron, Detlev von (1844–1909), author, wrote the poem *Cincinnatus*, with the lines: *"Meinen Jungen im Arm, in der Faust den Pflug und ein fröhlich Herz, und das ist genug"* ("On my arm, my young boy, in my fist the plow, and a happy heart, and that's enough").

Ludendorff, Erich (1865–1937), general and politician; served as a commander under Hindenburg in World War I. He subsequently was one of the main proponents of the antisemitic *Dolchstosslegende* (myth of the stab in the back), which alleged that a victorious German army was betrayed in WWI by its own politicians and their Jewish instigators. He participated in both the Kapp Putsch (a coup attempt in March 1920), and the Hitler-Ludendorff Putsch attempt against the Weimar Republic. After the failure of both abortive coups he led the anti-Jewish Deutschvölkische Freiheitspartei (German Völkisch Freedom Party).

Lustig, Dr. Dr. Walter (1891–1945), physician; worked in the 1920s in the Berlin police, head of the medical section there. He was dismissed in 1933 on the basis of the "Law for the Restoration of the

Professional Civil Service," in 1938 his license to practice medicine was revoked. In 1940 appointed as the functionary responsible for matters of healthcare in the Reich Association of the Jews in Germany (RV), and from 1940 appointed head of the health department in the RV. From 1941 director of the Investigative Department for Transport Claims in the Jewish Hospital, involving applications for deferment of deportations. In 1942, he was appointed director of the Jewish Hospital Berlin; after deportation of the staff workers of the Jewish community, he served from June 1943 as chairman and single remaining representative of the RV. Dr. Walter prevented the closing of the Jewish Hospital; on instructions from the Gestapo, he recommended persons for deportation. After liberation and the war's end, he was appointed director of the healthcare office in the Wedding area of Berlin. At the end of June 1945, following a legal complaint by inmates of the transit camp in the Jewish Hospital, Dr. Lustig was arrested by the Soviet occupying power, and due to his cooperation with the Gestapo, was put to death (not known precisely when).

Luxemburg, Rosa (1871–1919), social democratic politician, cofounder of the KPD; murdered on January 15, 1919, by a *Freikorps* officer in Berlin.

Mann, Thomas (1875–1955), writer, part of the well-known intellectual Mann family; he wrote inter alia the internationally famous works *Buddenbrooks: Verfall einer Familie* and *Tod in Venedig*. After the National Socialists assumed power, he immigrated to Switzerland, and, in 1938, on to the U.S. In 1952, he returned to Switzerland. During the war Thomas Mann tried with his radio program *Deutsche Hörer!* to persuade the German public to turn away from Nazism.

Markstahler, Wilhelm (1899–1944), economist, in 1936 convicted of preparations for high treason and sentenced to two years in prison. He was arrested on November 14, 1942, and sentenced on May 20, 1943, to three years imprisonment charged with crimes against the war economy; he died in prison.

Mecklenburg-Strelitz, Sophie Charlotte zu (1744–1818), the German-born wife of King George III of Great Britain and Ireland, and since 1814 also King of Hanover in Germany. For greater detail on Queen Charlotte, see Friederike Drinkuth, *Queen Charlotte. A Princess from Mecklenburg-Strelitz Ascends the Throne of England* (Schwerin: Thomas Helms Verlag, 2011).

Mendelsohn, Dr. Ludwig (1878–1948), head of the Infant Welfare Office in Berlin-Wedding and the Jewish Infant and Small Children's Care Home in Berlin Niederschönhausen. In the period 1933–1938 active in private practice; in 1938, his license to practice medicine was revoked. He immigrated via Portugal to Argentina in 1941, and after 1945 to the U.S.

Meyer, Gerhard (Gerd) (1919–1942), locksmith, married to Hanni Meyer, conscript forced laborer at Siemens in the same "section for Jews" as Herbert Baum, to whose group he belonged; executed on August 18, 1942.

Meyer, Hanni, née Lindenberger (1921–1943), wife of Gerhard Meyer; stenographer, milliner. She was a member of the Herbert Baum Group; arrested shortly after the attack on the "Soviet Paradise" exhibition in May 1942, sentenced to death in December, and executed on March 4, 1943.

Moratz, Ralph (1931–2016), son of Renate Moratz; sent in 1939 in a children's transport from the Auerbach Orphanage in Berlin to France, and in 1941 on to the United States.

Moratz, Renate (1908–1943), nurse. She provided members of the Herbert Baum Group with a place of refuge and for that reason was arrested; deported on October 14, 1943, to Auschwitz and murdered there.

Möller, Erich (1900–?), head of the Section for Jewish Affairs in Office IV D of the Berlin Gestapo; Möller visited the Grosse Hamburger

Strasse transit camp regularly and interrogated Jews in Schulstrasse camp who had previously been in hiding. Simultaneously he directed Section IV D 2 (responsible for revocation of citizenship). In the final days of the war he disappeared with no further trace, and in 1991 was declared dead by a Berlin court.

Neuweck, Fritz (1903–1944), banker and insurance agent; he went into hiding to avoid deportation in October 1942. He made a living selling counterfeit identity papers. He was arrested in August 1943, together with his fiancée Mary Bergmann, née Cahn; Fritz Neuweck betrayed persons involved with the procurement of counterfeit identity documents and was placed in a leading position as a "catcher" for Jews in hiding. He enriched himself from the property of his victims. On October 12, 1944, he eluded the deportation ordered for that reason, together with Mary Bergmann, whom he had married in the camp, by suicide.

Paech, Eva (Evchen) (b. August 21, 1933), daughter of Charlotte and Gustav Paech, today Chava Kürer, lives in Israel.

Paech, Gustav (1905–1945), Charlotte Holzer's first husband, technician; active in the communist Revolutionary Trade Union Opposition. On November 27, 1934, he was sentenced to fourteen months imprisonment. Due to his support for members of the Herbert Baum Group he was found guilty of acting as an accessory to treason and sentenced on July 16, 1943, to two years in prison. Following arrest he was imprisoned in Neuengamme concentration camp and escaped during camp evacuation. After liberation, he died of tuberculosis in August 1945.

Paul, Elfriede (1900–1981), physician, member of the KPD, from 1934 had a medical practice in Berlin. She made her office available as a meeting place for the group around Libertas and Harro Schulze-Boysen. In 1943, she was sentenced to six years in prison by the People's Court. From 1947 on, she participated in the development of the healthcare system in the GDR. Later published her memoirs, *Ein Sprechzimmer der Roten Kapelle* (Berlin: Militärverlag der DDR, 1982).

Pavlov, Ivan Petrovich (1849–1936), Russian physician and physiologist, Nobel laureate, investigated the physiological basis of behavior, particularly known for his experiments with dogs and their salivary responses (the well-known Pavlovian reflex).

Pikarski, Margot (b. 1932), archivist and author, published two books on the Baum Group: *Sie bleiben unvergessen (Widerstandsgruppe Herbert Baum, Berlin)* (Berlin: Junge Welt, 1968), and *Jugend im Berliner Widerstand. Herbert Baum und Kampfgefährten* (Berlin: Militärverlag der DDR, 1984).

Piscator, Erwin (1893–1966), theater director, producer, maintained his own theater 1927–1931, and relocated in 1931 to the Soviet Union.

Poelchau, Harald (1903–1972), Protestant prison priest in Berlin-Tegel, later a chaplain in the Plötzensee and Brandenburg-Görden prisons, pastor for many incarcerated opponents of the regime. He assisted Jews in finding a place for concealment, and belonged to the Confessing Church, the Kreisau Circle, and to the resistance group Onkel Emil. In 1949, his memoirs were published as *Die letzten Stunden. Erinnerungen eines Gefängnispfarrers, aufgezeichnet von Alexander Stenbock-Fermor* (Berlin: Verlag Volk und Welt, 1949). For his help provided under constant danger, and in particular for assistance in hiding a brother and sister who had escaped from the transit camp, Yad Vashem bestowed on Harald Poelchau and his wife Dorothea the title Righteous Among the Nations in November 1972.

Reisner, Larissa (1895–1926), Soviet writer, revolutionary, daughter of a Baltic–German father and Polish mother; she wrote both in Russian and in German.

Rehfeldt, Berthold, plumber; confined in the transit camp at the Jewish Hospital Berlin. He survived and was a witness in 1965, providing evidence in preparations for a trial against Otto Bovensiepen, the head of Berlin Gestapo from 1941 to 1943.

Reuber, Ursula (Ursel) (1921–1945), psychology student, was considered a *Mischling ersten Grades* (mixed race of the first degree) under Nazi racial legislation. She was confined from autumn 1943 in the Schulstrasse transit camp because she had assisted Konrad Latte, who had escaped from detention. She was released in spring 1944 and conscripted into forced labor in a street cleaning crew. Ursula helped several Jews in hiding to stay in her parents' house and perished together with one of her protégés during a bombing raid on March 22, 1945.

Römer, Joseph (Beppo) (1892–1944), lawyer, life companion of Cäcilie (Cilly) Bode. He was a career officer in World War I, and after that war a leader in the *Freikorps*. In 1932, he joined the KPD, and after the National Socialists came to power, was detained in several concentration camps. During the war he took part in several resistance actions together with Robert Uhrig and others; arrested in June of 1942, sentenced to death in June of 1944, and executed on September 25, 1944.

Rosenstein, Professor Dr. Paul (1875–1964), physician, from 1923 chief of the surgery department at the Jewish Hospital Berlin. He immigrated at the end of 1938 to Brazil and died in Rio de Janeiro.

Rosenthal, Hans (Hänschen) (1903–?), engineer at Osram, then appointed head of materials administration and purchasing in the Berlin Jewish community. Hans survived the war and then immigrated to the U.S., where he died. Not to be confused with the entertainer Hans "Hänschen" Rosenthal, who was a teenager at the time, survived in hiding in a Berlin community garden, and remained after the war in Germany, where he became famous as a TV gameshow host.

Roth, Wolfgang (Wölfchen) (1910–1988), stage designer; immigrated in 1933 via Prague to Vienna, 1934 to Switzerland, in 1938 to New York. The Berlin Academy of Arts houses his final papers, which in the main contain work of his after 1945 in the U.S.

Rotholz, Heinz (1921–1943), mechanic; from 1940 forced laborer at Siemens working in the same "section for Jews" as Herbert Baum, whose group he belonged to; arrested after the attack on the "Soviet Paradise" exhibition, sentenced to death in December 1942, and executed on March 4, 1943.

Saxe-Weimar-Eisenach, Augusta of (1811–1890), married to the Prussian king and later as consort to German Emperor Wilhelm I. Known for her liberal and antiwar views. She surrounded herself at court with thinkers of the same persuasion but had little impact on the great political decisions of the time.

Schanuel, Charlotte (1901–1948), prison warden; in 1944, she met Erich Honecker when he was sent from the Brandenburg-Görden prison to the Barnimstrasse prison in Berlin in order to help repair the roof. Honecker married her in 1946, and she died suddenly just a year later. In the GDR, the politically uncomfortable first marriage of Honecker as chairman of the Council of State and a leader of the SED was subsequently hushed up and largely kept a secret from the broader public during his long tenure.

Schiffer, Eugen (1860–1954), lawyer and politician; he stemmed from a Jewish family that had converted to Protestant Christianity. In the initial phase of the Weimar Republic, he served as finance minister, justice minister and vice-chancellor. He was confined shortly before the end of World War II together with his daughter in the Jewish Hospital Berlin. In 1945, the Soviet Military Administration appointed him president of the German Central Administration for Justice (1945–1948); he also served as chairman of the Constitutional Committee of the Provisional Volkskammer (People's Chamber) of the GDR (1949–1950). Dr. Schiffer lived from 1945 onwards in his former residence in Charlottenburg in West Berlin.

Schlesinger, Dr. Helena (Heli) (1911–2003), mathematician and physicist; born in Vienna, she earned a doctorate in physics from the University of Vienna and later worked in German industry in Berlin and

Dresden. She belonged to the group of Joachim Franke. Arrested on September 25, 1942, and deported to Auschwitz, she was transferred back to Berlin in March 1943, tried for treason as a communist, and sent as a prisoner and forced laborer to Leipzig. She survived and worked initially in Vienna after the war, later marrying Kurt Otley and immigrating to the U.S. in 1962. She passed away in Rockville, Maryland in 2003. As Helen Otley, she published her autobiography: *Wien, Auschwitz, Maryland. Meine Lebensgeschichte bis Kriegsende 1945* (Frankfurt a.M.: Haag + Herchen, 1995); in English: *Before and After Auschwitz: My Life Until 1945* (Riverside/CA: Ariadne Press, 2001).

Schulz, Robert (1900–1969), Communist politician, arrested by the Nazi authorities on numerous occasions. After the war he was officially installed by the Soviet occupation administration as mayor of Prenzlau between February and April 1946 and served again in this capacity from November 1946 to March 1950. In the Weimar Republic, Schulz was political head of the local local KPD and commandant of the paramilitary Roter Frontkämpferbund (Alliance of Red Front Fighters). He probably was not the individual whom Charlotte Holzer met in Prenzlau. See on this the entry above for Hermann Kolb.

Schmincke, Dr. Richard (1875–1939), physician, municipal council member, director of the health department in Neukölln; member of the KPD. After the Reichstag fire he was arrested and detained for several months; later active in private medical practice. After his license as a practicing physician was revoked, he committed suicide.

Schneider, Christa-Maria (b. 1920) (daughter of Dorothea), studied philology and (after the war) theology. She married the Swedish pastor Knuth Lyckhage. Declared a Righteous Among the Nations by Yad Vashem in 2002 for assisting Jews in hiding.

Schneider, Dorothea, née Ryssel (1889–1946), a pastor's wife active in youth work, member of the Confessing Church. She offered safe refuge to three Jewish women who had gone into hiding. Mother and daughter were honored by Yad Vashem in 2002 as Righteous Among the Nations. On Dorothea and Christa-Maria Schneider, see Daniel Fraenkel & Jakob Borut, *Lexikon der Gerechten unter den Völkern: Deutsche und Österreicher* (Göttingen and Jerusalem: Wallstein and Yad Vashem, 2005), pp. 244–245. It contains a brief description of how they assisted Charlotte Holzer (p. 245). For greater detail, see Beate Kosmala, "Zuflucht in Potsdam bei Christen der Bekennenden Kirche," in Wolfgang Benz, *Überleben im Dritten Reich: Juden im Untergrund und ihre Helfer* (Munich: Beck, 2003), pp. 113–130, in particular pp. 118–126. Based on comments by Christa-Maria, Kosmala points out several inaccuracies in Charlotte Holzer's memoirs.

Schumacher, Elisabeth, née Hohenemser (1904–1942), graphic artist; together with her husband, the sculptor Kurt Schumacher, she was active in the resistance circle around Libertas and Harro Schulze-Boysen. Arrested in September 1942, sentenced to death on December 19, and executed—together with her husband—on December 22, 1942.

Seelenbinder, Werner (1904–1944), top German wrestler, communist, and member of the resistance group of Robert Uhrig. As a leading sportsman, he was able to travel abroad and used the opportunity to operate as an illegal courier for the KPD. Arrested in February 1942, sentenced to death in September, and executed on October 24, 1944. See Walter Radetz, *Der Stärkere. Das Leben des Arbeitersportlers Werner Seelenbinder* (Essen: Verlag Neuer Weg, 1981); James McNeish. *Seelenbinder: The Olympian who defied Hitler,* (Wellington: Steele Roberts, 2016).

Steinbrink, Werner (1917–1942), chemical engineer, he worked at Kaiser Wilhelm Institute in Berlin-Dahlem; engaged to Hilde Jadamowitz. He did illegal work for the Communist Youth League. Arrested in 1936, he was acquitted and released due to a lack of evidence. Together with Joachim Franke he led a resistance group and was in contact with Herbert Baum. He prepared the incendiary devices for the arson attack on the propaganda exhibition "The Soviet Paradise." Arrested shortly after the attack, sentenced to death in July 1942, and executed on August 18, 1942.

Strauß, Dr. Hermann (1869–1943), *Geheimrat* (Privy Councillor), physician and internist; deported on September 16, 1942, to Theresienstadt, where he died on March 2, 1943.

Tau, Max (Mäxchen) (1897–1976), writer, editor, journalist; he published his memoirs *Glaube an den Menschen* in the West Berlin publishing house Verlag Herbig in 1948.

Teichmann, Ursula (Ursel), lived in Anklam, supported Jews in hiding, among them the later conductor and founder of the Berlin Baroque Orchestra, Konrad Latte. After the war she provided refugee children who had lost their parents a new home in the estate house Pentin. Shortly before construction of the Berlin Wall, she came with ten small children to West Berlin. Because she had not obtained the approval of church or state authorities prior to this decision, her right to care for the children was revoked. She then went on to work as a social worker in a boarding school for young girls. Later she relocated to West Germany, where she passed away in 1970.

Thälmann, Ernst (Teddy) (1886–1944), trade unionist and politician, initially in the SPD, then the USPD, then KPD. In the period 1924–1929, leader of the paramilitary Roter Frontkämpferbund; From 1925 to 1933 head of the KPD, Reichstag deputy, and twice unsuccessful as KPD candidate for Reich president. He positioned the KPD as a party in fundamental opposition to the socialist SPD. He was arrested in 1933 and without a trial was incarcerated in a series of prisons and camps. On instructions from Hitler, he was transferred on August 17, 1944, to Buchenwald concentration camp, where he was murdered the following day.

B. Traven, a pseudonym adopted by an anonymous bestselling novelist writing in English who wrote *The Death Ship* and *The Treasure of the Sierra Madre*. His stories bore similarities to those by Jack London and Mark Twain but featured protagonists from proletarian backgrounds. The identity of B. Traven remains controversial; the first generally accepted hypothesis was that he was identical with the actor and anarchist Ret Marut, another pseudonym. More recent biographical research leaves little doubt that both B. Traven and Ret Marut were pseudonyms employed by Otto Feige (1882–1969), a German metalworker born in Schwiebus, Lower Silesia (today Świebodzin, Poland).

Walther, Irene (1919–1942), office worker, partner of Heinz Birnbaum. She worked illegally for the Communist Youth League and was a member of the Herbert Baum Group; participated in the attack on the "Soviet Paradise"-exhibition. Arrested only days after the attack, sentenced to death in July 1942, and executed on August 18, 1942.

Waterstradt, Berta, née Wiener (1907–1990), journalist, writer, member of the Bund proletarisch-revolutionärer Schriftsteller (Association of Revolutionary–Proletarian Authors). After a short time in detention, she immigrated in 1933 to Great Britain and returned in 1934 to Germany; arrested once more in 1935 and sentenced to one year imprisonment. She was later active in the GDR particularly as a screenwriter. She later published her memoirs, titled *Blick zurück und wundre dich. Aus meinen zerstreuten Werken* (Berlin: Eulenspiegel Verlag, 1987).

Wesse, Suzanne née Vasseur (1914–1942), translator, member of the Herbert Baum Group, participated in the attack on the "Soviet Paradise" exhibition. Arrested several days later, sentenced to death in July 1942, and executed on August 18, 1942.

Zajdmann, parents Abraham and Brajna (?), **children Esther** (1924–?), **and Moritz** (1927–?); a Jewish family, originally from Breslau, connected with various Zionist organizations. Abraham, the father, arranged a Haitian passport through the Silberschein/Ladoś/Eiss network in Switzerland. Members of the Chug Halutzi group in Berlin, lived in hiding; Abraham and the children Esther and Moritz were arrested in 1943, after attending an opera performance, by the notorious Gestapo "catcher" Stella Kübler. They were imprisoned in the transit camp at Grosse Hamburger Strasse; father and son escaped on New Year's Eve of 1943/1944, and Esther managed to flee later. The entire family survived the rest of the war in hiding.

Zocher, Rita, née Resnik (1915–1982), in her first marriage wedded to Herbert Meyer; the sister-in-law of Gerd Meyer. Her second marriage was with Herbert Zocher. She was a member of the Herbert Baum Group; from 1940 in conscript forced labor. Arrested on October 7, 1942, she was incarcerated in Cottbus prison and the concentration camps Auschwitz, Ravensbrück, and Malchow; liberated in May 1945.

Zweig, Stefan (1881–1942), writer, born in Vienna, inter alia famous for his story *Schachnovelle*, numerous novels, and his autobiography *Die Welt von Gestern: Erinnerungen eines Europäers* (Stockholm: S. Fischer, 1942), in English: *The World of Yesterday* (New York: Viking, 1943). In the 1920s and 1930s, he was one of the most popular writers worldwide. Zweig immigrated in 1934 from Austria initially to England, later to Brazil, and committed suicide in exile in Brazil together with his wife Lotte on February 22, 1942.